# PRINCIPLES OF MODERN BUILDING

## Volume I

MINISTRY OF PUBLIC BUILDING AND WORKS
BUILDING RESEARCH STATION

# Principles of Modern Building

## Volume I

*3rd Edition*

Part I.  The Building as a Whole
Part II.  The Wall and its Functions

*LONDON*
HER MAJESTY'S STATIONERY OFFICE
1959

This publication was originally issued by the Department of Scientific and Industrial Research which is now dissolved and this *reprint* is issued by the Ministry of Public Building and Works—Building Research Station.

*First published 1938*
*Third edition 1959*
*Fifth impression 1970*

SBN 11 670295 8

# PREFACE

When the first edition of Volume 1 of this book 'Walls, Partitions and Chimneys' was issued in 1938 it was hoped that it would soon be followed by further volumes dealing with other parts of structures. The war, however, made a complete break in this work and by the time it became practicable to proceed with the work on the next volume it was evident not only that Volume 1 needed revision, but that the original plan for the further volumes needed some reconsideration.

This need arose from several causes. 'Principles' had been planned round a study of the function of the different elements of a building as self-contained units, and Volume 1 was concerned with the wall. When the same approach came to be applied to floors and roofs it was seen that considerable overlap, or repetition, of Volume 1 would be difficult to avoid since many of the general principles are common. The principles, for example, of heat loss, of strength, of dimensional stability, or of fire protection apply to a building as a whole as well as to the different elements of structure. The same applies to materials which in the old Volume 1 were discussed specifically in relation to their use in walls, but also more generally in relation to basic properties that are relevant to all uses. The years that have passed since 1938 have also seen a logical development of knowledge. Research starts with the materials and components and progresses to the study of the functional elements and then of the building as a whole. The efficiency of parts of a building cannot be fully assessed by treating them as isolated units; they act with one another in contributing to the functional efficiency of the whole building. Thus attention has been directed to the effect of the interaction between floors and walls on, for example, strength and sound insulation, and wider studies have appeared on particular types of buildings such as schools, hospitals and flats.

There has also been a change in general outlook. When Volume 1 was published in 1938 the novelty in its approach lay in its emphasis on functional requirements and on the principles that determine success in meeting them. This approach is now established. It found its first major application in the Report of the Interdepartmental Committee on House Construction (Burt Committee, 1944) and has since been developed in the Functional Series of Codes of Practice and in other books and publications. What in 1938 was unfamiliar has now entered into the common stock of ideas.

In this new edition of Volume 1, and in the first edition of Volume 2 which is to follow it, a modification of the original scheme has, for these reasons, been made. Part I of Volume 1 now deals with the principles of the functional performance of a building as a whole. As such it includes those parts of the old Volume 1 which have general application, leaving their specific application to walls and other vertical elements to be dealt with in Part II of Volume 1, which incorporates most of the remainder of the original volume. Volume 2 will deal similarly with their application to the horizontal elements, floors and roofs. The opportunity has also been taken to group together in Part I the discussion of the general properties of materials that determine the ways in which they can be used, leaving again to the later parts the more specific questions that arise in their use in the particular parts of a building. If on occasions this leads to the need for back-reference, it avoids what could easily have become excessive repetition.

This method of presentation does not represent any change in approach or purpose, but a development and broadening of the original conception of 'Principles'. This was, and still is, to weld together the knowledge of the Station and the accumulated experience of those engaged in the industry so as to provide as clear a formulation as may be of the functions of a building and of the elements of structure of which it is composed. The purpose is interpretative, to help the reader to grasp principles, to sense the interconnection of requirements, and to appreciate their relative importance in particular circumstances. It is to the conception of fundamental principles that the practitioner has to turn in adapting design to changing requirements, materials and methods. The reception given to the previous edition encourages the belief that this approach is of real service.

Although the application of principles to practice is described and illustrated by details, this book is supplementary to, and in no way a substitute for, a text book on building construction. It does not set out to cover all the details of construction and building practice that are covered in such books. In showing the application of principles to design and construction it is not practicable, nor for the purpose of this book even desirable, to attempt to refer to every material or method that could properly be used. It should therefore not be inferred that what is omitted may not be useful.

The first edition of Volume 1 was written essentially by one man, Mr. R. Fitzmaurice, with the full help of his colleagues in checking and criticizing the work. With the extension of the subject matter this method was no longer practicable and the rewriting and extension of Volume 1 and the preparation of Volume 2 is the work of numerous officers of the Station, each of whom has contributed those parts for which he was best fitted. It would be invidious in these circumstances to single out any small group of names as the authors. The volume is the collective work of the staff of the Station as a whole.

F. M. LEA,
*Director of Building Research*

Building Research Station,
Garston,
Watford, Herts.

July, 1959

# CONTENTS

## PART I

# The Building as a Whole

PART II

The Wall and its Functions

PART I

# The Building as a Whole

*Chapter* I

# STRENGTH AND STABILITY

THE basic requirements to be satisfied in structural design are that (i) the structure must have an adequate margin of strength above that necessary to support its normal loading and (ii) it must have sufficient stiffness so that its distortion does not offend the eye or reduce the efficiency of the structure for its normal purpose. These requirements must be given a quantitative significance by the designer, having regard to the particular circumstances relating to each design. Where the magnitude of the load is known with precision and its effect on the structure can be estimated accurately, the margin of strength need only be small; with variable loading involving the possibility of occasional serious overload, coupled with a structural resistance that is dependent on a material whose strength is liable to fluctuation over a wide range, the margin must be correspondingly high. The necessary stiffness of the structure is usually decided as a result of previous experience rather than from any fundamental consideration of distortion from an aesthetic or practical viewpoint.

## DESIGN METHODS

In the last fifty years the strength requirements of buildings have been met very largely by assuming, in the design calculations, that the imposed loading has a certain, rather arbitrarily chosen, value which is specified by the authority responsible for checking the structural adequacy of the building; the loading is usually related to the type of occupancy (see p. 8 and Table 1.1). The resistance of the structure to this imposed loading and to the weight of the building itself is calculated on the basis of permissible stresses specified for each type of material used in the building; these stresses vary, in relation to the ultimate strength of the material, depending on the variability of the material and on its behaviour under various conditions of stress (e.g. compression, tension, shear).

With this design approach, the requirement as to adequate stiffness is normally assumed to be met if the strength requirement is satisfied. Indeed, the permissible stresses are sometimes limited so as to ensure that the distortions of the building are not excessive. For example, the stresses in the tensile reinforcement of reinforced concrete are usually limited to 27 000 or 30 000 lb/sq. in. in order to avoid large cracks which would be unsightly and might lead to corrosion of the steel. Additional requirements are, however, occasionally introduced. The deflection of steel girders is commonly limited to 1/325 of the span in order to avoid damage to partitions or to finishes. The span/depth ratio of reinforced concrete beams and slabs may be limited for the same reason.

Design on the basis of permissible stresses involves an assessment of the stress conditions in the structure at working load. This assessment is

3

commonly made on the assumption that the materials are elastic and homogeneous. Research has shown that this assumption is often far from the truth for many building materials. The actual stresses are modified considerably by plastic deformations (see p. 20) as well as by the effects of moisture or thermal changes. Again, the behaviour of the structure in its resistance to load usually changes as the load increases, and particularly when failure is incipient; the margin of safety must be chosen with these changes of behaviour in mind, and the permissible stresses have been continually modified to allow for them. It has become increasingly clear that a more logical design method is needed which bears a closer relationship to the true behaviour of a structure and can be extended rationally as new knowledge becomes available.

In recent years a new design philosophy has been suggested, the main principles of which are as follows:

(1) The load that will just cause failure of the structure shall be sufficiently greater than the working load, so that the probability of failure during the required life of the structure is less than a specified limit;

(2) for working-load conditions throughout the required life, the deformations of the structure shall not be such as to impair its safety or efficiency;

(3) economic considerations in the design of structures shall include full allowance for the need for, and cost of, maintenance during the life of the structure.

With regard to the first principle, the ratio of the load that will just cause failure to the working-load is now commonly referred to as the 'load factor against failure'. The value chosen for this factor must depend on the extent to which the loading on the structure, the strength of materials used in it, and the standard of workmanship adopted both in its design and in its construction, may vary from the conditions assumed in the design calculations. Much research is being done, in this country and abroad, to provide data that will enable designers to decide on suitable load factors for various types of structure. The present indications are that the load factors to be used should range from about 1·7 for buildings constructed from materials of closely-controlled strength with careful design and competent supervision during construction, to perhaps 4·0 for buildings constructed with materials of variable strength and rather poor workmanship.

The use of load-factor methods may result in smaller structural members than those determined by older methods, resulting in a reduced stiffness of the structure. Greater care is therefore necessary to ensure that the stiffness is adequate in accordance with the second principle given above. It is difficult to formulate specific rules for so limiting deformations that the safety or efficiency of the structure is not thereby impaired, and considerable research into the effects of distortion is required before the load-factor basis of design can be fully exploited.

## THE STATISTICAL APPROACH TO DESIGN

The load-factor method is based on considerations that can be dealt with statistically. No method of design, even if wildly extravagant, can assure that there is no risk of failure under any circumstances that can arise. All

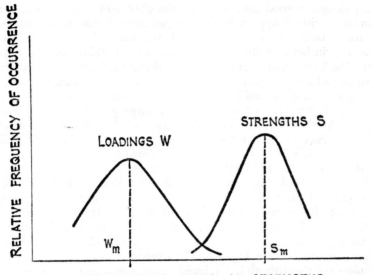

MAGNITUDE OF LOADS OR STRENGTHS

(a) LOADING AND STRENGTH CHARACTERISTICS

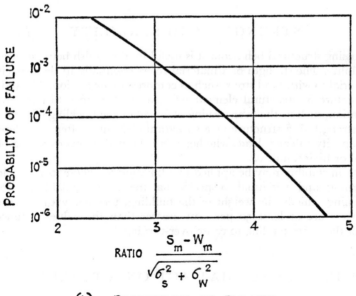

RATIO $\dfrac{S_m - W_m}{\sqrt{\sigma_s^2 + \sigma_w^2}}$

(b) PROBABILITY OF FAILURE

FIG. I.I

*The relationship between loadings, strength and probability of failure*

In this figure, $S_m$ and $W_m$ are the mean values for the strengths and loadings, respectively; and $\sigma_s$ and $\sigma_w$ are the corresponding standard deviations (see Glossary, p. 279)

that any design method assures is that the chance of failure is sufficiently low. In the statistical approach, the designer must decide more consciously what risk of failure he can accept as reasonable and arrange to have a suitable margin between the likely strength of the building and the normal loading. The inter-relationship between loads, strength and risk is indicated for a simple idealized structural system in Fig. 1.1. The load and strength characteristics are illustrated in Fig. 1.1(a) in the form of frequency diagrams which show (i) the relative frequencies of occurrence of various load intensities to which the system is subject; and (ii) the probable variability of strength for all such structures designed to the same requirements. The probabilities that the structure will at some time be subjected to loading in excess of a specified amount, and that its strength will be less than a certain value, can be deduced from such diagrams. The probability that the load will exceed the strength and hence cause failure can also be assessed and is shown in Fig. 1.1(b) on the assumption that the frequency diagrams are of the normal form. In statistical terminology this is known as the Gauss-Laplace form.

For most practical examples, the conditions are much more complicated than has been assumed in Fig. 1.1. The loading does not follow a normal distribution and the strength is developed by the interaction of many elements of the structure, each of which may have very variable characteristics. At present, therefore, and probably for some time to come, the choice of load factor must be left largely to the intuition of the designer, rather than follow from a statistical study of loading and strength.

## STRENGTH AND STABILITY

In discussing structural behaviour it is useful to distinguish between strength and stability. The strength of a material refers essentially to the capacity of the material to withstand stress, such as compression or tension. The stability of a structure or structural element refers to its resistance to large overall deformation, such as the over-turning of a wall or the buckling of a column.

The strength of a structure or a structural element is often considered to be its capacity to carry load, whether this is limited by overstressing of the material or by instability.

The term stability may be applied to a building to denote its resistance to over-turning, and it is usual to specify that the forces available to prevent over-turning (chiefly the weight of the building, together with any special anchorages) are at least 50 per cent greater than the values assumed in design of the forces tending to cause over-turning.

## THE FORCES THAT ACT ON A BUILDING

The principal forces that act on a building are the constant vertical 'dead' loads comprising the weight of the building fabric, the vertical imposed loads comprising the weight of furniture and of articles stored in the building, the variable 'live' loads which include both the weight and the dynamic effect of machinery or people or articles being moved about within the building, and wind loads acting against the walls and roofs. Snow loads, earthquake shocks and other mechanical agencies may also have to be taken into account. Usually, for purposes of design, the live loads are included in the allowance made for imposed loads.

The 'dead' loads can be estimated with fair accuracy. Other loading, however, varies considerably and it is necessary therefore to adopt certain arbitrary design rules which have been shown by experience to be satisfactory when associated with calculations of the resistance of a structure on a permissible-stress basis. These rules must also be used at present for load-factor methods of design.

*Design loadings: vertical*

The use to which from time to time the floor space of many buildings will be put is uncertain and some probable maximum loading must be assumed by the designer. Loadings based on long experience have been embodied in building regulations, but the recent trend has been to regard former requirements as unduly conservative and to reduce them. For instance, whereas the London Building Act of 1930 required the designer to provide for an imposed load of 70 lb/sq. ft on a domestic floor, and of 56 lb/sq. ft on a flat roof, the current B.S. Code of Practice (CP.3, Chap. V) calls for only 30 lb/sq. ft in each case, and reduces this to 15 lb/sq. ft for a flat roof to which no access is provided (see Table 1.1).

TABLE 1.1

*Typical imposed floor loadings to be assumed in the design of buildings according to CP.3, Chap. V (1952)*

|  | lb/sq. ft |
|---|---|
| Floor used for domestic purposes in a building not more than two storeys high . . . . . . . . . . . . | 30 |
| Floor used for domestic purposes in a building more than two storeys . | 40 |
| Offices on upper floors not used for storage or filing . . . . | 50 |
| Workroom or retail shop, church, restaurant . . . . . | 80 |
| Flat roof (accessible) . . . . . . . . . | 30 |
| Flat roof (if no access is provided) . . . . . . . | 15 |

It could be argued that a loading even of 30 lb/sq. ft for the floor of a dwelling as normally used is excessive. The weight of furniture, divided by the whole area of the floor of a room, would seldom exceed 5 lb/sq. ft; and if twenty grown-up persons were crowded into a room measuring 15 ft by 12 ft—an extreme case—the average loading would be under 20 lb/sq. ft. Similarly, normal office loadings seldom amount to anything like 50 lb/sq. ft. Local or occasional loading may, however, far exceed the normal average. A room may contain a heavy bookcase, or may be used to store documents; boxes and cases packed for removal may be stacked in the middle of a floor, or a heavy safe may have to be moved across the floor to its final position. Nor can it be forecast on what part of which floor such an ususually heavy load will at some time be placed in the course of the life of a building.

Although, therefore, it is necessary in the design of an individual floor panel to assume a high value for the imposed loading, it would be unreasonable to assume that *all* panels are so heavily loaded. The bigger the floor area that is considered, the smaller the average imposed load will be. This effect would not, however, be expected to be so great in buildings used solely for storage purposes.

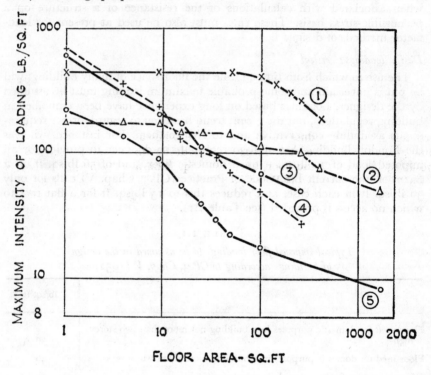

FIG. 1.2

*Floor loadings*

In a survey of actual loads in buildings of various types, data were obtained by the Building Research Station on the effect of the area of floor considered, on the average intensity of loading. Some results are shown in Fig. 1.2, which indicates clearly that for such structures as those examined the maximum intensity of loading is closely dependent on the area of floor taken into consideration. The curves in this figure relate to

(1) a food store,
(2) a seed-merchant's store,
(3) the stock-room of a large shop,
(4) the sales-floor of a large shop,
(5) the show-room of a house furnisher.

To ensure safety against the very high loading intensities associated with small areas, Code CP.3 (Chap. V) specifies minimum imposed loads that must be used in place of those given in Table 1.1 when the floor span is short.

For example, in a two-storey dwelling, the load on a floor panel must be assumed to be at least 240 lb (uniformly distributed over the span) per ft width of floor for all spans less than 8 ft. Similarly, the total load on a beam supporting a floor panel must be assumed to be at least 1920 lb uniformly distributed over the span. This amounts to saying that for any floor of less than 64 sq. ft in area the assumed load shall be that required for 64 sq. ft.

To allow for the reduced loading intensities corresponding to large areas of flooring, the Code provides that, where a single span of a beam supports not less than 500 sq. ft of floor, the imposed load may in the design of the beam be reduced by 5 per cent for each 500 sq. ft supported, subject to a maximum reduction of 25 per cent. Similarly, in designing columns, walls and foundations, reductions in assumed imposed load are allowed in relation to the number of floors carried by the member under consideration. These reductions are, however, not at present permitted where the floors are used for storage purposes.

*Design loadings: wind*

Wind loadings are based on measurements of wind velocities, and of the pressures exerted when the velocity of a mass of air is checked by an obstruction. The pressure is proportional to the square of the velocity. The greatest wind velocity that may be expected in any particular locality will depend upon its exposure, that is its nearness to the sea coast, elevation above sea level, and the shelter provided by hills, woods and neighbouring high buildings. It would be extravagant to design a building in the middle of a town, surrounded by other buildings of a similar height, as though it had to resist the same wind forces as a tower built on a high hill overlooking the open sea. The surface of the ground, and objects growing or built on it, considerably reduce the velocity of wind at low levels. The B.S. Code (CP.3, Chap. V) therefore tabulates basic wind pressures to be used in design according to both exposure and 'effective' height of building, as shown in Fig. 1.3.

In considering the stability of a building as a whole, the horizontal forces to be resisted are:

(i) the horizontal component, at the height of a point halfway up the slope of the roof from the eaves to the ridge (the 'effective height'), of the wind forces and suctions on the roof (Fig. 1.4), and

(ii) the pressure corresponding to that height, considered to be acting uniformly over the whole height and length of the wall.

The recommendations of the Code embody the results of experiments made both on models in wind tunnels and on actual buildings, particularly those made for the Building Research Station by the National Physical Laboratory. Earlier recommendations for the pressure exerted by wind on roof surfaces had been based on the forces exerted on small isolated plates exposed at the top of a tower to winds of measured velocity. Since, however, the wind force is the pressure effect of a moving mass of air when deflected from its path by the obstruction offered by a building, this cannot be the same as it would be on a number of isolated plates of equivalent area at the same slopes as the parts of the building, but with ample room between for the air to escape (hence the way cricket screens are constructed). The air striking the wall of a closed building is deflected upwards and at eaves level is moving

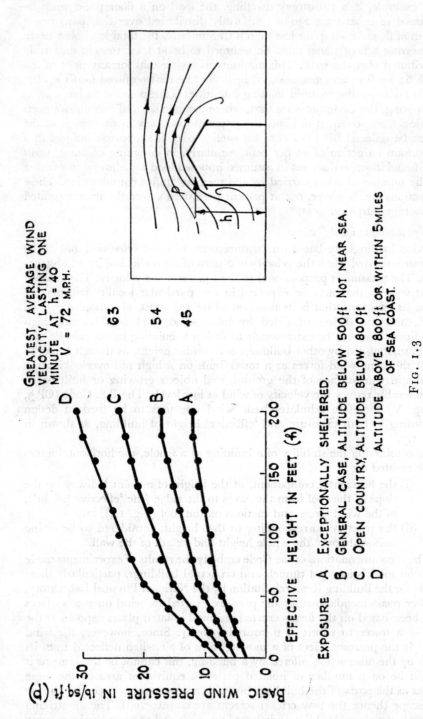

GREATEST AVERAGE WIND
VELOCITY LASTING ONE
MINUTE AT h = 40
V = 72 M.P.H.

D    C    B    A
     63   54   45

FIG. 1.3

EXPOSURE A EXCEPTIONALLY SHELTERED.
         B GENERAL CASE, ALTITUDE BELOW 500ft NOT NEAR SEA.
         C OPEN COUNTRY, ALTITUDE BELOW 800ft
         D ALTITUDE ABOVE 800ft OR WITHIN 5MILES
           OF SEA COAST.

*Relationship between wind pressure and height of building for various severities of exposure*

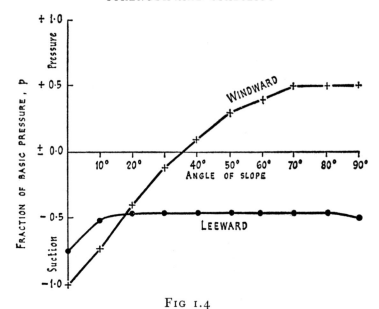

FIG 1.4

*Wind pressure and suction on roof slopes, as a fraction of the basic pressure, p, given by Fig. 1.3*

almost vertically, so driving up, clear of the roof, that oncoming mass of air which would otherwise have exerted a positive pressure on the roof. The result is that with low-pitched roofs the air pressure above the roof is less than that inside the building, and the wind in effect exerts a *suction* on the roof. Suction is likely to be greater on the leeward slope of the roof than on the windward, and on the leeward wall it may amount to about half the basic pressure acting outwards. That the suction effect does occur is shown by the frequency with which, in very high winds, roof coverings are stripped off; indeed the lifting or tearing off of whole roofs is by no means unknown. Many modern lightweight roof constructions need anchorage against this uplift since, particularly at small slopes, the dead weight may be less than the suction force exerted by a high wind. The intensity of the pressure or suction, which, for purposes of calculation, may be taken to be evenly distributed over the whole sloping surface of one side of a pitched roof, is shown in Fig. 1.4. It is shown as a proportion of the basic pressure appropriate to the effective height of the roof and to the exposure of the site.

As has already been observed for loads on floors, the local intensities of pressure due to wind may be considerably greater than the average intensity over the whole wall or roof of a building. Allowance for this effect must be made, in accordance with the provisions of the Code, in the design of individual wall panels and in the anchorage of roof sheets, particularly near the eaves and at the ends of buildings.

*Impact and fatigue*

The sudden application of a load to a structural element results in stresses that are momentarily higher than those due to the same load at rest.

Vibration similarly causes stress fluctuation. If certain critical values are exceeded, this fluctuation may in time cause a material to lose strength—a phenomenon known as 'fatigue'.

The specified design loadings given in Code CP.3 (Chap. V) are sufficient to provide for normal effects of impact or acceleration. Special dynamic effects from machinery must be dealt with individually. In general, it is unlikely that structural elements of a building will be weakened as a result of vibration due to machinery or traffic. However, in special members such as crane girders, the stress changes may be important and the possibility of fatigue must be considered. With the modern tendency to reduce the assumed imposed loads and to increase permissible stresses, the likelihood of fatigue is becoming a subject for greater consideration than in the past. Impact resistance is not normally of much importance in buildings.

# RESISTANCE OF BUILDINGS
# TO THE FORCES ACTING UPON THEM

*Elements of the structure and their interaction*

The structural behaviour of complete buildings is very complex, and any assessment of the resistance of buildings to the forces acting upon them must necessarily involve considerable simplifying assumptions, which are based to a large extent on the intuitive judgments of structural engineers.

The usual procedure in design is to consider the structure to be composed of a number of elements, to estimate the loading on each element, including possible restraints from other elements, and to proportion them accordingly. Only the so-called structural members are considered, elements such as internal partitions being ignored. In this procedure considerable errors in assessing the behaviour of the structure arise from inadequate allowance for the interaction between the various structural elements. For example, it is commonly assumed for design purposes that the beams in a steel framework for a building are not restrained, by their connection to the stanchions, from rotation at their ends; in fact, the restraint may be sufficient to reduce the stresses at mid-span of the beam by 50 per cent or more, particularly if the steelwork is encased in concrete. Again, floor slabs are usually designed as though the supporting beams were rigid, whereas the beams in fact bend, with considerable effect on the stresses throughout the slabs.

The designer has long been aware of some of the deficiencies of his basic design approach, but a more rational and accurate assessment of structural behaviour involves so much additional time in making the design calculations that it can rarely be justified on economic grounds, particularly as the permissible stresses in the simple design method have been progressively increased as designers have realized that their structures were unnecessarily strong. Although the weight of steel in a building framework can be considerably reduced if rigid welded joints are used to connect the beams and stanchions, little advantage will be taken of this until a method of design is developed which is both accurate and as simple and quick to use (or nearly so) as the method now adopted of designing steel frameworks as though the members were connected by hinges. Work at the Building Research Station over a period of several years gives some hope that this problem will be solved before long.

In reinforced concrete buildings, it has been the practice to allow for some structural continuity between the members of a framework; moreover, it is easier than in steel frameworks to vary the strengths of the members, or of the various parts of a member, so as to be adequate for the local conditions of direct load, bending moment and shear. However, the assessment of the bending moments throughout the framework depends closely on the distribution of the load transmitted by the floors to the beams, but no accurate analysis of this distribution is yet available in a form convenient for design use.

*Lateral stability*

Until well into the present century the majority of buildings were constructed with loadbearing walls of masonry or brickwork and, unless they

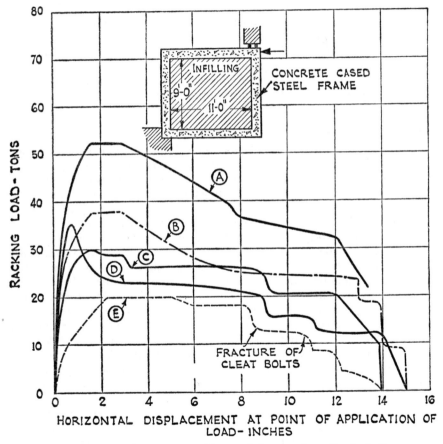

A. $4\frac{1}{2}$-in. brick; B. $4\frac{1}{2}$-in. brick with central door opening; C. 3-in. hollow clay block panel; D. 3-in. clinker block panel; E. Open frame

FIG. 1.5

*Effect of infilling panels on concrete-cased steel frame subjected to racking load*

were great halls or monumental buildings, were divided into rooms of moderate size. The walls and floors, constructed on traditional lines, could generally be relied upon to provide both adequate support and a sufficiently box-like construction to ensure stability as well. In modern framed buildings, however, the internal partitions and even some or all of the external walls may be of light panel construction only. In such buildings the framework itself must usually be designed to resist the bending due to lateral forces such as wind. However, tests at the Building Research Station have shown that even lightweight panels can appreciably stiffen and strengthen the main framework of a building against racking (i.e. distortion in the plane of the panel). Some results are shown in Fig. 1.5 of racking tests on a series of simple frameworks, each consisting of two steel beams and two steel columns, all encased in concrete, within which various types of panel were built. In one test the encased steel frame was tested without any infilling, and in another the bare steel frame alone was tested. It will be observed from the curves that the stiffness and strength of the frame were considerably increased as a result of the concrete encasement and the block infilling, even when weak lightweight concrete blocks were used for the latter.

Unless, therefore, a building is very lofty for its depth or breadth, it is seldom necessary to resort to special bracing or connections in the framework to resist wind forces and sway. At present, however, it is not possible to specify the minimum amount or distributions of cross-walls to give adequate 'box-action' to a building.

*Encasement of steelwork*

Concrete encasement of steel beams and columns, provided essentially for fire protection, serves two structural functions. First, it stiffens the member, reducing the deflection under load and increasing the load that can be carried before lateral or torsional buckling takes place. Secondly, the concrete can support load. Allowance for these effects is being made progressively in Codes of Practice as experimental data become available. A simple allowance for encasement to beams has been in use for many years, whereby with a prescribed encasement the stress in the beam may be suitably increased. For stanchions, however, it was not until 1948 that B.S. 449, 'The Use of Structural Steel in Building', introduced an allowance for the stiffening effect of the encasement in resisting buckling of the stanchion. The 1959 revision of this British Standard allows the designer to assume also that direct load is supported by the concrete encasement of stanchions. Tests at the Building Research Station have shown the importance of the concrete encasement in strengthening steelwork and Fig. 1.6 gives a comparison between the loads that may be permitted on axially-loaded stanchions on the basis of recommendations from the Station and those corresponding to the allowances in B.S. 449.

It is well to remember that the primary purpose of the encasement is to protect the steelwork from fire. Precautions must therefore be taken to enable the cover of concrete over the steel to continue to give such protection for the required period, and for this purpose suitable binding or wire mesh should be wrapped round the stanchion to hold the concrete cover in place, even if it cracks and separates from the steel. It is necessary also to design the stanchion so that, after a fire, the strength without any assistance from the concrete is adequate to prevent collapse; the margin of strength beyond the probable applied load need not, however, be so great as for normal circumstances.

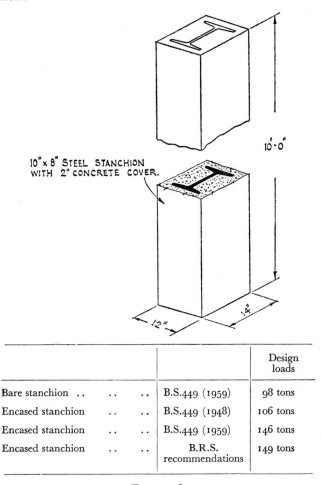

10" × 8" STEEL STANCHION WITH 2" CONCRETE COVER.

| | | Design loads |
|---|---|---|
| Bare stanchion .. .. .. | B.S.449 (1959) | 98 tons |
| Encased stanchion .. .. | B.S.449 (1948) | 106 tons |
| Encased stanchion .. .. | B.S.449 (1959) | 146 tons |
| Encased stanchion .. .. | B.R.S. recommendations | 149 tons |

FIG. 1.6

*Concrete encasement of steelwork—increase in permissible axial load*

## INTERACTION BETWEEN SUPERSTRUCTURE, FOUNDATION AND SOIL

The stresses in any structural system are dependent not only on the dead and imposed loadings, but also on the way the system is supported. The forces acting on a building superstructure include those developed between it and its foundation. These in turn are dependent on the behaviour of the foundation in resisting the forces from the building and the reactions from the soil. The superstructure, foundation and soil form a complex system, and any complete study of the strength and stability of a building must include an assessment of the behaviour of this whole system.

A simple basis of design of the superstructure is to assume that the foundation is rigid. Although deformation of the foundation and settlement due to soil movement are bound to occur, the assumption is equivalent to ignoring any *differential* settlement of the foundation, and may be reasonable if suitable precautions are taken. The load should be spread over a sufficient area for safe bearing and should be distributed as evenly as possible between different parts of the foundation.

It is impossible to eliminate all differential settlement, however carefully the loads are distributed, particularly as the soil properties themselves may vary considerably over a building site. It may be assumed roughly that the likely differential movements are proportional to the average settlement of a building, which can be estimated fairly accurately according to the established principles of soil mechanics. For a multi-storey block of flats, for example, the differential movements are not likely to be serious if the theoretical average settlement is no greater than 1 inch.

Although differential settlement can lead to appreciable increases in stress in parts of a building structure, e.g. at the junctions of beams and columns in framed structures, these changes will often have no important influence on the ultimate resistance of the structure to collapse. However, the distortions of the building can result in the cracking of partitions or finishes and it is this effect which must particularly be guarded against.

Differential settlement of structures on shallow foundations, such as houses, may also occur as a result of shrinkage or swelling of the soil (particularly clay), as discussed on p. 30.

The choice of type of foundation depends upon the disposition of the load-bearing elements of the structure and the bearing capacity of the soil. If the loads from floors are transmitted to the foundation by walls, strip foundations are usually adequate. On poor soil, these strips may need to be much wider than the wall footings, and transverse reinforcement must be used to spread the load over a sufficient area.

If the building is of framed construction, the columns are normally supported on isolated pad foundations, reinforced if necessary. These isolated foundations are usually proportioned so that the bearing pressures on the soil are approximately the same for all of them; the possibility of differential settlement can be further reduced if allowance is made for the fact that the settlement under a foundation pad is dependent, not only on the average pressure on the soil, but also to some extent on the area of the pad.

Raft foundations may be desirable, whatever the type of superstructure, on sites where the soil is weak and the load from the building must be spread over a large area. If the soil is particularly weak, it may be necessary to transfer the load to a lower stratum better able to support it, and piled foundations are used. Fairly short piles (8–10 ft) can also be used to avoid supporting the building on unstable soil such as clay at shallow depths (see p. 30).

## SELECTION OF TYPE OF STRUCTURE

The choice of type of structure for a particular building is largely a matter of experience and judgment on the part of the architect, having regard to the requirements of his clients, the internal planning, the need or otherwise to reduce site labour, the importance of sound and thermal insulation or protection from fire, the availability of materials, and last, but by no means least, the cost.

From the engineering aspect, the type of structure is to a great extent dependent on considerations of dead weight. Even where spans are short it is necessary to reduce the dead weight as much as possible so that the imposed loads can be carried with the utmost economy of structural material; where spans are large, the weight of the structural element bridging the gap is of over-riding importance. Apart from arches or domes, this structural element is, in a building, essentially a beam or truss. For simplicity certain standardized structural forms are used for short spans, e.g. rectangular reinforced concrete beams or slabs, rectangular timber beams, and I-section steel beams. As the spans are increased, it is necessary to increase the structural efficiency by removing parts of the system that do not contribute greatly to the strength. Thus the rectangular form for reinforced concrete section is changed to the T-section, largely eliminating the concrete in the tension zone where it is of little value, and open-web beams, lattice girders and trusses replace the simple I-section in steel systems. As the span increases, more and more attention is given to the need for as much of the beam as possible to be stressed to the limit permissible for the material. The refinements can be costly in construction or prefabrication and are introduced only when the spans and imposed loading are such that the improvements are worth-while.

In general, the structural efficiency might be expected to increase as the strength/density ratio of the material used is increased. Often, however, considerations other than strength may intervene to prevent full advantage being taken of a light strong material. For example, aluminium alloys can be obtained with strengths similar to that of steel and a much reduced weight; their modulus of elasticity is, however, lower, so that their use is sometimes restricted because of excessive deflections. Cost is, of course, frequently the over-riding consideration.

Prestressed concrete has two main advantages over reinforced concrete that enable it to be used for longer spans. First, the strength of the concrete is usually appreciably greater in prestressed concrete, with little increase in density, and the strength of the prestressing steel is considerably higher than that of ordinary reinforcing bars. Second, as a result of prestressing, the whole of the concrete area can be utilized to resist the applied forces.

For large spans, concrete can be used in its most effective structural form in shell construction, which combines the structural advantages of the deep T-beam and the arch. With prestressed edge-beams, this system provides an efficient structural solution to the problem of covering a large area free from columns or walls.

The dead weight to be carried includes not only the weight of the structural elements but also the weight of other permanent construction, such as partitions and external cladding which are considered to be non-loadbearing. Considerable reductions in the weight of such elements are being made in the present trend towards lightness in construction. Although these changes are to be welcomed as helping towards structural economy, it is necessary to remember that so-called non-structural members have in the past provided stiffening to the building, particularly against lateral forces such as wind, and that removal of this stiffening may require special treatment of the connections between vertical and horizontal load-bearing members.

A general principle for obtaining overall economy in building is to attempt to design the elements of the structure to serve several functions. A floor slab can be proportioned so as to be capable not only of supporting the imposed loads, but also of acting as a barrier to sound or fire. The encasement of a steel stanchion can protect it from fire and corrosion, stiffen it against buckling and also carry direct load. A wall can divide separate occupancies, providing a sound and fire barrier and can be given a structural function also. In multi-storey flats, for example, the usual framework of columns and beams can be dispensed with. Floors and walls are necessary to divide the building and these are sufficient, when properly designed, to form the structural system. The use of concrete cross-wall construction, in which the floors are supported directly by cross-walls, has architectural advantages, allowing freedom of planning of the rooms between the cross-walls (which, as party walls, have no openings to reduce their structural efficiency) and freedom of treatment of the external faces of the building. In maisonette construction, consideration of overall functional requirements suggests that only the alternate floor slabs acting as horizontal divisions between maisonettes need be of concrete, designed to have adequate fire and sound resistance; the intermediate floors within the maisonettes can be much lighter.

*Chapter 2*

# DIMENSIONAL STABILITY

## DEFORMATIONS IN BUILDINGS

UNTIL comparatively recently, dimensional changes in building materials were recognized and allowed for only when these changes were visible and capable of measurement by crude methods. For example, wood was known to change its dimensions appreciably and this was taken into account in the methods of fixing it; on the other hand, materials such as brickwork and masonry and the plaster and allied finishes applied to them were assumed to be dimensionally stable and were treated as such, not always with satisfactory results.

With modern developments in building materials and particularly the advent of Portland cement, cracking of building elements has become commonplace. The cracking, at best, is unsightly and, at worst, may lead to serious structural weakening. Whilst knowledge of the dimensional changes of building materials is still imperfect, there is now a large fund of information available and it is possible by careful design and construction to avoid many of the troubles that are liable to arise.

There are four principal causes of dimensional changes of building materials and structures. These are:

(1) Elastic and inelastic deformation due to applied loads.
(2) Expansions and contractions due to changes in temperature.
(3) Expansions and contractions due to changes in moisture content.
(4) Movements due to chemical reaction between building materials in contact or between building materials and moist air (see p. 85).

*Deformations due to applied load*

When any material is subjected to a force it deforms. Within certain limits of loading, it is convenient and (usually) sufficiently accurate to assume that the deformation due to simple compression or tension is directly proportional to the load, the constant of proportionality being expressed as the modulus of elasticity, $E$, so that

$$E = \frac{\text{load per unit area}}{\text{deformation per unit length}} = \frac{\text{stress}}{\text{strain}}.$$

With most building materials the immediate deformation under load is elastic, i.e. the material returns to its original shape when the load is removed. However, many materials also undergo an inelastic deformation when a load is sustained for a long time. This movement, called 'creep' or 'plastic flow' is not fully recoverable when the load is removed. For design purposes it is often possible to adopt an 'effective' modulus of elasticity that takes these effects into account.

Of the major structural materials, steel has a very small creep at normal working stresses, and the deformations under load can usually be considered to be wholly elastic. At high stresses, however, plastic deformations become very large, influencing considerably the behaviour of a steel framework as the load approaches that which would cause collapse; this effect is of great importance in modern design methods based on a load factor against failure (p. 4).

Concrete tends to deform continuously with time, however small the applied load. For normal conditions, the effect of creep of the concrete is to increase the deformation of a structural member to two or three times the initial elastic movement. The creep is comparatively large during the first month or so after application of the load, and continues at a decreasing rate for several years.

### Deformations due to changes in temperature

With very few exceptions, materials expand when heated and contract when cooled. For a solid material, the increase in length per unit length, for one degree rise in temperature, is known as the coefficient of thermal expansion. (It should be remembered that the numerical value depends on whether the increase in temperature is measured on the Fahrenheit or on the Centigrade scale.)

As a very rough guide to the magnitude of the effect with building materials it may be said that a 100-ft length whose temperature rises to 100°F will expand between one tenth of an inch and one inch, if unrestrained. More detailed values are given in Part II (p. 184).

### Deformations due to changes in moisture content

Materials capable of absorbing water expand as they do so, and contract again as they dry out. This movement, termed the moisture movement, like thermal movement is generally reversible, but with one important exception concerning concretes, mortars and most plasters. Such materials may have an initial drying shrinkage, when they dry out for the first time after setting, that exceeds any future reversible movement. Clearly it may be this initial shrinkage that is most important with work cast or applied in situ.

Moisture movement is discussed in more detail in Chapter 13.


## CRACKING IN BUILDINGS

Cracking occurs wherever the tensile stress in a material exceeds its tensile strength. In composite materials such as brickwork the tensile strength may be determined by the limiting adhesion or connection between the constituent elements (brick and mortar) or by the strengths of the elements themselves. The stress may be due to the effect of externally applied loads or may be induced by internal movements due to temperature or moisture changes, or by the effects of chemical reactions such as corrosion of metals.

The load on a structural member may cause stretching of part of it, e.g. the lower part of a beam, and cracking of the member may result. This cracking leads to a redistribution of the stresses in the member and the size of the individual cracks depends very much on the new structural system which forms within the member to resist the applied load. In a reinforced concrete beam, the reinforcement does not prevent cracking and in fact it plays little part in supporting the load until a crack forms in the concrete.

Once cracking has occurred, however, most of the tension previously developed in the concrete must be provided by the steel bars, which effectively tie together the concrete on the opposite faces of each crack. The concrete tends to slide along the bars on each side of the crack and the extent of this movement, which largely determines the crack width, depends on the stress in the steel and on the bond between the bar and the concrete. To take advantage of the higher strength of special reinforcement, as compared with ordinary mild steel, it is common for the bars to have suitable surface characteristics (obtained by twisting the bars or by forming them with projections or indentations) so that they develop a good bond with the concrete and prevent cracks from becoming very wide.

The deformation of a structural member may also lead to cracking of other elements of a building. In a framed structure, the deflection of a beam, due to elastic deformations and perhaps also to creep, may crack a partition that is built up to the underside of the beam. The sag of a suspended concrete floor may result in a high compressive force in tiling laid thereon; if this leads to a failure of the bond, the tiles will part from their base. Plaster and other finishes may also be cracked by excessive distortions of the building structure.

Most cracking in buildings is probably due to induced stresses arising from restraint to shrinkage and thermal movements. In reinforced concrete, cracking commonly occurs also as a result of expansion when reinforcement corrodes. The corrosion may itself be due to the presence of cracks that allow access of the corrosive agents to the metal, but more often occurs because the cover of concrete over the bars is inadequate and the quality of the concrete poor.

The stresses induced in building materials by temperature or moisture changes are dependent on four factors:

(1) the magnitude of the movement in the material if unrestrained;

(2) the modulus of elasticity of the material;

(3) the capacity of the material to creep or flow under load;

(4) the degree of restraint to the movement of the material by its connection to other elements of the structure.

The interdependence of these factors is illustrated in Fig. 2.1, from which it is seen that the unrestrained movement is equal to the sum of the actual movement (which depends inversely on the degree of restraint), the elastic movement (which is proportional to the induced stress and inversely proportional to the modulus of elasticity) and the creep (which increases with the induced stress and depends on the time during which the movement takes place).

The quantitative assessment of the liability of a building component to crack is complicated by the fact that change in any one of the first three factors is often accompanied by compensating changes in the others and by changes in the strength of the material. For example, additional water in a concrete mix would increase the unrestrained shrinkage movement, but this is compensated by a reduced modulus of elasticity (allowing a larger elastic movement for a given stress) and increased creep (thus reducing the elastic movement necessary). The shrinkage stresses for a particular degree of restraint are in fact less with the concrete of higher water content, but, nevertheless, since the tensile strength is also reduced by the addition of water to the mix, the final result is a tendency for greater shrinkage cracking with wet mixes.

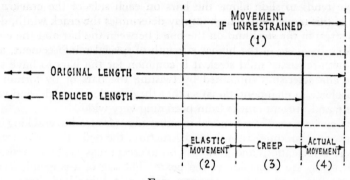

FIG. 2.1

*Factors influencing stresses due to temperature or moisture changes*

As with cracking due to externally applied load, the effect of reinforcing the material is to distribute shrinkage cracks, so that there are more of them but they are individually finer than in an unreinforced member. But the reinforcement does not prevent cracking; in fact, it acts as a restraint to the movement and so contributes to the development of induced stress in the material. In a heavily reinforced concrete beam, shrinkage cracking can sometimes occur even though there are no external restraints to the shrinkage of the concrete; the internal restraint due to the steel bars leads to compressive stresses in these bars (the 'actual movement' shown in Fig. 2.1 corresponding to the elastic compression) and tensile stresses in the concrete.

It is evident from the foregoing remarks that it is impossible to give precise recommendations for reducing cracking due to induced stresses in building materials. It is probably reasonable to assume, however, that the likelihood of serious cracking can be reduced by:

(1) Avoiding materials that, when unrestrained, deform considerably as a result of moisture or temperature changes.

(2) Avoiding unnecessary restraint to shrinkage or expansion of the material.

(3) Using materials or combinations of materials in a building element in such a way that the extensibility (i.e. the total elastic and creep deformations before cracking occurs) is as large as possible.

## THERMAL MOVEMENTS

Although thermal movements and movements due to moisture changes are of similar importance in causing cracking, only thermal movements will be considered in detail in this chapter, since these often need to be allowed for in the overall design of the building; movements due to moisture changes are more appropriately considered in relation to the various elements.

The amount of movement that an unrestrained element of a building will undergo with change of temperature depends upon the range of temperature, the coefficient of thermal expansion of the material, and on the length of the element. It is the outer shell of a building, and particularly the roof, that is usually exposed to the greatest changes in temperature. It is important to realize that there are two main types of temperature variations; a slow seasonal change and a more rapid daily change. In temperate climates, the former has the wider range.

The seasonal variation in temperature of walls in Britain may attain a range of over 50°F. But as regards the likelihood of structural damage, the fluctuations between night and day in summer may be more important—in seven or eight hours the temperature of a wall may rise by 15–20°F. This rapid change may set up very high stresses when the movements of a long wall or roof are restrained, and it remains to consider the conditions under which failures are liable to occur.

Where the arrangement of the walls is such that they are free to expand in any direction, the likelihood of serious failure becomes remote. This applies to a building of fair size up to, say, 100 ft in length and with the normal type of rectangular plan. If, however, the arrangement is such that the expansion of a long length of walling is restricted then the possibility of fractures must not be overlooked. Two examples are shown diagrammatically in Fig. 2.2. These cases had certain features in common. The walls were

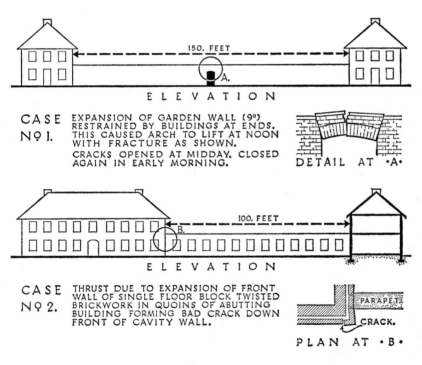

ELEVATION

CASE Nọ 1. EXPANSION OF GARDEN WALL (9") RESTRAINED BY BUILDINGS AT ENDS. THIS CAUSED ARCH TO LIFT AT NOON WITH FRACTURE AS SHOWN. CRACKS OPENED AT MIDDAY. CLOSED AGAIN IN EARLY MORNING.

DETAIL AT •A•

ELEVATION

CASE Nọ 2. THRUST DUE TO EXPANSION OF FRONT WALL OF SINGLE FLOOR BLOCK TWISTED BRICKWORK IN QUOINS OF ABUTTING BUILDING FORMING BAD CRACK DOWN FRONT OF CAVITY WALL.

PLAN AT •B•

FIG. 2.2

*Thermal movement of brickwork causing damage under conditions of restraint*

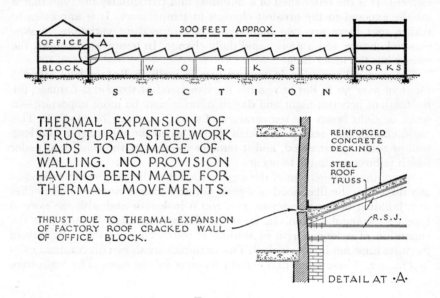

THERMAL EXPANSION OF
STRUCTURAL STEELWORK
LEADS TO DAMAGE OF
WALLING. NO PROVISION
HAVING BEEN MADE FOR
THERMAL MOVEMENTS.

THRUST DUE TO THERMAL EXPANSION
OF FACTORY ROOF CRACKED WALL
OF OFFICE BLOCK.

FIG. 2.3

*Thermal movement*

exceptionally well built; cement mortar was used and every joint was carefully filled so that there was little possibility of expansion being taken up in
the vertical joints. The combination of a thin external cavity shell with a
slight set-back where the wing walls abutted on the main buildings was a
form of construction that enabled the thrust due to thermal expansion to
cause quite serious damage. It would have been difficult indeed to foresee
the trouble in this case, since simple structural forms resembling this in
outward appearance have been traditional in England for centuries, though,
after the event, one may reflect that the traditional buildings did not include
strong cement mortar nor the thin external wall in cavity construction.
Another failure due to restrained thermal movement is sketched in Fig. 2.3:
here the trouble might have been foreseen and avoided.

In the layout of areas surrounding monumental buildings it is not unusual
to make use of walls and balustrades substantially constructed in themselves
but yet, nevertheless, lacking support from other structural elements, which
makes them liable to become displaced relatively easily. Moreover, these
features are often very long in comparison with the buildings they surround.
One or two typical examples may be mentioned.

The parapet wall to a terrace was strongly constructed in masonry, with
an unbroken length of more than 300 ft. This wall showed indications of
considerable distress at a point at about a third of its length. Stones were
spalled and broken and the wall was seriously disfigured.

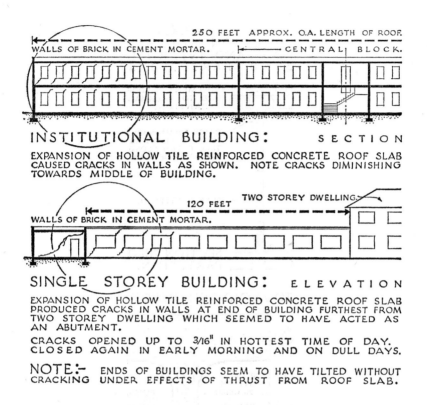

**INSTITUTIONAL BUILDING:** SECTION

EXPANSION OF HOLLOW TILE REINFORCED CONCRETE ROOF SLAB CAUSED CRACKS IN WALLS AS SHOWN. NOTE CRACKS DIMINISHING TOWARDS MIDDLE OF BUILDING.

**SINGLE STOREY BUILDING:** ELEVATION

EXPANSION OF HOLLOW TILE REINFORCED CONCRETE ROOF SLAB PRODUCED CRACKS IN WALLS AT END OF BUILDING FURTHEST FROM TWO STOREY DWELLING WHICH SEEMED TO HAVE ACTED AS AN ABUTMENT.

CRACKS OPENED UP TO 3/16" IN HOTTEST TIME OF DAY. CLOSED AGAIN IN EARLY MORNING AND ON DULL DAYS.

NOTE:— ENDS OF BUILDINGS SEEM TO HAVE TILTED WITHOUT CRACKING UNDER EFFECTS OF THRUST FROM ROOF SLAB.

FIG. 2.4

*Roof movement: examples of buildings where movement of roof slab cracked external walls*

Dwarf walls bounding formal gardens had natural stone copings. These were placed with a fine joint, and several of the stones were spalled and broken by thermal expansion in hot weather.

In both these cases it would have been a comparatively simple matter to provide expansion joints to accommodate the movements. An open joint in every 50-ft length would be sufficient safeguard as a rule.

When different parts of a structure are heated to a different extent, failures are very liable to occur. The most important site of trouble is the junction of a rigid, concrete roof slab with walls and partitions. The roof receives radiation from the sun during the hottest part of the day at more nearly normal incidence than the vertical surfaces, and gets hotter and expands more; meanwhile the wall that supports the north edge of a roof will receive no sun at all. When the roof is a continuous slab of strong concrete it is not

## CRACK AT JUNCTION BETWEEN ROOF AND INTERNAL SLAB PARTITIONS

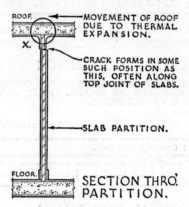

ROOF.

MOVEMENT OF ROOF DUE TO THERMAL EXPANSION.

X.

CRACK FORMS IN SOME SUCH POSITION AS THIS, OFTEN ALONG TOP JOINT OF SLABS.

SLAB PARTITION.

FLOOR.

### SECTION THRO. PARTITION.

## TO AVOID THIS DEFECT

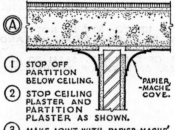

Ⓐ

(1) STOP OFF PARTITION BELOW CEILING.

(2) STOP CEILING PLASTER AND PARTITION PLASTER AS SHOWN.

(3) MAKE JOINT WITH PAPIER-MACHÉ COVE MOULD, SECURED WITH ADHESIVE.

PAPIER -MACHÉ COVE.

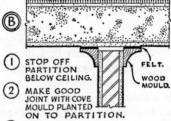

Ⓑ

(1) STOP OFF PARTITION BELOW CEILING.

(2) MAKE GOOD JOINT WITH COVE MOULD PLANTED ON TO PARTITION.

(3) MAKE TIGHT JOINT WITH STRIP OF FELT TO STOP SOUND LEAKAGE.

FELT.

WOOD MOULD.

## DETAILS AT POINT ·X·

### FIG. 2.5

*Roof movement*

difficult to see that its expansion may cause damage to the supporting structure which does not get as hot or expand to the same extent. With framed buildings, where the frame is usually rigidly connected with a roof slab, the expansion is generally distributed uniformly in each bay of the walling; with buildings of load-bearing brickwork and masonry the tendency is for the roof slab to exert a thrust at the ends of the building. With long buildings this produces failures of the kind shown in Fig. 2.4.

Another type of failure associated with the thermal expansion of a roof slab occurs at the junction of top-floor partitions with the ceiling. This seems to happen in all kinds of buildings, whether of framed construction or of load-bearing brickwork. Cases have been reported where repeated attempts have been made to repair the cracks that formed, but every summer they reopened. The cracks are usually horizontal and form at the top of the partition, just below the ceiling; they may be expected to be worst at the ends of a long building. The reason for their formation is, of course, that the roof slab is being heated up relative to the walls and floor into which the partitions are bonded. A typical example of failure of this kind is sketched in Fig. 2.5, with various ways of avoiding such trouble.

Failures of this latter kind are best avoided by the use of some form of treatment that reduces the temperature rise in the roof slab. A white colour of the exposed surface is the best safeguard, since this reflects much of the solar radiation and so reduces the amount of heat absorbed by the roof system. With long expanses of roof, say over 100 ft, expansion joints are necessary in addition to the white surface treatment.

The provision of a movement joint in a building is often difficult. Consider the case previously discussed. This is a troublesome one in practice owing to the necessity of providing for the differential movement between concrete roof slab and supporting walls of brickwork or masonry. The problem can be solved in two ways:

(1) By forming a continuous movement joint in roofs, supporting walls and floors. To be effective the structural break must be complete. Some suggested details are given in Fig. 2.6.

(2) By arranging for the roof slab to slide on the supporting walls and by breaking the slab by suitably designed movement joints at convenient intervals. To be effective, the sliding bearing of the roof slab must be so contrived as to provide a complete break. It is not satisfactory to attempt to plaster solid over the junction of the walls with the roof slab; either the plaster will fracture or the sliding joint will be ineffective. Similarly, provision must be made for the roof-covering material to move relative to the walls, and again this involves elaboration in detailing.

## SOIL MOVEMENTS

Mention has already been made (pp. 15–16) of the interaction between the building, its foundation and the soil. Whereas in that chapter attention was focused on the loading conditions and their effects, it is necessary here to consider soil *movements* and the stresses and cracking in the building that may result from them.

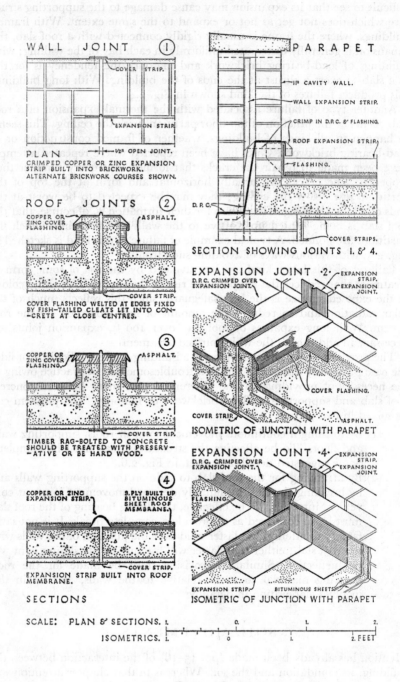

WALL   JOINT   (1)

COVER  STRIP.

EXPANSION  STRIP

PLAN      ←—→1/2" OPEN JOINT.
CRIMPED COPPER OR ZINC EXPANSION
STRIP BUILT INTO BRICKWORK.
ALTERNATE BRICKWORK COURSES SHOWN.

ROOF   JOINTS   (2)
COPPER OR                    ASPHALT.
ZINC COVER
FLASHING.

                  COVER STRIP.
COVER FLASHING WELTED AT EDGES FIXED
BY FISH-TAILED CLEATS LET INTO CON-
-CRETE AT CLOSE CENTRES.

(3)
COPPER OR                    ASPHALT.
ZINC COVER
FLASHING.

                  COVER STRIP.
TIMBER RAG-BOLTED TO CONCRETE
SHOULD BE TREATED WITH PRESERV-
-ATIVE OR BE HARD WOOD.

(4)
COPPER OR ZINC        3.PLY BUILT UP
EXPANSION STRIP.      BITUMINOUS
                     SHEET ROOF
                     MEMBRANE.

                  COVER STRIP.
EXPANSION STRIP BUILT INTO ROOF
MEMBRANE.

SECTIONS

PARAPET

11" CAVITY WALL.
WALL EXPANSION STRIP.
CRIMP IN D.P.C. & FLASHING.
ROOF EXPANSION STRIP.
FLASHING.
D. P. C.
COVER STRIPS.

SECTION SHOWING JOINTS 1. & 4.

EXPANSION  JOINT ·2·    EXPANSION
D.P.C. CRIMPED OVER         STRIP.
EXPANSION JOINT.           EXPANSION
                          JOINT.

COVER FLASHING.

COVER STRIP.              ASPHALT.
ISOMETRIC OF JUNCTION WITH PARAPET

EXPANSION  JOINT ·4·    EXPANSION
D.P.C. CRIMPED OVER         STRIP.
EXPANSION JOINT.           EXPANSION
                          JOINT.
FLASHING

EXPANSION STRIP.    BITUMINOUS SHEETS
ISOMETRIC OF JUNCTION WITH PARAPET

SCALE:  PLAN & SECTIONS. 1.    0.           1.          2.
        ISOMETRICS. 1.    0           1        2. FEET

FIG. 2.6

*Movement joints continuous in roof and walls*

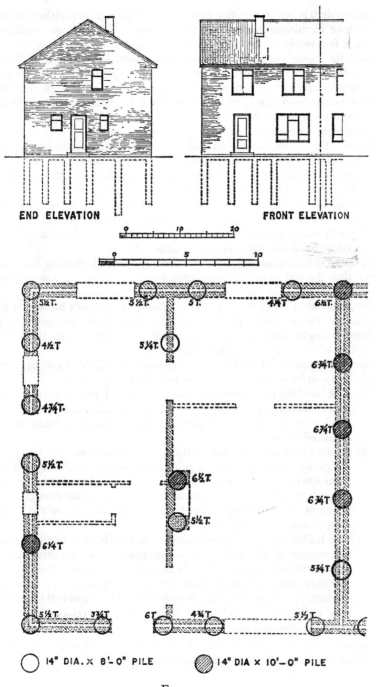

END ELEVATION                                    FRONT ELEVATION

○ 14" DIA. × 8'-0" PILE       ◉ 14" DIA × 10'-0" PILE

FIG. 2.7

*One arrangement of piles to suit a typical semi-detached house : the design
load (in tons) is indicated against each pile*

The problem arises in practice mainly with housing, built either on shrinkable clay or in mining areas liable to subsidence. For average conditions, a spell of a few weeks of dry weather in the summer will cause certain clays to shrink for a depth of about 8 ft from the surface. The amount of shrinkage and the depth to which it occurs depends on the shelter that the ground has from the sun and the presence of vegetation which through its root system removes water from the clay. The shrinkage is greatest near the surface, involving a settlement often of the order of an inch, and is usually of little importance at a depth of 4 or 5 ft.

Houses built on the traditional shallow strip foundations on such clays are liable to serious distortion and consequent cracking since, as a result of the protection from climatic changes afforded to the soil within the periphery of the house, there will be differential settlement between the clay on the inside and that on the outside of the external walls. The effects can be considerably worsened if trees are growing close to the house. Although during the winter the clay will swell, the cracks only partially close and there may be progressive increase in the widths of the cracks each year.

The incidence of cracking can be avoided or reduced by using foundations so deep that the soil movements are unimportant, or by keeping trees so far from the building that the roots do not reach the foundations. It is often cheaper, instead of using deep strip foundations, to support houses on bored pile foundations as shown in Fig. 2.7, the piles being designed to have adequate strength and sufficient resistance to settlement so that relative movements of the piles are unimportant.

Where, as in mining areas, large soil settlements are liable to occur, damage to buildings can be minimized in three very different ways:

(a) The building can be strengthened, by reinforcement or otherwise, so that it can act as a single structural unit which may tilt but will not crack even though its support by the ground is reduced to a few localized areas.

(b) As an alternative to this method, the foundation can be specially designed, either as a strong reinforced concrete raft, or as a structural system of beams and slabs with three-point support from the ground, so that soil movements cause tilting of the foundation and hence of the building, but not relative movements of the building such as will cause cracking.

(c) The building can be so constructed that is is very flexible, relative movements of the soil being accommodated in the structure in a predetermined manner, details of connections and cladding being carefully worked out so that the movements can occur without damage to structural elements or finishes. Provision is then made for easy replacement of cladding units when the relative movements exceed a specified amount.

Whatever method is chosen, the risk of cracking is reduced by making the individual structures as small as is convenient.

*Chapter* 3

# EXCLUSION OF WATER

APART from the obvious desirability of the interior of a building being dry it will be made clear in the chapter on durability (p. 81) how many types of deterioration are associated with the presence of moisture. This emphasizes the importance of keeping moisture outside the outer skin, or at least of ensuring that it cannot penetrate to materials whose deterioration it may hasten. Account must first be taken of the conditions of exposure on the site and of the movement of groundwater.

## RAINFALL AND WIND

A rainfall map, such as is shown in Fig. 3.1, is quite a useful guide to the severity of weather for which a building has to be designed. It does not tell the whole story, however. Wind has a very important influence on rain penetration through lapped joints on pitched roofs and with almost every type of wall construction.

Wherever possible, meteorological information should be supplemented by study of traditional building habits in a given locality, including any evidence of special maintenance dictated by conditions of exposure. Thus, along the sea-front of any seaside resort with a south or west aspect we find external renderings carefully maintained and usually heavily painted. Further inland it is quite common to see the end house of a terrace painted with bitumen or rendered, indicating that the exposure was more severe and the original method of construction inadequate. The designer of a building in a locality with which he is unfamiliar needs to ascertain whether his own favourite forms of construction are in fact adequate for the particular site on which he has to build.

## GROUNDWATER

Except in basements below groundwater level, there is no positive pressure forcing water into a building from the soil on which it stands. Any water entering the fabric from the ground has to rise against the force of gravity. This it may do in two ways: by capillary action in the pores of a material and by diffusion in the form of vapour.

If there are continuous pore paths, groundwater may rise several feet in materials laid in contact with the soil. On the other hand the air in an enclosed space immediately above the soil, such as that below a suspended ground floor, may become saturated with water vapour unless it is ventilated.

## METHOD OF CONSTRUCTION

Most building materials are permeable to water. A broad division between permeable and impermeable materials would not be very helpful, as much

31

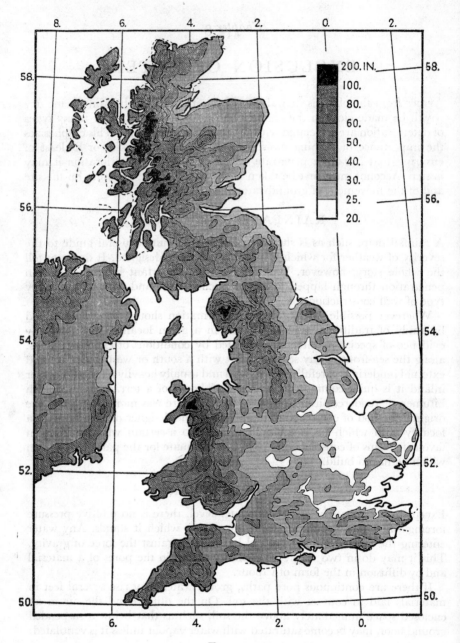

FIG. 3.1

*Average annual rainfall*

depends on questions of degree. Slow penetration of water through a barrier may do no harm if the water can evaporate and be carried away by ventilation as fast as it gets through (although the possibility of efflorescence (p. 83) needs to be kept in mind). But if it can collect on the far side of the barrier, trouble is very likely to arise.

It is safest to regard only metals, glass, hot-poured asphalt or bitumen, and some synthetic resins (plastics) as being *completely* impermeable building materials. Paint films, bituminous emulsions and dense cement products may be impermeable to liquid water but sufficiently permeable to water vapour to be inadequate where a perfect barrier is required.

There are three main principles by which the interior of a building may be kept dry:

(a) the provision, at the outer face or somewhere within the fabric, of a skin of material that is completely impermeable, or impermeable for all practical purposes (but see p. 42, regarding condensation);

(b) the use of materials that are permeable to water, but allow it to pass so slowly that, under the site conditions of wind and rainfall, it will not reach the inner face before a drying-out period ensues;

(c) the provision, behind the outer skin, of a continuous cavity to break the capillary paths along which the moisture travels.

All three principles are commonly employed: asphalt and metal roofing, paint on woodwork, damp-proof courses, window glazing and sheet metal curtain walling are examples of impermeable skins; masonry and roof tiling employ relatively permeable materials; cavity walling, suspended ground floors and roof spaces avoid continuous capillary paths.

The impermeable skin is restricted in its usefulness by the difficulty, with many materials, of designing it to accommodate thermal and other movements without cracking. If such a skin does crack, the consequences are generally serious. Rain water running off adjacent areas pours in through the crack and is then trapped in the fabric; the skin prevents it drying out quickly in fine weather. For the same reason, joints in impermeable skins have to be carefully designed, especially if they are required to accommodate thermal movement. Impermeable materials *must* be used, however, wherever direct *downward* penetration of moisture is to be prevented.

The safety with which permeable materials can be used without cavity construction depends upon exposure conditions, as well as on the permeability of the materials themselves. An important aspect of exposure is the extent to which vertical surfaces can be protected by projecting features such as eaves and string courses, which can be surprisingly efficacious in throwing water clear of the wall surface below. Systems of design whose efficacy depends on this action, and which may have been found completely successful for small buildings, are liable to prove quite inadequate for high buildings; besides the more severe exposure to wind at the top of a high building, there is the reduction in eaves protection.

Cavity construction, in one form or another, is now almost a universal feature of external walling. Besides being, in certain circumstances, the surest form of protection against damp penetration it offers other advantages, such as enhanced thermal insulation.

Dampness caused by condensation can more conveniently be dealt with in the chapter on heat insulation.

## Chapter 4

# HEAT INSULATION

## THE FUNCTION OF HEAT INSULATION

ONE of the main objects in most buildings is to keep fairly constant the temperature of the internal environment independently of the varying climatic conditions externally. The temperature that is needed will depend on the use to which the building is to be put. It may be determined only by the need for human comfort, or by the need for an environment in which certain processes can be carried on satisfactorily, or it may be determined by the requirements for the storage of goods, as in refrigeration chambers. Thus, the internal temperature may be higher or lower than that outside the building and accordingly it may be necessary to introduce heat into or to abstract heat from the building. The natural tendency is for heat to flow from the hotter to the colder zones, partly through the enclosing structure of the building and partly by air change or ventilation.

Any external wall, floor or roof construction will offer some resistance to this heat transfer, but will not entirely prevent it. By providing good heat insulation in the construction, the rate at which the heat transfer takes place can be restricted and the demand on the heating or refrigeration plant can be kept to a reasonable minimum. Insulation may also be used for other purposes, such as the prevention of condensation, the reduction of the risk of water freezing in pipes and the reduction of heat loss from hot-water systems.

In the climate of the British Isles the usual function of structural heat insulation is the reduction of the rate of heat loss from inside to outside the building, but in refrigerated stores the reverse function is served.

The three processes by which heat transfer occur are:

*Conduction*, by which heat flows through or along a material or from one material to another in contact with it.

*Convection*, by which the transfer of heat occurs through the movement of a liquid or a gas.

*Radiation*, by which heat is emitted from a body and transmitted through space as energy without the aid of a solid, liquid or gaseous medium.

## HEAT LOSS FROM BUILDINGS

When heat has to be provided in a building, the conservation of this heat is necessary if excessive consumption of fuel is to be avoided. We have to consider, therefore, the manner in which heat is lost from a warmed building.

Whatever the form of construction, the following factors influence the heat loss:

(1) the climate of the locality;

(2) the degree of exposure of the particular building on the site.

34

*Effect of climate*

There are considerable climatic variations in Great Britain. Some parts are notably colder than others and a quantitative estimate of these variations can be seen in the map, Fig. 4.1.

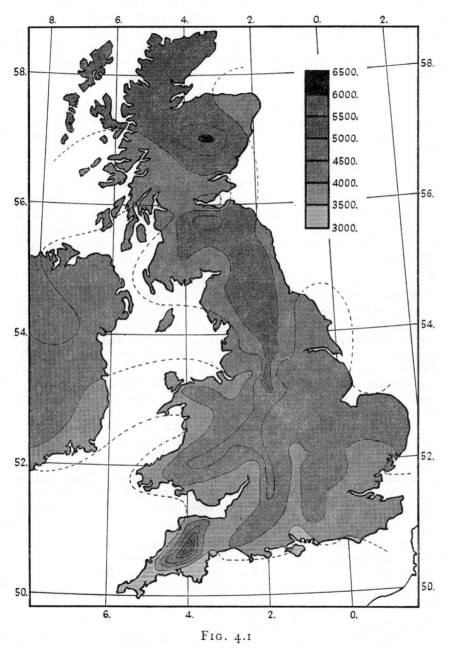

FIG. 4.1

*Variation in annual heating requirements, as measured by 'degree-days'*

The contouring of the map is based on the product of the number of days on which, and the amount by which, the daily mean temperature falls below 60°F. It is assumed that heating is required in buildings when the mean daily outside temperature falls below 60°F.

The map is based on data published by the Meteorological Office and only two of the stations for which information has been collected are more than 1000 ft above sea-level (Princetown on Dartmoor and Braemar). The effects of altitude are not fully taken into account and the map does not truly show the coldness of Snowdon or of Ben Nevis. The effect of altitude amounts to an increase of roughly one degree-day per foot increase in height above sea-level.

The map suggests that for buildings in the north of Scotland or high up on the Yorkshire Moors, the standard of insulation provided may justifiably be better than the standard which is adequate for a building in the Home Counties.

*Effect of site exposure*

Exposure varies between different building sites. A house on high ground with full exposure to the prevailing winds and rain will lose more heat than one sheltered by trees or other buildings. Sunshine gives a marked diminution in the heat requirements. Any form of shelter that encroaches too closely on the building and cuts off the sun will increase the heat requirements, though it is likely that a good wind-break may be beneficial.

*Thermal conductivity*

Measurements are made in laboratories of a physical property usually termed the 'thermal conductivity' ($k$) of a material. This is a rate of heat transfer, usually expressed as the number of heat units (B.t.u.) conducted through unit thickness (in.), over unit area (sq. ft) in unit of time (hour) under the action of unit temperature difference between the faces. The British Thermal Unit (B.t.u.) is defined as the quantity of heat required to raise the temperature of 1 lb of water from 63°F to 64°F. The $k$-value of a material varies with its density, porosity and moisture content and also with temperature.

Thermal conductivity alone, however, does not determine the rate of heat flow between the air inside an enclosure and the air outside.

*Thermal resistivity*

In calculations it is often convenient to use the reciprocal of thermal conductivity, i.e. $1/k$, a quantity called 'thermal resistivity'. This value is a measure of the resistance to heat flow provided by unit thickness of a material.

*Surface resistance*

Generally, resistance will be offered to the transfer of heat between the surface of a material and the adjacent air. This resistance may vary with the emissivity of the surface (rate of radiant heat emission), its roughness, the rate of air movement across it, its orientation or position, and with the temperature of the air and of other bodies facing it.

*Air-to-air heat transmission coefficient 'U'*

The flow of heat from the warmed air inside the building to the cold air outside is governed by the resistance to heat transfer from the warm air to the inner surface of the building shell, the resistance to conduction through the shell, and the resistance to transfer from the external surface of the building to the cold outer air (influenced by wind and evaporation) or to the ground. Radiation loss (on balance) depends on the emissivity of the surface and on the surroundings—e.g. clear sky, clouds, other buildings. With these complexities the problem of heat transfer would become almost insoluble under everyday conditions of design practice, and it is customary to make use of certain broad simplifications, basing calculations on overall 'air-to-air' coefficients of heat transmission.

The heat loss through a wall, for example, is computed from the following simple equation:

Loss of heat $= UA\,(t_1 - t_0)$

$U =$ overall coefficient of heat transfer, an empirical value depending on the situation and exposure of the wall and on the materials of which the wall is built and their thickness,

$A =$ area of the wall,

$t_1 =$ temperature of inside air,

$t_0 =$ temperature of outside air.

It should be clearly understood that what is nowadays widely referred to as the '$U$-value' of a construction, although commonly expressed to two places of decimals (suggesting considerable exactness), is not a constant value. In practice the rate of heat flow through a construction bounding a building will vary with solar radiation, wind and moisture conditions.

With some constructions, particularly those with open joints through which wind can penetrate into the overall thickness of the construction (into a roof space, for example), the variation in the $U$-value may be considerable throughout the year. In other constructions such as solid masonry walling, the variation is comparatively small. The $U$-value is useful, however, for comparing the insulation values of various wall, floor and roof constructions and for estimating the heat loss from a building in order to design the heating plant or to estimate the fuel consumption necessary for heating the building.

In general, for estimating fuel consumption for space heating over the period of a heating season, an appropriate heat-transmission coefficient to use is the average value for the season. For designing the heating plant, it may be necessary with some constructions to use a value typical of the days on which heat loss through the construction is greatest.

As already mentioned, it is possible to measure, in the laboratory, the thermal conductivity of a homogeneous material; in a similar manner, the thermal conductance of a composite structure can be measured. There are difficulties in applying these measurements, however. The moisture content of a material at the time of testing may have a considerable effect on the value obtained, and it is not by any means a simple matter to ensure that test specimens are conditioned to a moisture content which is fairly representative of their condition in service.

Special wall and roof laboratories were constructed at the Building Research Station to measure the heat transmission coefficients of various wall and roof constructions under the normal exposure conditions at the Station; in these laboratories, test walls or roofs form part of the external structure.

The *U*-values of many wall, floor and roof constructions that are either basically homogeneous (such as a monolithic concrete wall) or that consist of a number of continuous parallel homogeneous layers (such as a solid concrete wall, rendered externally and lined internally with cork and plaster) can be calculated easily from a knowledge of the appropriate thermal conductivities and thicknesses of the materials and the external and internal surface resistances (see p. 36 and Part III).

In other constructions, such as those with posts and panel infilling, calculation is much more complex and a measured value is often desirable.

*Thermal capacity*

In the general problem of the heating or cooling of buildings the thermal capacity of the enclosing walls, floor and roof and of the interior of the building sometimes plays an important part.

Thermal capacity is a measure of the quantity of heat required to raise the temperature of a mass of material; looked at another way, it is the capacity of a body to store heat. Thermal conductivity and thermal transmittance are concerned with the rate at which heat will flow through a material or construction when a difference exists between the temperatures on either side and when this differences remains constant. Under these conditions there is a progressive decrease in temperature, a temperate gradient, across the material or construction from the warmer to the cooler side.

In practice these steady temperature conditions seldom, if ever, occur in buildings. The external temperature is continually varying with weather conditions and the internal temperature, particularly with intermittent heating, is also variable. Under these changing temperature conditions surrounding a material or construction, the natural flow of heat from a warmer to a cooler area tends to adjust the temperature gradient accordingly. The absorbing or giving up of heat by a material is not instantaneous and a delay or time-lag is inevitable. Under the influence of a rise or a fall in the surrounding temperature, a material or a building of high thermal capacity will take longer than a material or building of low thermal capacity to follow this temperature change.

These characteristics may be beneficial; for example in hot climates, very thick and heavy wall constructions buffer the effect of very high external daytime temperatures on the internal climate of the building. On the other hand, in buildings that have to be heated, if the building is cold, the rate of warming will depend partly on the thermal capacity of the structure and its contents. With intermittent heating, allowance has to be made for this, either in the sizing of the heating plant to give adequate output, or in the running of the heating system to provide a suitable preheating period.

In rooms that are used occasionally and therefore require only intermittent heating for comfort, lining the interior surfaces with material of low thermal capacity will reduce the heat input required to warm the room; as less heat is stored in the enclosing structure, however, the room will cool more rapidly when the heat input is stopped.

For many buildings in the British Isles, thermal capacity is unlikely to be a deciding factor in the choice of construction. In multi-storey buildings particularly, the general mass of the whole structure is likely to be the determining influence on the time lag. In a small single-storey building the thermal capacity of the walls and roof is likely to have a greater significance, although even in these cases other considerations may predominate and the heating system and heating schedule may be adapted to the thermal capacity of the structure.

*Ventilation heat loss*

Air change or ventilation of a heated building, whether deliberate or fortuitous, involves the replacement of warm air within the building by colder air from outside. It therefore contributes to the total loss of heat and to the demand on the heating plant. The proportion of heat lost by ventilation to that lost by conduction will depend on the ventilation rate and on the thermal transmittance and area of the external shell. In a typical two-storey semi-detached house of normal brick wall and tiled roof construction the ventilation heat loss may be about one-third of the total.

The amount of heat required to raise the temperature of 1 cu. ft of air through 1 °F is about 0·019 British thermal unit. Therefore the heat loss from a building due to ventilation is calculated as follows:

$$\begin{matrix} \text{Ventilation} \\ \text{heat loss} \\ \text{per hour} \\ \text{(B.t.u.)} \end{matrix} = \begin{matrix} \text{Internal volume} \\ \text{of building} \\ \text{(cu. ft)} \end{matrix} \times \begin{matrix} \text{No. of air} \\ \text{changes} \\ \text{per hour} \end{matrix} \times 0\cdot019 \times \begin{matrix} \text{Temperature} \\ \text{difference between} \\ \text{inside and outside} \\ \text{(°F)} \end{matrix}$$

## THE ECONOMICS OF HEAT INSULATION

In some heated buildings the heat input may be restricted by the capacity of the heating plant or by the willingness of the owner or occupier to supply heat. Under such conditions, improved insulation may contribute partly to reducing fuel consumption and partly to providing a higher internal temperature; its value must take both into account.

For buildings in which a specified internal temperature is to be maintained the standard of insulation will directly influence the quantity of heat to be put into or extracted from the building; it will thus influence the size of the heating or cooling plant and the consumption of fuel.

An economic appraisal of heat insulation for a heated building must consider

(a) the cost of providing insulation additional to that inherent in the structure as designed to satisfy other requirements,

(b) the rate of heat loss from the building, taking account of the areas and U-values of the exposed parts,

(c) the difference in temperature to be maintained between inside and outside,

(d) the capital cost of the heating plant required,

(e) the continuing expenditure on fuel, which will depend on the cost of the fuel and the efficiency of the heating system.

It is unlikely that the details of heat insulation will play an important part in the formative stages of the design for many new buildings, when broad considerations of aesthetic, economic and structural requirements are predominant. It is important, however, that it should be properly considered at an early stage during the detailed preparation of a building design. At this stage the cost and insulation values of possible constructions for the external walls, roof and ground floor can be compared and any extra cost in providing a higher standard of insulation weighed against the possible savings in capital and running costs of the heating installation.

No simple rigid appraisal of the economic limits of insulation can be applied generally to all buildings. The addition of a given amount of insulation to constructions with different $U$-values does not give equal reductions in those values. The cost of reducing the $U$-value of a construction is not necessarily proportional to the reduction achieved. Individual buildings and constructions should therefore be judged on their merits; in general, good insulation will be economic where a high temperature is maintained and the cost of heating is high.

As assessment of the reduction in the heat requirements for, say, a factory, by improving the insulation of the roof may be obtained as follows:

| Reduction in the heat requirements for a heating season (B.t.u./ sq. ft roof area) | = | Reduction in $U$-value (B.t.u./ sq. ft h °F) | × | Mean difference in temperature between inside and outside (°F) | × | No. of hours in heating season. |

Thus, if the $U$-value of the roof is reduced from $1 \cdot 40$ to $0 \cdot 40$ B.t.u./sq. ft h °F, if the mean seasonal inside and outside temperatures are 55°F and 45°F respectively, and the length of the heating season is 5500 hours, the reduction in heat flow through 1 sq. ft of the roof for the season is 55 000 B.t.u., i.e. approximately $\frac{1}{2}$ therm. In this way the cost of improving the roof insulation can be considered against the heat saving.

The mean outside temperature is obtainable from meteorological data. The mean inside temperature will be governed by the type of heating system and the method of operation, particularly where occupation of the building is intermittent and the temperature requirement for the building is reduced during the unoccupied periods. The extent of such a reduction will depend on the flexibility and controllability of the heat output from the system, and of course on the effectiveness with which these features are operated in practice. The building designer should obtain the advice of the heating engineer on these matters so that a combined appraisal of the economic aspects may be obtained. This appraisal should take into account future running costs over a selected period of years, and the possibility of variation in fuel prices should not be overlooked.

# CONDENSATION

Moisture is present normally in the atmosphere in the form of water vapour; the quantity in external air depends on climatic conditions, and the quantity in the air inside a building depends on these and also on the ventilation rate and the water-vapour production or extraction rate in the building.

The amount of water vapour that a given quantity of air can hold increases with the temperature. When air at any particular temperature contains as much water vapour as it can hold, the air is said to be saturated. The temperature at which air with any particular moisture content is saturated is known as its dew point. If its temperature is increased and no further vapour added, the air is no longer saturated; alternatively, if its temperature is decreased, the excess vapour that can no longer be held by the air will be deposited as condensation.

The humidity or moisture content of air is the amount of water vapour present in unit volume or unit weight of that air; it is usually expressed as grains per cu. ft or as lb per lb of air. The relative humidity is the amount of vapour present in air expressed as a percentage of the maximum amount that the air could hold at the same temperature. Thus the relative humidity alone does not specify the amount of water vapour present in air; to do this the temperature also must be known.

Another measure of the water-vapour content of air is the vapour pressure. This pressure increases with the vapour content of the air; it is often expressed as millibars. Of the total pressure exerted by air (a mixture of gases), the vapour pressure is that portion that is contributed by the water vapour present in the air.

*Transfer of water vapour*

Movement or transfer of water vapour will take place with the movement of air. Thus, if the air inside a building has a higher water-vapour content than the external air, as is usually the case, ventilation will remove water vapour from the building. Provided the removal rate is greater than the rate of production of vapour inside the building, the ventilation will reduce the water-vapour content of the internal air.

The water vapour present in a region of high vapour pressure will tend to spread to an adjacent region of lower vapour pressure independently of any gross movement of the air. When the vapour pressure inside a building is higher than that outside, the enclosing walls and roof will generally act as an obstruction to this vapour movement. The effectiveness of this obstruction will depend partly on the materials and partly on the presence of through-gaps or openings in the walls and roof.

Water vapour can diffuse through permeable materials when the moisture content of the air, and hence the vapour pressure, is greater on one side than on the other. In general, the quantity of vapour transferred through unit area of a homogeneous material in unit time will be governed by the difference in the vapour pressures on the two sides, by the diffusion characteristic of the material (i.e. its vapour diffusivity) and by the thickness of the material. Materials impermeable to moisture vapour can serve as a barrier to its transfer; obviously their effectiveness in this respect will be reduced if there are gaps at joints or if cracks develop in the material.

*Surface condensation*

When the temperature of any surface within a building, such as the internal face of a wall, floor or roof construction, is at a temperature below the dew point of the adjacent air, some of the moisture in the air will condense on that surface. Depending on the nature of the surface, the condensate may either be absorbed by the material (perhaps remaining unnoticeable) or it may appear as liquid water on the surface.

Surface condensation will not occur if

(i) the temperature of the surface is kept above the dew point of the adjacent air by adequate heating or by sufficient insulation behind the surface, or if

(ii) the humidity of the air is limited so that its dew point is below the temperature of the surface.

With occasional or intermittent surface condensation, an absorbent surface is advantageous, as it can retain a limited quantity of condensate until conditions change and re-evaporation can take place.

*Condensation within the thickness of a construction*

Condensation in buildings is not necessarily confined to exposed surfaces, but may, under certain conditions, occur within a material or on a surface within the thickness of a wall, roof or floor construction; this has sometimes been referred to as interstitial condensation.

In the discussion of thermal insulation, reference has been made to the temperature gradient across a construction when there is a difference between the temperatures on either side. When the air temperature inside is higher than that outside, the internal room surface of an external wall will usually be above the dew point in the air in the room. If the inside-to-outside temperature drop is great enough, then at some positions within the thickness of the wall the temperatures will be below the dew point of the room air. Broadly speaking, if that room air penetrates the wall construction without any reduction in its vapour pressure, condensation will occur where it meets temperatures below its dew point.

Many constructions, such as the traditional brick wall, do not offer a complete barrier at any point in their thickness to the transfer of water vapour and when, as is often the case, the inside vapour pressure is greater than that outside the building, vapour will diffuse through the construction to the outside air. A progressive reduction in vapour pressure then occurs across the wall. Although the temperature within the wall may fall below the dew point of the room air, the reduction in vapour pressure across the wall may prevent any condensation within the wall thickness. Whether interstitial condensation will occur depends, therefore, on both the temperature and the vapour-pressure gradients across the construction.

Modern constructions often include materials that are impervious to moisture vapour and they stop the diffusion of water vapour from the inside to the outside air and prevent the progressive reduction in vapour pressure across the construction. Metal, asphalt, and bitumen-felt finishes to roofs, metal and glass claddings to walls are examples, their primary function generally being the exclusion of rain. Their position is therefore usually on the external face which, for a heated building, is the colder side of the construction; the temperature at this external face during the heating season may often be below the dew point of the internal air, and condensation may then be expected within the construction. The condensate may be absorbed or held by the material in the construction and as the external temperature rises again it may re-evaporate without causing any trouble. If, however, the internal air has a high moisture content, as in a humidified factory, and if the condensation period is sufficiently long, then trouble may arise from saturation of part of the construction; dripping of condensate into the building space may also result.

A vapour barrier may, however, be provided internally, i.e. on the warmer side of the construction, to prevent the entry into it of moisture vapour; with certain constructions the vapour barrier may be provided at some position within the thickness of the construction.

The principles discussed under the section on surface condensation (p. 41) may be applied in considering the question of condensation on a vapour barrier used as an internal surface or at some intermediate position within the construction.

In practice, the provision and maintenance of a perfect and complete barrier on the internal surface may frequently be difficult. Where it is likely that vapour may pass the barrier, either by movement through the material or through joints or cracks, it is a reasonable safeguard to require that this vapour may be able to escape to the external air. For this purpose, ventilation or diffusion gaps may be provided or, alternatively, the materials on the colder side (normally the external side) of the barrier should offer less resistance to moisture vapour transfer than the barrier itself.

# Chapter 5

# VENTILATION

VENTILATION may be required for a number of reasons. In inhabited buildings the air-change rate must be sufficient to dilute odours, smoke, etc., to an acceptable level (the air supply required for this will more than suffice to meet the air required for breathing). Suggested minimum rates of air supply to buildings for human habitation are given in the British Standard CP.3 (Chap. I (c) (1950) 'Ventilation'). In industrial buildings where heat or moisture is liberated, the standard of ventilation may be based on the need to limit the rise in temperature or humidity and this to maintain comfortable conditions; in buildings where dust or fumes are produced by some manufacturing process, ventilation may be used to limit the concentration of such contaminants and thus reduce possible health hazards. Reduction in humidity, dust and fumes may also help in the general maintenance of the building structure. Buildings in hot climates may call for different treatment: in hot dry climates copious ventilation at night with low ventilation during the day will help to limit the rise of temperature in the building; in hot humid climates the aim may be to provide high ventilation rates at all times so as to promote air movement within the building. Consideration of such aspects will lead to the formulation of desirable standards, and the general design problem then is to provide the required flow of air, either by natural or by mechanical means.

Where close control of the rate of air supply and its distribution, or of the rate of extraction, is essential, a mechanical system will be adopted. For most buildings, however, natural ventilation will be adequate; in many types, e.g. dwellings, offices, the areas and dispositions of the openings provided will be largely based on previous experience, but where high rates of ventilation are necessary, as in factories where considerable quantities of heat and steam are liberated, the areas of the openings required should be calculated. The calculation is made in terms of the two forces causing natural air flow: the differences in wind pressures on exposed surfaces, and the flue or stack pressure due to a difference in the temperatures of the air inside and outside the building.

## VENTILATION DUE TO WIND PRESSURE

When wind blows at right-angles to one face of a rectangular building on an exposed site, a positive pressure is produced on the windward face, and a negative pressure on the leeward face. Negative pressures will also occur on the other sides and, if there are openings in the surfaces, the general air flow will be inwards through the windward openings and outwards through the openings in the other three sides. If the wind direction is at 45° to one of the faces, positive pressures will be produced on the two windward faces and negative pressures on the two leeward faces. The pressures at openings

44

in a simple pitched roof will depend on the pitch of the roof and to some extent on the length of the roof in relation to the height. Wind-tunnel tests have shown that roof pressures are generally negative, except on the windward side of a roof with a pitch greater than 30°. With a flat roof, the largest negative pressures will occur at the windward end of the roof and there may be a tendency, particularly with a large roof, for air to eddy down and give positive pressures farther along the roof; with such a roof, ventilators in the windward end of the roof would extract air which could enter in turn through openings in the leeward end of the roof. With more complex roof constructions, such as monitor roofs, local positive pressures will occur on windward upstands and local negative pressures on the leeward ones, and these pressures will be superimposed on the general pressure pattern. Where positive pressures are expected on the roof surfaces and extraction is required, vertical stacks carried up above the roof may be used.

In calculating the air flow through a building, it is not possible to make exact allowances for all the effects of local disturbances and some simplifications must be adopted. The simplest pressure pattern is that occurring around an isolated rectangular building with the wind at right-angles to one face. If the outlets have the same total area as the inlets on the windward face the rate of air flow is given by

$$V = 3150 \, Av$$
where $V$ = rate of air flow in cubic feet per hour
$A$ = area of inlets in square feet
$v$ = wind speed in miles per hour.

If the direction of the wind is not at right-angles to the face of the building, the wind pressure developed across the building will be less than assumed in the above calculation, e.g. if the wind is at 45° to the face of the building, the air flow will be reduced by about half.

In either case, if the total area of the outlets is appreciably different from the total area of the inlets, then another value must be substituted for the figure 3150 in the equation. The value to be adopted is given in the following table:

| $\dfrac{\text{Total area of outlets}}{\text{Total area of inlets}}$ | Value to be used |
|:---:|:---:|
| 1 | 3150 |
| 2 | 4000 |
| 3 | 4250 |
| 4 | 4350 |
| 5 | 4400 |
| $\frac{3}{4}$ | 2700 |
| $\frac{1}{2}$ | 2000 |
| $\frac{1}{4}$ | 1100 |

As an example, consider the ventilation caused by a wind of 10 m.p.h. blowing at right-angles to one face of an isolated rectangular building which has openings of 10 sq. ft in each side. There will be 10 sq. ft of inlet on the windward face and a total outlet of 30 sq. ft in the other three sides. From the table, the value 4250 should be used in the expression for calculating air flow, i.e.

$$V = 4250 \times 10 \times 10 = 425\,000 \text{ cu. ft per hour}$$

If the wind were at 45°, the openings in the two windward faces would act as inlets and the other two as outlets, so that allowing for the 50 per cent reduction due to the wind being at 45°, the air flow would be calculated as

$$V = \tfrac{1}{2} \times 3150 \times 20 \times 10 = 315\,000 \text{ cu. ft per hour.}$$

The effect of sheltering by adjacent buildings must now be considered. Wind pressures on buildings in built-up areas are much reduced by general screening, and measurements have shown that wind speeds are generally about one-third of those in open country. Wind speeds in suburban areas lie between these extremes, and can probably be taken as about two-thirds of the speeds in open country. In estimating ventilation caused by wind, the wind speed appropriate to the site must be chosen.

## VENTILATION DUE TO STACK PRESSURE

Natural ventilation may also occur when the air inside a building is at a different temperature from the air outside. The extreme case of stack pressure is, of course, the 'pull' of a heated flue, but even the comparatively small differences between the general air temperature inside a building and the temperature of the outside air can induce high rates of air flow through openings at different heights. In a heated building, in the absence of wind, cold air from outside will tend to enter through any openings at low level and warm air will tend to leave through openings at high level. The rate of air flow will increase with the difference in level of inlet and outlet, the areas of the openings, and the temperature difference. The rate of air flow when the outlet area is equal to that of the inlet can be calculated from the equation

$$V = 540\ A\sqrt{ht}$$

where $V$ = air flow in cubic feet per hour
$\quad\quad A$ = area of inlet in square feet
$\quad\quad h$ = height in feet between inlet and outlet
and $t$ = temperature difference in °F between the air inside and outside the building.

Again there will be a change in the multiplier if the total area of the outlets is different from that of the inlets. The values to be used are given below.

| $\dfrac{\text{Area of outlets}}{\text{Area of inlets}}$ | Value to be substituted for 540 |
|:---:|:---:|
| 1 | 540 |
| 2 | 680 |
| 3 | 720 |
| 4 | 740 |
| 5 | 745 |
| $\tfrac{3}{4}$ | 455 |
| $\tfrac{1}{2}$ | 340 |
| $\tfrac{1}{4}$ | 185 |

In the example of the calculation of air flow due to wind, a building with openings of 10 sq. ft in each face was considered. Assuming that these openings are half at high and half at low level, the difference in heights being 20 ft, the air flow due to a temperature difference of 20°F will, in the absence of wind, be

$$V = 540 \times 20 \times \sqrt{20 \times 20} = 216\ 000 \text{ cu. ft per hour.}$$

## VENTILATION DUE TO WIND AND STACK PRESSURES COMBINED

The examples of the calculation of air flow have shown that for a given building, a wind of 10 m.p.h., acting alone, would produce an air flow of 425 000 cu. ft per hour, and that the air flow due to a temperature difference of 20°F would, in the absence of wind, amount to 216 000 cu. ft per hour. When both wind and stack pressures are acting, the air flow should strictly be estimated by combining the pressures, but in practice it is generally sufficient to calculate the air flow caused by each pressure acting by itself, and to take the larger estimate. In the example, the wind of 10 m.p.h. would swamp the flow due to stack pressure and the total air flow would be approximately that caused by wind alone. If the building were in a built-up area, the effective wind speed would be reduced to one-third of the free wind speed in open country and the air flow would be reduced proportionately. In this case, the calculation of air flow due to wind gives 140 000 cu. ft per hour. This is lower than the air flow caused by a temperature difference of 20°F, so that under these conditions, stack pressure would predominate and the air flow could be taken as 216 000 cu. ft per hour.

## VENTILATION OPENINGS

The ventilation rate obtained by these natural forces with fixed openings in a building will show large variations throughout the year. In some cases this may be acceptable, and the areas required for a given average rate of ventilation can be estimated from the above type of calculation. For many buildings, however, more constant rates will be required and provisions for either manual or automatic control of the areas of the openings must be made. The lower the wind speed or the temperature difference the larger will be the openings required for a given rate, and it is obviously difficult to have openings large enough for the odd occasions when the forces are extremely low. The approach to design is therefore best done on the basis that the ventilation should be equal to or greater than a given standard for a reasonable proportion of the time. It is also important at the design stage to ensure that incidental ventilation through gaps in the construction will not be excessive when wind speeds or temperature differences are high, e.g. an openable window with 25 ft of crack around it will be equivalent to openings of 12 and $4\frac{1}{2}$ sq. in. if the face clearances are $\frac{1}{16}$ in. and $\frac{1}{32}$ in. respectively, but with weather stripping the equivalent opening would be as low as $\frac{1}{2}$ sq. in. Air flow through masonry or plastered walls is negligible.

For estimating the maximum areas required for openings the local variations of wind and temperature difference have to be taken into account.
Fig. 5.1 shows the percentage of the time when the wind speed in a typical
open inland area in Britain is above a given value. It will be seen, for instance,
that for about 80 per cent of the time the speed is above 3½ m.p.h.; for 50
per cent of the time it is above 7 m.p.h.; and for 20 per cent it is above
11 m.p.h. The choice of wind speed for design purposes must depend on the
percentage of time for which ventilation rates below a given minimum can
be tolerated; it may be sufficient to provide a rate which for 50 per cent of
the time is above a given value; where the ventilation requirements are more
demanding it might be preferable to ensure that rates are above a given
standard for 80 per cent of the time.

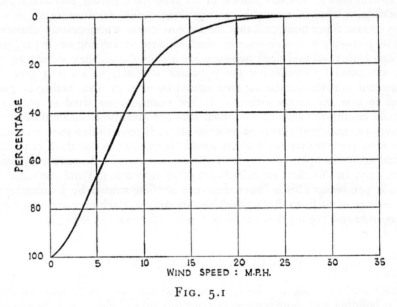

FIG. 5.1

*Percentage of time when wind-speed is above a given value in a typical
inland area in Britain*

It may be that the prevailing wind is at right-angles to one side of a
building in open country, in which case the above wind speeds might be
adopted; for buildings in suburban and built-up areas the corresponding
design wind speeds would be two-thirds and one-third, respectively, of the
wind speed in open country as given above. The lower wind speeds are,
however, more variable in direction and particularly in built-up areas it
becomes more difficult to assess the appropriate mean wind direction. This
variability reduces the effective wind speed by about a further one-third,
giving design wind speeds in suburban and built-up areas of four-ninths and
two-ninths, respectively, of the speed in open country.

Similarly, systems using stack pressures can be designed in terms of the
difference between the temperatures of the air inside and outside the building.
In Great Britain in winter, the maximum temperature difference for heated

buildings can exceed 35°F, and this figure could be used to check that incidental ventilation is unlikely to be excessive in cold weather. The size of openings required for winter ventilation in mild weather should be evaluated, using a temperature difference of about 5°F; then, when the outside temperature rises above 60°F, with an inside temperature of 65°F, it should be possible to bring the summer ventilation system into action. Temperature differences during working hours in summer are likely to be small unless heat is generated inside the building or there is considerable solar gain. In such cases, the rate of air flow required to limit the temperature rise to a given value can be estimated in terms of the rate of heat liberation (one cubic foot of air with a temperature rise of 1°F will carry away 0·019 B.t.u.) and the size of openings required can then be obtained from the above calculation.

The positioning and distribution of the openings required is particularly important in occupied buildings. For winter ventilation using wind pressure, the openings should be at a fairly high level and well distributed so that the entering cold air can, as it falls, mix more thoroughly with the heated air in the building and thus reduce the risk of draughts. When using a system designed on stack pressure for winter ventilation, the outlets should be as high as possible, but it will not usually be practicable to make use of the full height of the buildings to promote stack pressure by having the inlets at ground level. In occupied buildings it will be better to raise the inlets and reduce risk of draughts, the reduction in the distance between inlets and outlets being compensated by using rather larger areas. For summer ventilation, particularly where personal cooling is important, the openings utilizing wind pressures can be at low level so that air movement can be induced in the working zone; similarly, inlets for systems using stack pressure can be at ground level.

## Chapter 6

# SOUND INSULATION

## THE PROBLEM

THE need for special attention to sound insulation in buildings has increased over the last half-century, owing to increasing population densities, changing habits of the community and changes in building practice. Flat-dwelling is an outstanding example of a trend that greatly increases the vulnerability to noise; moreover, nearly every home now has its radio, television or gramophone. Reasonable sound insulation in buildings can be obtained only by due regard to the principles underlying sound transmission.

Sound insulation cannot be considered with reference to isolated walls and floors as if the problem reduced to the screening effect of a given barrier between a source of noise and an observer. The sound may travel from one part of a building to another, or from outside the building to the inside, by any clear air paths, open windows or doors, or narrow cracks, such as the spaces round ill-fitting doors; it may be transmitted through a wall or floor dividing two rooms; it may travel along parts of the structure—for instance, a continuous wall or floor common to several rooms—or along pipes. The structural problem of sound insulation must therefore be considered first in terms of the whole planning and construction. It is also necessary to consider two types of noise: that which has its origin as airborne sound, e.g. from voices, radio, typewriters, and that which originates in contacts with the structure, e.g. footsteps, hammering and many machinery noises.

Considerable advances have been made in recent years in research into sound insulation, and for details reference should be made to the technical literature. Here it is practicable only to sketch the main outlines and principles of the subject. A word of explanation should be added, however, on certain omissions that may be apparent in comparing the treatment of the subject here with that given in earlier editions of this work. Among the first fruits of an extensive programme of laboratory and field investigation commenced since the last war, has been the discovery that the problem of sound transmission is in practice a good deal more complex than was previously realized, or is not amenable to the forms of analysis previously used, and that several ideas and design rules corresponding to the pre-war stage of knowledge now need to be discarded or modified. Current investigations have not, however, reached the stage where more satisfactory design rules can confidently be formulated. This applies particularly to indirect sound transmission. Details are available of many measurements made in actual buildings of specific types of construction, and these will give the designer some guidance, but it must be recognized that a host of sociological, psychological and economic factors are involved; physical measurements do not by any means tell the whole story.

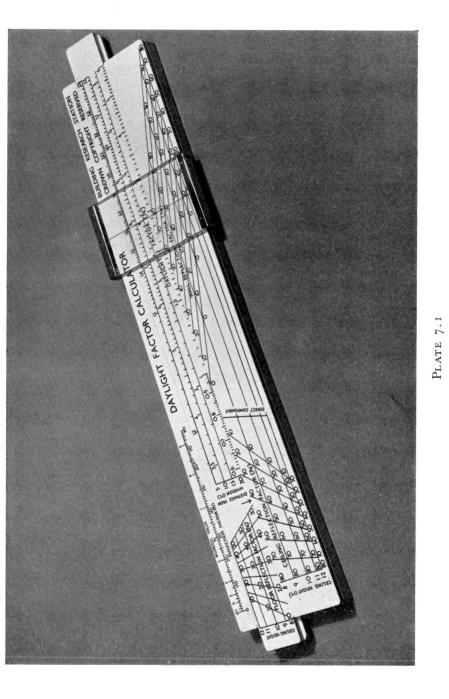

PLATE 7.1

B.R.S. daylight factor slide rule

C*

PLATE 7.2

*Horizontal window baffle (See also Fig. 7.6)*

PLATE 7.3

*Opposite-side lighting in classroom in Sweden*

PLATE 7.4
*Heliodon table with model in position*

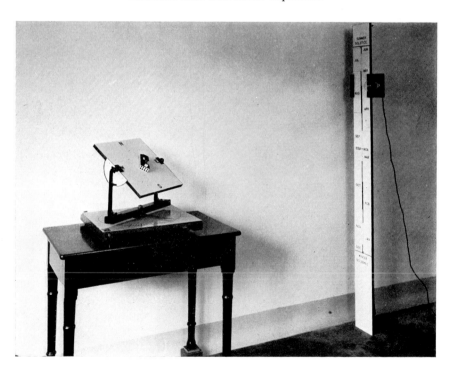

PLATE 7.5
*The heliodon in use*

PLATE 7.6
*Use of light surfaces to reduce glare*

PLATE 7.7
*Daylight factor meter*

*Planning*

The problem of sound insulation is one of ensuring adequately quiet conditions in the various parts of buildings. The first essential is good planning; details of construction and the choice of materials are important but cannot compensate for errors in the plan. It is essential that every precaution should be taken in the layout of a building, so that those parts in which quiet is needed shall be as remote as possible from sources of noise. This, coupled with the prevention of the noise at its source, is often the most useful weapon at the designer's disposal in reducing the problem of noise in a building; but, even so, in most cases structural precautions will be needed in addition.

## UNITS OF MEASUREMENT

Sound is a form of energy, and its transmission in a building can be studied by measuring the energy levels, at different locations or in different rooms, of sounds of a number of specific frequencies. The ratio of the energy of the sound at its source to that at any other location is known as the sound-reduction factor and is expressed as a number of decibels (dB). The sound-reduction factor is used as a measure of the comparative efficiencies of different forms of construction as insulators to sounds of different frequencies (pitches). For general purposes, the average of the reduction factors at all the frequencies may be an adequate criterion. The decibel scale is also used for defining noise level by basing it on an arbitrary zero approximating to the threshold of audibility of sounds of 1000 cycles per second (c/s).

The decibel, being an objective measurement obtained by physical instruments, is only approximately related (by resorting to a logarithmic scale) to the sensation of loudness registered by the human ear. To express this sensation of loudness with greater accuracy the unit of the 'phon' has been adopted (see Appendix I). Phon readings of noise level are useful on occasion, but the phon is unsuitable for general use in defining noise because it is not directly related to physical measurements of sound energy.

There is an unfamiliarity about the decibel scale of measurement which sometimes causes misunderstanding. It is logarithmic. This means, for example, that an increase of 10 in the sound-reduction factor on the decibel scale (e.g. from 40 dB to 50 dB) corresponds to a reduction of the sound energy transmitted to one-tenth; an increase of 20 decibels corresponds to a reduction to one-hundredth, and so on. This relationship corresponds roughly to that between loudness as heard by the ear and intensity as measured in terms of energy; a sound where intensity is successively doubled (or multiplied by any constant figure) will be *heard* to increase in loudness by roughly equal steps; in other words, loudness varies as the logarithm of the intensity.

Neither the insulating value of a structure nor the sensitivity of the ear is constant for all frequencies of sound. To simplify matters of sound insulation, use has generally been made of an 'average sound reduction factor', which is the average of a representative number of sound reduction factors (in decibels) over a frequency range from 100 to 3200 cycles per second. The loss of accuracy involved in using this figure is often more than offset by the convenience it affords, but in some circumstances it is advisable to design more exactly for sound reduction at specific frequencies.

## MECHANISM OF SOUND TRANSMISSION

An airborne sound may travel direct to the ear of the observer by a continuous air path. In addition, the compression wave in the air due to a noise source in a room may set up vibrations in the surrounding structure, which in turn create compression waves in the air in the room where the observer is situated.

This leads us immediately to three basic principles of sound insulation:

(1) Continuous air paths enable sound to travel with very little fall-off in intensity.

(2) The more massive the structure the less will be the intensity of vibration imparted to it by a compression wave in the air.

(3) Any break in the continuity of the structure, whether a complete gap or a cushioning layer, provides a more or less efficient barrier to the transmission across the gap of any vibrations in the structure. On the other hand, a break in continuity may leave some parts of the structure more free to vibrate and to radiate sound; also, the thin layer of air in normal cavity walls act as a fairly stiff 'cushion', capable of transmitting quite a lot of vibration from one leaf to the other.

To these may be added a fourth principle:

(4) Sound waves in air, or vibrations in a structure, can be transmitted with little loss of intensity along what might appear to be very insignificant paths. An uncovered keyhole may noticeably reduce the insulating effect of a heavy door; a few wall ties of the heavy strip pattern may transmit vibrations at almost full strength from one leaf of a cavity wall to the other.

The chief principles for practical purposes are those of mass and of freedom from 'short-circuits', especially air paths. A definite relationship has been established between the sound-reduction factor and the weight of single homogeneous barriers: the reduction factor increases roughly in direct proportion to the logarithm of the weight per unit area of the barrier—provided there is no direct air path. With excessive air leakage the insulation may be very considerably reduced.

The curve showing the approximate relationship between the average sound-reduction factor and the logarithm of the weight per sq. ft, as derived from tests carried out at the National Physical Laboratory, is shown in Fig. 6.1. From this curve it will at once be apparent that whereas weight alone is, for practical purposes, the factor determining the sound insulation of single walls, nevertheless, for all but the very lightest partitions, small differences in actual weight have little significance. Each doubling of the weight is seen to have equal significance—increasing the insulation by steps of about 5 dB. This relationship applies approximately to all forms of barrier that are more or less solid, including walls of hollow masonry blocks, and indicates that the nature of the material used is of little significance provided there are no air paths right through it.

The third of the basic principles referred to the effect of a break in continuity within a structure. Different considerations govern the application of this principle according to whether a wall or a floor is concerned, and detailed discussion is therefore deferred to the appropriate later parts of this book. Here it will be sufficient to point out that structural discontinuity at once conflicts with stability requirements; the two must be considered together if a satisfactory compromise is to be achieved.

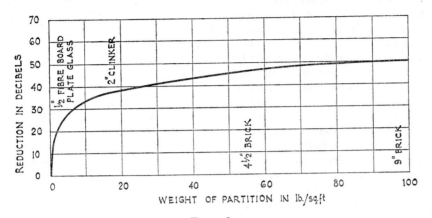

FIG. 6.1

*Graph showing transmission of sound related to weight of structures*

## SOUND ABSORPTION

Sound insulation and sound absorption are very often confused. The function of a sound-absorbent material is to reduce sound reflected from a surface, whereas the function of a sound-insulating construction is to reduce sound passing through it. If, for example, a porous absorbing quilt were to be hung up as a partition between two rooms, only 10 per cent of the sound energy falling on it would be reflected back, so it would be an excellent acoustic absorbent. Sixty per cent of the sound energy would be dissipated within the quilt, as heat; this amount of energy would cease to exist as sound, it is true, but the remaining 30 per cent transmitted as sound to the next room is far more than enough to classify the quilt as a very poor *insulator* —it is equivalent to a reduction of only 5 dB.

Sound-absorbent materials, then, may be applied to the wall, floor and ceiling surfaces of a room, or introduced as furnishings, to reduce the build-up of sound levels by reflection within that room. They may also be used to line corridors, ducts, etc., to attenuate the transmission of airborne sound along them.

## MASKING NOISE

One level of noise may mask other noises, and this often needs to be taken into account in design. The obvious example is when one 'cannot hear oneself speak', but a lower noise level, to which the hearer has become so accustomed that it may be hardly noticed, can also have a masking effect. Many sounds are heard at night that would escape notice by day. Noise transmitted through a party wall will be less obtrusive if there is also noise from traffic or from something going on in the room in which the hearer is situated.

## PRACTICAL TREATMENT

The difficulties in the way of providing very high degrees of sound insulation in a building structure are so great that it is of the utmost importance to minimize the amount of objectionable noise at the source. Silence in running would be the first consideration in the choice of mechanical equipment. Lift motors, ventilating fans, blowers to heating boilers, and the like are devices where care is essential. Similarly with sanitary appliances and plumbing.

The same arguments apply as regards layout or planning. Rooms where quiet is desirable should be grouped both horizontally and vertically, and sources of noise should, wherever possible, be well separated from these rooms.

Having reduced the requirements for sound insulation to a minimum by careful planning and by choice of silent equipment, the next step is to take the design of the building as it stands and to estimate the amount of sound insulation required between various parts. Account must be taken here of the nature of the occupancy of rooms and the amount of masking noise with various types of occupancy. For some types of problem, such as walls and floors separating houses and flats, enough investigation has been done to reduce the design data to a limited range of recommended standards, as described later. With other problems the closest possible estimate should be made from experience and from such advice as can be obtained.

It then remains to select methods of construction that will supply the necessary insulation. In considering the transmission of sound between two rooms it must be borne in mind that the dividing wall between them is not the only path by which sound can be transmitted. Floor systems and flanking walls common to both rooms contribute, sometimes preponderantly, to the sound transmission. Transmission is likely to be highest when the flanking structures are light and easily set in vibration.

It is obvious that the efficiency of the sound insulation in a continuous building structure of the type implied here can be comparatively readily brought up to the standard 9-in. brickwork or a concrete floor, or thereabouts, but that to improve it beyond this point involves such massive construction that it is economically not feasible. One can assume, therefore, that there is a clear limit of efficiency of sound insulation which can be attained in continuous building structures.

### Examples

Some examples are shown in Fig. 6.2. The following discussion may perhaps be followed more easily after studying the relevant chapters on walls and floors (pp. 224–9 and Part III).

CASE 1. A flat or office building with massive external walls, reinforced concrete or hollow tile floors. The dividing wall between rooms A and B is a solid structural wall, 9 in. thick, and a relatively light clinker concrete partition is provided against the corridor. It is required to determine what will be the factor governing the sound transmission from room A to room B.

The external wall, being the most massive, will be the least readily set in vibration.

The 9-in. dividing wall and the floor system, being of much the same order of weight, will be very similar in the extent to which they are set in vibration.

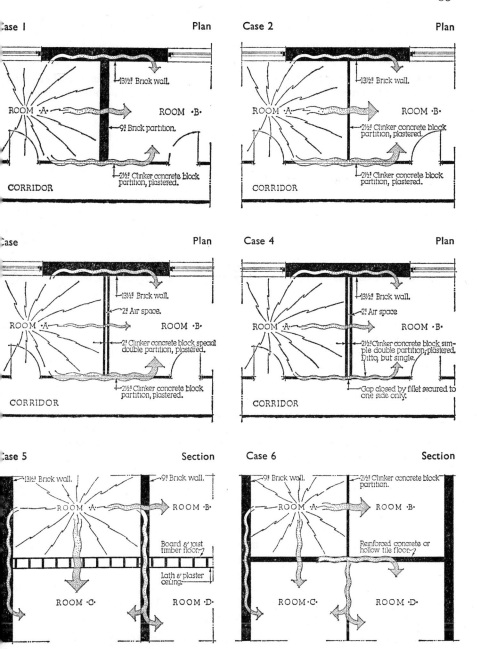

**Note:** Arrows indicate paths of sound, in roughly relative amounts. The broadest arrow in each case shows the path offering least resistance to the transmission of sound.

FIG. 6.2

*Examples of the transmission of air-borne sound by indirect paths*

The 2½-in. clinker concrete partition is obviously much lighter. It is bonded, however, into a 9-in. brick wall and its transmission into room B will be reduced thereby, so that the overall transmission of the system would approximate that of the 9-in. dividing wall.

CASE 2. As Case 1 but with a light clinker concrete dividing wall between the rooms. Here it seems likely that the sound transmission would be approximately equally shared between the dividing wall and the corridor wall, though the latter may be slightly improved by its connection to the relatively heavier floor and ceiling. The overall transmission would be greater than in Case 1.

CASE 3. As Case 2 but it is proposed to improve the insulation between the rooms by erecting a special double partition with edge isolation.

With this arrangement the weak feature will probably be the light corridor wall, which will not be stiffened by the partition owing to the edge isolation of the latter. Consequently this arrangement is unlikely to show any appreciable advantage over the conditions in Case 2 and there is no definite justification for the expense of the special construction of the partition.

CASE 4. A double partition between the rooms, but without edge isolation: the continuity of the corridor partition is broken where it meets the double partition.

By doing this the transmission along the corridor partition is overcome, except in so far as it is carried across the gap by the floor or ceiling, and the overall insulation between room A and room B will probably be that of the floors or outer wall. In this case the floors are less massive than the outer wall and will be the factor deciding the transmission.

This construction should be efficient and light in weight.

CASE 5. This shows the method of approach to the problem of vertical transmission of airborne sound. Solid structural walls not less than 9 in. in thickness carry board and joist timber floors with lath and plaster ceilings.

The timber floors are supported by, but not rigidly connected to, the walls, and the transmission horizontally between room A and room B will be largely determined by the wall system since the floors are discontinuous.

Considering room A as the source of the noise, what will be the condition in room C immediately below? The floor is far less massive and rigid than the walls and, consequently, the sound transmission will be determined by the floor. The floor could be improved by pugging or by inserting a false ceiling, but it would not be possible by any treatment of the floor to obtain insulation greater than that offered by the walls.

Still considering room A as the source of noise, it will be seen that the conditions in rooms B and D (diagonally below A) will be very similar, but slightly better than in room C.

CASE 6. Solid structural walls, with continuous reinforced concrete or hollow tile floors, and light clinker concrete partitions between rooms.

Considering the transmission of sound between room A and room C it is evident that the lower partition is unlikely to vibrate to any greater extent than the floor, and the insulation, therefore, will be determined by that of the floor system.

## Chapter 7

# DAYLIGHTING

It is only recently that daylighting has come to be regarded as a functional requirement that lends itself to deliberate design based on physiological and psychological criteria. By and large, this development had to await the freeing of fenestration from restriction imposed by structural necessity.

Good lighting is necessary to enable work to be done well and in comfort. A building with bad lighting is an inefficient building, even if it may look attractive superficially. It will be judged a bad building by those who have to live and work in it. Poor lighting can certainly be combated by good sight and by keenness on the work, but at the eventual expense of efficiency, comfort, and well-being. The designer of a building has, therefore, to ensure from the start that he will be able to provide good lighting.

Good lighting is not merely a lot of light—that is the mistake that has been made in the past. Good lighting is sufficient light free from glare, and it should come from the right direction. It should also combine a sufficient amount of general diffused light to soften harsh shadows. 'Shadowless' lighting, however much praised in the past, is rarely good. Shadows are one of the many aids to good seeing which the skilful lighting engineer uses to produce a satisfactory result.

The crux of the daylighting problem is how to admit enough light for good seeing without setting up uncomfortable glare. No simple solution has yet been achieved, or is likely to be achieved. This is because the sky varies so much in its brightness from hour to hour, and from season to season. A window large enough to admit sufficient light on a winter afternoon would give intolerable sky glare on a bright summer day.

Even if lighting considerations were the only ones to be taken into account, the problem would be difficult, but in addition the designer has to balance lighting with, above all, heat insulation. Single panes of glass have a much greater thermal transmission than most wall constructions, so that the larger the area of single-glazing window provided the greater the loss of heat (though a larger window also admits more solar heat). On the other hand, the larger the window, the less use needs to be made of artificial lighting, and this saving may partly offset the cost of heat loss. A careful balance has therefore to be struck for any given circumstances, and it is by no means always in favour of smaller windows.

## THE AMOUNT OF LIGHT REQUIRED FOR GOOD SEEING

Different tasks need differing amounts of light for the same visual efficiency, but very little close work can be done with less light than that equivalent to one candle one foot away from the work. Most tasks require about ten times this amount, and many need twenty, fifty, or one hundred times as

57

much. The foot candle, or (in Great Britain) the 'lumen per square foot', is the unit of illumination which is in general use (the corresponding metric unit being the 'lux', which is one lumen per square metre and approximately one-tenth of a lumen per square foot).

The correct amount of light for any task is determined by

(a) the characteristics of the task—size of significant detail, contrast of detail with background, how close it is to the eyes;

(b) the sight of the worker—for example, older people need more light;

(c) the speed and accuracy necessary in the performance of the work— if no errors are permissible, much more light is needed; and

(d) the ease and comfort of working—long and sustained tasks must be done easily, whereas the worker can make a special effort for tasks of very short duration—the light needed to enable an elderly person to thread needles all day long would be much greater than that for ordinary sewing—she can make the effort to thread an occasional needle without undue strain.

These factors have been made the subject of a careful analysis, as a result of which tables of necessary levels of illumination have been drawn up. A simplified version is given in Table 7.2 (p.64). A fully detailed table is given in the Code of Practice for Interior Lighting of the Illuminating Engineering Society of Great Britain. These values are nowadays expressed, not only in terms of the visual difficulty of the task, but also in terms of the standard of performance of the average person. The I.E.S. values refer to a standard of performance of 90 per cent of that possible with ideal lighting. Work that can be done easily with such levels can, in fact, still be done, but with greater difficulty, in only one-thirtieth the amount of light, so it is clear that the eye and the intelligence behind the eye are capable of a great degree of adaptation. But this adaptation should not be called upon too much and too often.

*Lighting and colour*

Levels of lighting determined analytically from first principles must be translated into levels of daylight, and thence into sizes of window openings. One of the many important factors involved in this translation is the lightness of the room surfaces; the same amount of daylight will go much further in a light-coloured room than in one with dark surfaces.

It is necessary, therefore, at an early stage to consider the colouring of the rooms of the building, and not to leave this until later. *This is a new departure in design*. Lighting is not merely a matter of window openings. Quite half the eventual level of lighting may be dependant on the decorations in the room. Consequently any special requirements in colour of the surfaces must be known before the daylight calculations are made, in order to inject the necessary values of reflection factor into the calculations at the appropriate stage.

## THE CALCULATION OF DAYLIGHT

The calculation of daylight nowadays is undertaken in two stages, first the calculation of the direct light from the sky, and second, the calculation of the indirect light reflected from exterior buildings and the ground, and inter-reflected from the surfaces in the room. The total of direct and indirect light gives the total daylight. This is usually expressed as the *daylight factor* in the room, that is, the *ratio* of the light in the room to the light of the unobstructed sky.

## Direct daylight

The direct light from the sky which reaches any given point in a room is determined by how big a patch of sky can be seen from that point, or, more strictly, the projected solid angle subtended by the patch of visible sky at the point. It is also determined by the brightness of the patch of sky. If the brightness of sky can be assumed to be uniform, the ratio of direct internal light to the external light from the sky is known as the *sky factor*, and it is proportional to this projected solid angle.

In practice, plotting diagrams and other calculating devices, or tables, are used. Of the diagrams, the Waldram diagram consists of a plotting web such that equal areas of the diagram correspond to equal values of the ratio of internal illumination to the total illumination from the hemisphere of sky of uniform brightness. The configuration of the patch of sky as seen from the point in the room can be plotted on the diagram, and the area of the patch so enclosed on the diagram is a direct measure of the ratio of the internal to external illumination from the sky. The diagram can be modified to take into account the loss of light through the glazing, and it can also be modified to allow for the non-uniformity of the brightness of the sky.

A simpler method of determining the direct light from the sky is by means of the B.R.S. protractors, which can be laid directly on to the working drawings. Fig. 7.1 shows the use of the protractors.

An alternative method is the use of tables. Published tables differ in their accuracy and complexity. References to sets of tables are given in the bibliography (p. 291).

Formulae have also been worked out to enable the ratio of direct internal light to external light from a sky of uniform brightness to be computed. One such formula is:

Internal direct light expressed as a percentage of external light from the

whole sky (sky factor) $= \dfrac{30WH^2}{d(d^2+H^2)}\%$

where $2W$ is the width of the window ($W$ is thus the half-width of the window),

$H$ is the height of the window above the point under considera-tion,

$d$ is the distance from the plane of the window to the working point.

This formula only applies to points on the same horizontal plane as the window-sill at some distance from the window, which is vertical. In spite of these limitations, it is a useful formula to memorize for use when tables, protractors or diagrams are not available.

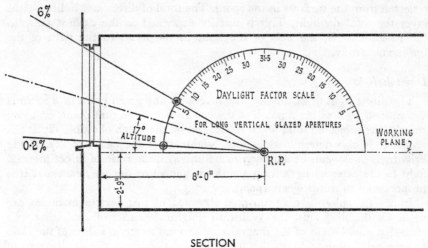

SECTION
Reading 6% − 0·2% = 5·8%

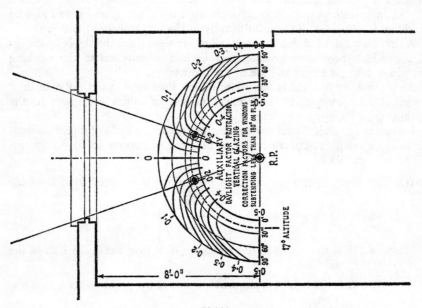

PLAN
Reading 0·18 + 0·18 = 0·36
Sky factor at R.P. = 5·8 × 0·36 = 2·08%

FIG. 7.1

*Use of B.R.S. protractors for determining sky factor*

*Indirect daylight*

The indirect light in the room can be expressed by the formula:

Average level of indirect light in room expressed as a percentage of external light from whole sky $= \dfrac{0 \cdot 85S}{A(1 - R)} (CR_{fw} + 5R_{cw})$ %

where $S$ = area of window (actual glazed area),

$A$ = total area of ceiling, floor and walls,

$R$ = *average* reflectance of ceiling, floor and all walls, expressed as a fraction,

$R_{fw}$ = *average* reflectance of the floor and those parts of the walls *below* the plane of the mid-height of the window (excluding the window wall),

$R_{cw}$ = *average* reflectance of the ceiling and those parts of the walls *above* the plane of the mid-height of the window (excluding the window wall),

$C$   is a constant having values dependent on the degree of obstruction outside the window. Table 7.1 gives values of $C$ for various obstructions.

TABLE 7.1

| Angle of obstruction as seen from centre of window (degrees above horizontal) | $C$ |
|---|---|
| no obstruction | 39 |
| 10 | 35 |
| 20 | 31 |
| 30 | 25 |
| 40 | 20 |
| 50 | 14 |
| 60 | 10 |
| 70 | 7 |
| 80 | 5 |

In practice, the indirect component can be obtained from the B.R.S. nomograms (Figs. 7.2–3) or more simply (but less accurately) from tables. The total daylight factor can be determined. The steps are as follows:

(1) Determine the direct daylight from the appropriate diagrams, protractors, or tables, making the allowances there indicated for glazing (single or double, dirtying, area of window bars, etc.), and for the brightness distribution of the sky (e.g. either uniform brightness, or the C.I.E. International Overcast Sky).

(2) Determine the indirect daylight from the nomograms or tables, for the same sky conditions as for the direct daylight.

(3) Add the direct and indirect daylight. The total is the *daylight factor*.

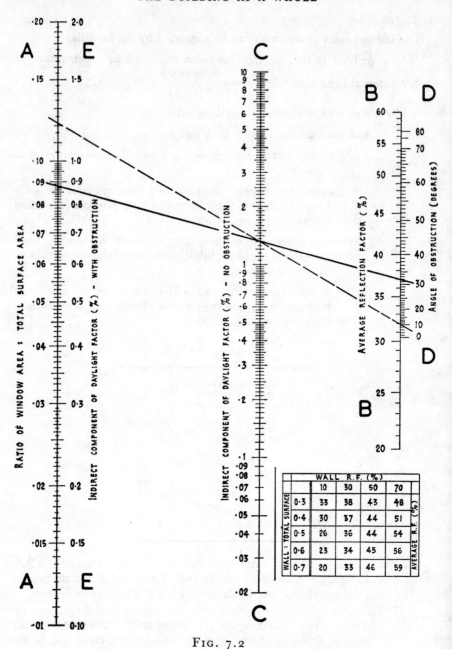

FIG. 7.2

*Nomogram I. Average indirect component of daylight factor*

Lay a straight-edge across the nomogram between the Scale A (ratio of window to total surface area) and Scale B (average reflection factor of the room). Then the intercept on Scale C gives the unobstructed indirect component. If there is an obstruction,

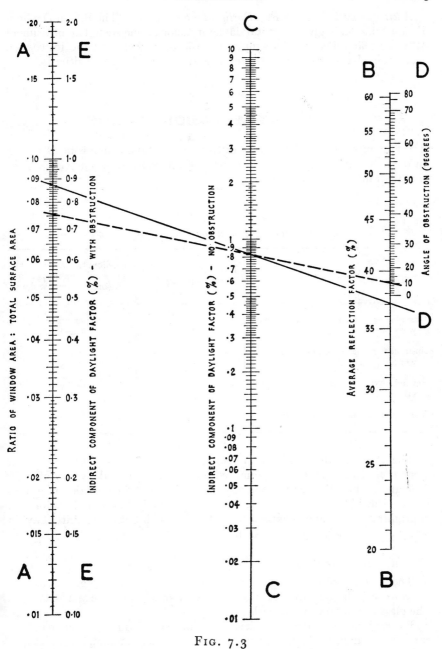

FIG. 7.3

*Nomogram II. Minimum indirect component of daylight factor*

lay the straight-edge from the unobstructed indirect component on Scale C to the angle of the obstruction on Scale D. Then the intercept on Scale E will give the indirect component allowing for the obstruction.

*Alternative method—the B.R.S. Daylight Factor Slide Rule.* The B.R.S. Daylight Factor Slide Rule gives the total daylight factor in one step. The instrument (Plate 7.1 and Fig. 7.4) is simple in basic operation, and the instruction manual explains its use in both simple and more complicated situations.


## NECESSARY LEVELS OF DAYLIGHT

The amounts of light necessary for different visual tasks can now be expressed in daylight factors. Table 7.2 lists some of the more common visual tasks met with in interiors of buildings.

TABLE 7.2

*Amounts of daylight for adequate visual performance*

| Visual task | Level of illumination (lumens per sq. ft) | Daylight factor when sky gives 500 lumens per sq. ft (bright overcast sky) |
|---|---|---|
| | | (per cent) |
| Casual reading, ordinary factory bench work . . . . . . | 7–10 | 1·4–2 |
| Sustained reading, school and office work . . . . . . | 10–15 | 2–3 |
| Sewing, typing and other difficult visual work . . . . | 15–25 | 3–5 |
| Very fine work or in poor contrast . | 25–50 | 5–10 |

The values in the third column relate to a 'standard sky' of 500 lumens per square foot, such as is experienced on bright overcast days very often in England and N.W. Europe generally. It is also approximately the brightness of the clear blue sky, and is therefore a useful practical datum. A sky of such a brightness or greater is experienced at noon on all but about thirty days in the year over most of the British Isles.

### The efficiency of fenestration

The amount of glass necessary to realize the given daylight factor (or more) everywhere in the room depends very much on the exact placing of the glass in relation to the work.

For example, in order to achieve the Ministry of Education's demand for a minimum daylight factor of 2 per cent in a school classroom, it is necessary, if conventional side lighting is employed, to use glass to the extent of about 25 per cent of the area of the floor. By careful placing of windows, however, the result can be achieved with only 15 per cent, or, if top-lighting is the main illuminant, with even as little as 10 per cent glass/floor area.

In general, the higher a window is placed, the more efficiently it admits light. There are two reasons for this.

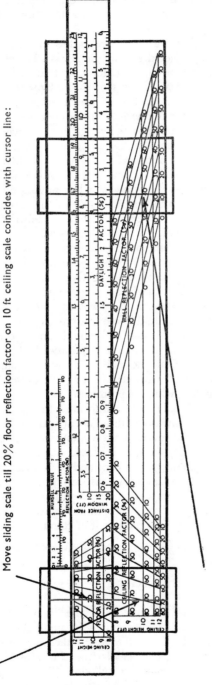

Set cursor line against 70% ceiling reflection factor on 10 ft ceiling scale

Move sliding scale till 20% floor reflection factor on 10 ft ceiling scale coincides with cursor line:

(i) Then set cursor line against 40% wall reflection factor on 10 ft ceiling scale:
read off, on daylight factor scale, values of daylight factor at distances of 5, 10, 15 and 20 ft from window, i.e. 16·9, 8·2, 4·3, 2·6 respectively.

(ii) Alternatively, set the cursor line against, say, 2% daylight factor at 20 ft from window: read off, on 10 ft ceiling scale, the required wall reflection factor, i.e. 17%.

FIG. 7·4

*Example of operation of the daylight factor calculator*

First, the sky is usually brighter near the zenith than near the horizon. On fully overcast days the horizon is about one-third as bright as the zenith. Consequently a window which looks on to the horizontal sky will admit the least light for its area.

Second, light coming at glancing incidence is less effective than light coming perpendicularly (the projected solid angle is less). Hence low-placed side windows are less effective for lighting horizontal surfaces than high-placed side windows or roof lights. Fig. 7.5 gives daylight factor contours for two arrangements of fenestration, one of which employs glass to the extent of one-eighth and the other of one-fifth of the floor area.

Tall windows admit light farther into the room than do wide windows, but give rise to greater glare. Some of the advantages of a tall window without the attendant glare can be obtained by means of a baffle. The screen extends outwards from the main window, and reduces substantially the view of sky as seen by an observer near the window, while having little effect on the amount of light admitted to the remoter parts of the room (Plate 7.2 and Fig. 7.6). The worst glare is thus reduced, while the level of daylight is maintained where it is most needed.

In general, windows in one side only of a room give harsher contrasts than are usually desirable. While often satisfactory if one can choose where to sit and work, as in a dwelling-house, single-side lighting can be uncomfortable if one is faced continuously with a bright sky view. Lighting coming from another side reduces glare by lighting up the walls adjacent to the window, but it is preferable that the light should come from an adjacent side rather than an opposite side, unless one side can be made distinctly the dominant side. Plate 7.3 shows a successful design of opposite-side lighting which enables the darker areas remote from the main window to be supplemented by diffused lighting from the roof, without affecting the dominance of the main window and the modelling which it produces.

A complete window wall is usually more comfortable than a large window in the wall, because no harsh contrasts with adjacent wall areas arise. This is not true on very bright days however, and a window wall should either be provided with efficient blinds or louvres, or it should be glazed with glass of a transmission to daylight of about 30 per cent and of neutral colour. (The 'neutrality' of the colour of the glass is not critical. Provided there is no other glass in the walls to permit comparison, the eye adapts to an off-neutral colour, such as the green of heat-resisting glass, and is unaware of any abnormality except, perhaps, for the critical judgment of colour.)

## SUNLIGHT

Direct sunlight in a room can be a source of intense discomfort from overheating and from glare, but it is often wanted in small measure and at certain times. The study of sunlighting is therefore linked with a study of the orientation of buildings and of the correct placing of windows, and is best undertaken either on models placed in a heliodon (Plates 7.4–5), or by diagrammatic study. The heliodon consists of a table rotating on a vertical axis, illuminated by a fixed lamp which represents the sun. The tilt of the table is adjusted to correspond to the latitude of the locality. The table turns about a vertical axis, this movement relative to the fixed lamp corresponding to the earth's daily rotation. The height of the lamp above and its distance from the axes of the table are adjusted to correspond to the season of the year. The table with the model placed upon it is rotated on its vertical axis,

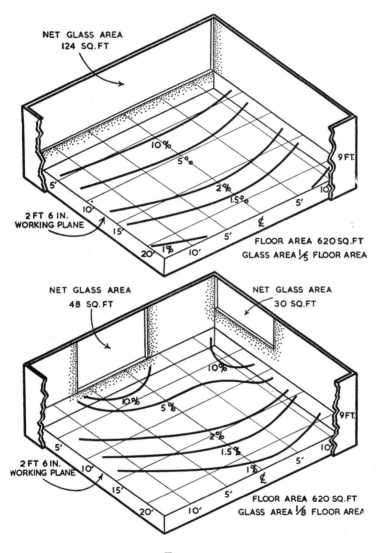

FIG. 7.5

*Daylight factor contours for two arrangements of window. The glass/floor ratio in the lower room is ⅛. It is shown that a level of daylighting similar to that produced by conventional windows can be achieved with a smaller glass area if the windows are carefully placed*

(138029)

D

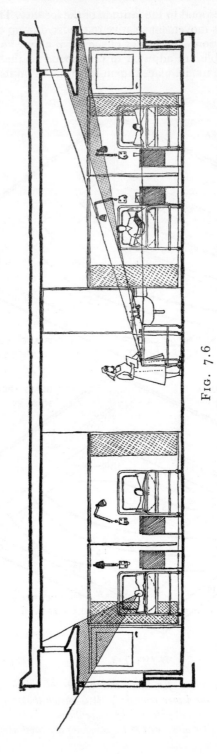

FIG. 7.6

The horizontal window baffle used in the ward unit at Larkfield Hospital, Greenock: This shows how the baffle reduces the area of sky visible to patients in beds near the window without seriously reducing the level of daylight near the middle of the room (see also Plate 7.2) and the shadowing and the sun penetration can be studied for different times of day. The model may, for example, consist of blocks of buildings, the problem being to study the effectiveness of a town plan in allowing sufficient access of sunlight to the façades of the various blocks. The illustration shows the use of the heliodon in the study of the over-shadowing caused by a row of very tall trees.

In the absence of a model, sun penetration must be studied by one or other of the diagrammatic methods. One such method, that of Graham and Nicklin, permits the hours of insolation of a building façade to be assessed directly from the working drawings. Pleijel's method permits the assessment of total solar and sky irradiation of a building façade to be made as well as the hours of insolation.

The elimination of unwanted sunshine is best achieved by blinds or curtains, rather than by the use of glass blocks, prismatic glass, or diffusing glass, which 'flash' to uncomfortably high brightness when they receive direct sunlight.

In regions where sunlight is to be expected for long periods, the deliberate use of reflected sunlight as the illuminant for a building should be considered. It has been shown by experience that sufficient reflected sunlight may be received from the ground and from opposing façades to give an adequate level of illumination in a building. In the United States (Texas and California) many schools have been designed to receive all their natural light by reflection. The result is comfortable and free from glare.

## GLARE

The failure to avoid glare is the root of most of the criticism of the lighting of modern buildings. Glare arises when some parts of the field of vision are excessively bright. Although the eye has a power of adaptation from starlight to full daylight, this power is not limitless, and most people feel some discomfort from glare on bright days out of doors—even to the extent of using dark glasses to combat the discomfort. Besides being related to the saturation of the power of adaptation, glare is also a matter of contrast, and one of the best ways of reducing glare is to reduce the contrast between the sky and the interior of the room.

To reduce sky glare to an acceptable level, the *average* brightness in the room must have a minimum value determined by the brightness of the sky through the window and by the total *apparent* size *of those windows which are within the observer's field of view*. For example, glare will be caused by a window of 100 sq. ft area located 15 ft from the observer, who sees through it a normal overcast sky of 500 ft-lamberts brightness, unless the room itself has a brightness of at least 50 ft-lamberts. The theoretical calculation is somewhat complex, and the average brightness requirement is therefore usually estimated from a calculator or from tables.

In practice, since room brightness is itself dependent on the brightness of the sky, some rooms can never be free of glare in bright daylight for, if the sky gets brighter, the glare gets worse because the increase in room brightness is insufficient to combat the glare from the brighter sky. The only way to combat the glare is to let in light from an opening that is outside the observer's field of view. Such light increases the brightness of the room without increasing the area of visible sky, and thus helps to restore the comfortable balance between room brightness and sky brightness. This is one of the advantages of two-side lighting. In the example given in the last paragraph, the comfortable interior level of 50 ft-lamberts would have to be obtained by assistance from 'booster' light from windows behind, and hence invisible to, the observer.

Other obvious methods of reducing glare are the use of louvres or blinds to limit the direct view of the sky, while retaining as much light as possible on the work and on the surroundings. If the sky is known to be bright for a large part of the year (as in some tropical and semi-tropical regions) it is sound policy to use low-transmission neutral glass, better lighting being given by large windows glazed with such glass than by small window openings through which the brilliant sky can be seen. This somewhat unorthodox expedient, first advocated some years ago by the Building Research Station by direct derivation from the fundamentals of glare, is now becoming widely accepted in the southern U.S.A. as good building practice.

Glare is reduced by the avoidance of sharp contrasts between the sky and the immediate surroundings to the windows. The walls near the windows should be as bright as possible. Ways of achieving this are by splaying the window bars and the reveals, and painting them a light colour, by directing light on to the window wall from another opening, and by making full and intelligent use of reflected light and the configuration of the room (Plate 7.6).

## THE MEASUREMENT OF DAYLIGHT

The accurate measurement of daylight in buildings calls for skilled photometric technique. Two simultaneous measurements are required, of the outdoor and of the indoor illumination. The outdoor measurement must give, either directly or by derivation, the total illumination that would be yielded by the unobstructed hemisphere of sky. The indoor measurement must be made simultaneously by an instrument in complete accord, as regards calibration and sensitivity over the whole visible spectrum, with that measuring the outdoor illumination. The daylight factor is the ratio of the two measurements.

Daylight photometry is essentially a matter for the specialist, but it frequently happens that approximate measurements of the strength of daylight are needed to only a moderate degree of accuracy. Such measurement can be made with the aid of the daylight factor meter developed by the Building Research Station. The instrument (Plate 7.7) consists essentially of a conventional photoelectric illumination meter provided with

(a) an adjustable sensitivity control, and

(b) a mask to restrict the view of the sky.

In operation the meter is held horizontally, with the mask in position, facing the sky, preferably through an open window. It is then in position to measure the illumination from a zone of sky at a mean elevation of 42°, which is known to give, fairly accurately, a measure of the illumination from the whole overcast sky. The sensitivity control is then adjusted until the meter pointer comes to the mark X1. The meter is then taken indoors and placed at the point where the daylight factor is to be measured, the mask being swung out of the way. The meter then reads directly the daylight factor at the given point.

*Chapter 8*

# FIRE PROTECTION

THE ideal way of making buildings safe against the danger from fire would be to make sure that fires do not start, but the designer cannot rely on this because a large proportion of the 50 000 or so fires that occur each year in buildings in this country are attributed to causes that can never be eliminated. Some precautions can be taken to prevent fires starting by attention to the design and maintenance of plant and equipment and by proper design of parts of the structure, e.g. around chimneys. Some fires can also be prevented by using building materials that cannot be readily ignited, but that method has obvious limitations, as the contents of many buildings are more easily set on fire than the materials used in their construction. The designer has therefore to resort to other methods of achieving the necessary standards of safety. These are:

(1) To provide means for the occupants to leave the building safely and quickly if a fire starts.

(2) To design the building so as to reduce, as far as is practicable and economic, spread of fire, both within the building and through its external walls (in either direction).

In meeting these requirements, the availability of fire brigades and the provision of automatic and manual extinguishing and alarm equipment inside the building may have to be taken into account. The total fire protection in a building is made up of a combination of some or all of these measures, depending on the height and size of the building and use to which it is put.

Specific requirements for various buildings are set down in Building Acts, byelaws and other legislation relating to the construction of buildings and safety of their occupants, e.g. the Factories Acts. In addition, fire insurance offices lay down certain standards of construction, and extinguishing and alarm equipment, on which fire insurance premiums are in part based.

## INCIDENCE AND CAUSES OF FIRES

Of all the fires that start each year in buildings in this country, more than half occur in houses and flats. The majority of the fires are relatively small; for example, most of those in houses and flats are extinguished before they spread beyond the room in which they started, by the efforts either of the occupants or of the fire brigades. Only a small proportion of fires become big enough to threaten adjacent buildings seriously.

The most frequent cause of fires is the domestic fire in a grate; this is responsible for about one-half the fires in houses and flats. Otherwise fires are usually started by small high-temperature sources, such as sparks from defective electrical equipment or wiring or from welding operations, matches, or blowlamps, igniting some easily ignitable material.

Full details of the numbers and causes of fires are given in the Annual Reports of the Joint Fire Research Organization.

*Development of fires*

Once some material has been ignited, the fire tends to spread to other material until all ignitable material in the room is set on fire. Unless extinguishing equipment is brought into operation, the subsequent development depends on what material there is to burn and on the construction of the walls and floors enclosing the room. If there are openings in the walls and floors the fire can spread unchecked to other parts of the building. Even if there are no unprotected openings, the structure itself may burn, or be so affected that the fire can pass through holes and cracks that form, or sufficient heat may be conducted through wall or floor to ignite material on the opposite side. The fire may then spread through the building.

A fire in a building, like an ordinary fire in a grate, creates a strong draught which helps to spread the fire; staircases and lift shafts act as flues unless they are cut off from the rest of the building. Ahead of the fire itself, hot gases and smoke may be carried throughout the building. Many lives have been lost by asphyxiation by these gases without any signs of burning.

Structural precautions in building aim at preventing the spread of fire and smoke in this way; walls, floors and other barriers must remain effective long enough, in the first place, to allow occupants to escape in safety and, subsequently, to confine the fire until it has burnt itself out or is extinguished. The effects of a fire on the various parts of a structure depend on how hot the fire becomes and how long it burns.

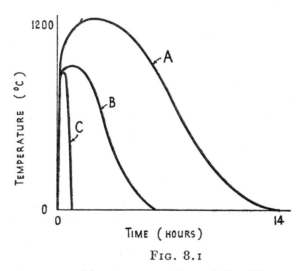

FIG. 8.1

*Time-temperature characteristics of fires*

Fig. 8.1 shows roughly how the temperature in fires varies with time. Curve A is for a fire in a heavily loaded warehouse; curve B is for a fire in a compartment with much less material and curve C shows how fire-fighting affects the characteristics of a fire in a compartment similar to B. Apart from the effects of fire-fighting, clearly the more material there is to burn, the longer and hotter will the fire be. The amount of material is called the 'fire load', and is more precisely defined as the number of British thermal units that could be liberated per square foot of floor area by the combustion of the contents and any combustible part of the building itself. It is determined by multiplying the weights of all combustible materials by their several calorific values and dividing by the floor area under consideration.

The calorific values of some materials are given in Table 8.1. A more comprehensive list is given in Post-War Building Study No. 20, 'Fire Grading of Buildings'.

TABLE 8.1

*Calorific values of some materials*

| Material | Calorific value (B.t.u./lb) |
|---|---|
| Timber (average with approximately 12 per cent moisture content) . | 8 000 |
| Paper  .    .    .    .    .    . | 7 000 |
| Straw  .    .    .    .    .    . | 6 000 |
| Bitumen  .    .    .    .    . | 15 200 |
| Oils  .    .    .    .    .    . | 17 000–20 000 |
| Rubber  .    .    .    .    . | 17 000 |

Fire load is, in some respects, analogous to a floor load specified for structural design and just as the actual numerical value of a structural load is not the only factor, e.g. it may be a vibrating load, so other characteristics of fire loads have to be considered. For example, a fire load of celluloid presents a much greater danger than the same fire load of heavy timber. For this reason special regulations apply to the storage and handling of many materials, such as celluloid and petrol.

## DESIGN OF BUILDINGS TO REDUCE SPREAD OF FIRE

The underlying principle of all structural precautions to reduce spread or smoke, hot gases and fire is simply that of dividing up the interior by walls and floors so constructed that they help to confine the fire within any room, group of rooms or compartment and thus reduce as much as possible the size of the fire that can develop. The way in which this is done depends on the size and type of the building, the use to which it is put and the purpose of the separation, i.e. whether to prevent spread of smoke and hot gases so that occupants can escape before the fire really develops, or to prevent spread of fire.

Where limitation of size is considered necessary, building regulations specify the maximum sizes of buildings or parts of buildings according to the construction of the buildings and the nature of the occupancy.

*Materials*

Although there is usually more to burn in the contents of a building than in the structure, the designer should aim, other things being equal, at selecting materials that would contribute as little as possible to a fire if an outbreak occurred. To do this it is first necessary to know whether a material will burn or not. The distinction is self-evident for some materials but not for others, and the combustibility test in B.S. 476 has been devised to enable this distinction to be made. The classification, on the basis of this test, of some building materials that are not obviously combustible or non-combustible is given in Table 8.2.

TABLE 8.2

*Combustibility of some building materials*

| Non-combustible | Combustible |
|---|---|
| Asbestos insulation board. | Plastics (roof and wall sheeting). |
| Fibrous plaster. | Timber, even if impregnated with fire-retardant material. |
| Glass wool or slag wool not having an organic binder (e.g. bitumen) or covering (e.g. paper). | Bitumen felt (either asbestos or organic fibre base). |
| | Compressed straw slabs. |
| | Fibreboard, even if impregnated with fire-retardant material. |
| | Gypsum plasterboard. |
| | Glass wool or slag wool quilts if bonding agent or covering is combustible. |
| | Hardboard. |
| | Protected metal sheeting (bitumen protected). |
| | Wood-wool slabs. |

Composite materials about whose classification the user may have some doubt are of three kinds: (1) those consisting of an intimate mixture of combustible and non-combustible material, e.g. wood-wool slabs; (2) sheet or board materials with a non-combustible core and a combustible covering, e.g. gypsum plasterboard; (3) sheet or board materials with a combustible core and a non-combustible covering, e.g. fibre-board with asbestos-paper or thin metal covering. The behaviour of materials in group (1) depends on the nature and relative proportions of the constituents and on the way in which they are combined. Wood-wool is combustible. It is not possible to say without test to which class materials in this group belong. Materials in groups (2) and (3) will always be classed as combustible.

For some purposes, e.g. in the construction of chimneys, it is essential to use non-combustible materials, but many combustible materials burn so slowly or contain so little combustible material that they do not contribute materially to fire, and these can be used in construction without creating undue hazard. The actual behaviour of a material in fire depends on both its composition and the way in which it is incorporated in buildings. Thus plywood burns quickly, large baulks of timber burn very slowly. For this reason no general test method can be established covering all material and methods of use, but sheet materials used as wall linings can be classified by test, since they are all used in much the same way. This test and the classification of various wall and ceiling linings are discussed on pp. 141–2.

Although non-combustible building materials do not contribute to a fire they are all affected in one way or another by heat: there is, in fact, no 'fireproof' material. Some materials are decomposed by heat, e.g. limestone is converted to lime; others lose strength at high temperatures, e.g. the strength of steel falls from 27 tons/sq. in. to about 8 tons/sq. in. at 600°C; others melt, e.g. lead and aluminium.

*Structural elements and fire resistance*

In this section the term 'structural element' is used to describe any part of a building intended to act as a barrier to fire spread, and any part, such as a column or beam, that supports the barrier.

To achieve proper fire separation in buildings it is essential that these structural elements should continue to function throughout the fire, or at least for a sufficient time to allow occupants to escape or the fire to be extinguished. For the period in question the element should not collapse, crack, or allow enough heat to be conducted through it to ignite material on its opposite side.

It takes time for the heat to be conducted into the interior of an element, so the temperatures within it at a given moment will be less than those on the surface. Fig. 8.2 shows the temperature attained in a brick wall during a fire in an actual building (an office block), and Fig. 8.3 shows the temperatures in a reinforced concrete column during a warehouse fire. Neither

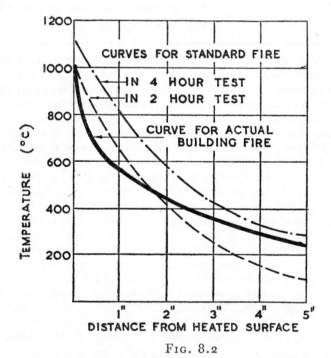

FIG. 8.2

*Average temperature gradients in walls exposed to fire*

element failed in the fire, and it is evident that only the outermost surface exposed to fire reached temperatures sufficient to weaken the material seriously.

A thinner wall or column more quickly attains high temperatures throughout its thickness and might therefore have only a short life as a fire barrier. The time for which a structural element continues to function satisfactorily in fire is known as its fire resistance period or, simply, its fire resistance. Fire resistance is a property of *a structural element*, and it is not related to the combustibility of the materials of which it is made. Thus a heavy timber column is combustible, but will have a higher fire resistance than an equivalent steel column, which is non-combustible. The fire resistance of a timber stud partition depends mainly on the protection afforded by the cladding on each side. To compare accurately the behaviour of different elements, a standard test has been devised (B.S. 476) in which an element is subjected to a standard fire, with other conditions such as loading comparable with those to which the element would be subjected in practice. An element is thus classified as having $\frac{1}{2}$-, 1-, 2-, 3-, 4-, or 6-hour fire resistance, according to the time for which it complies with specified conditions. The fire conditions are controlled by a standard time-temperature curve (Fig. 8.4) and full-size structural elements are tested. The fire resistance of various structural elements are given in subsequent sections dealing specifically with them (p. 231 and Part III).

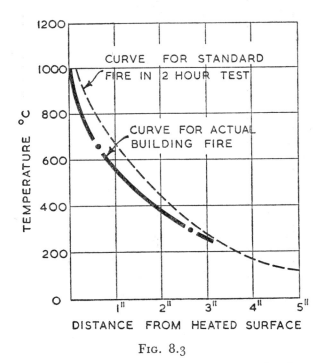

FIG. 8.3

*Average temperature gradients in columns exposed to fire*

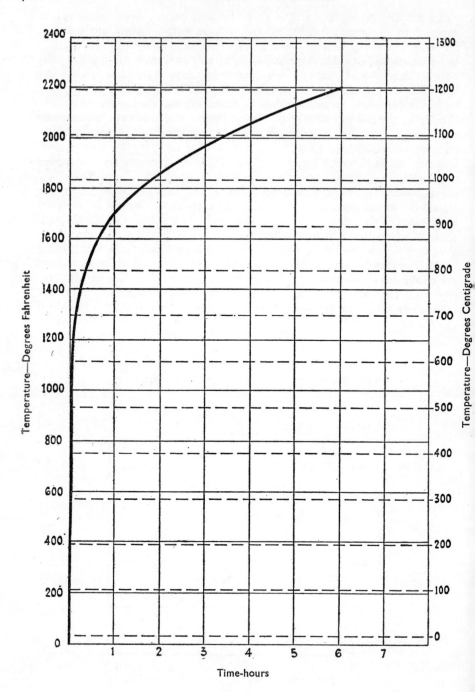

FIG. 8.4

*Standard time-temperature curve for fire-resistance tests*

*Assessment of fire-resistance requirements*

By comparing the effects in buildings of fires, caused by known fire loads, with the effects of various periods of the standard test, the fire resistance periods required in the structural elements, if they are to function satisfactorily, can be determined. They are given in Table 8.3.

TABLE 8.3

| Fire load (B.t.u./sq. ft) | Period of fire test giving equivalent fire (h) |
|---|---|
| Up to 100 000 | 1 |
| 100 000–200 000 | 2 |
| 200 000–400 000 | 4 |
| More than 400 000 | more than 4 |

This means that any wall, column or beam having a fire resistance of one hour will withstand without failure the effects of a fire caused by a fire load of 100 000 B.t.u./sq. ft, and so on. If, however, it can be assumed that any fire will be extinguished before the structure is exposed to the full potential effects of the fire load, the fire resistance can be reduced. There is, at present, no precise information on the effects of water in reducing the severity of a fire due to a certain fire load, but building regulations take account of the effects of fire-fighting by allowing a lower fire resistance than that based on the fire-load relation, on the assumption that the smaller and lower the building the sooner will the fire be extinguished by fire-fighting. For example, existing building byelaws in England require a 2-h fire resistance in the columns, floors and beams in a warehouse class of building 'not predominantly used for storage', if it exceeds 75 ft in height or 250 000 cu. ft in capacity, or 7500 sq. ft on one floor. In a smaller building of the same class, 1-h fire resistance is regarded as sufficient and ½-h for a still smaller building. In some regulations an allowance is made for increased sizes if a sprinkler system is installed.

The fire resistance of structural elements whose sole function is to protect means of escape need not be based on considerations of fire load, as the protection is required only for a short period; elements having a fire resistance of half an hour or one hour will be sufficient. On the other hand, if a staircase is to be used as access for firemen, or if in a large building it is necessary to ensure that fire cannot spread from storey to storey via the stairwell, the higher grade of resistance is needed.

## MEANS OF ESCAPE

In all buildings occupied by people it is necessary to provide means whereby they can leave the building in safety if a fire breaks out. Legal requirements apply only to certain classes or sizes of buildings, but it is the designer's duty to ensure that there are ways of getting out of all buildings, even though in a small building it may mean no more than the provision of an accessible window with an opening light sufficiently large to allow a person to get through. In some multi-storey buildings one staircase only is permitted, though, more generally, it is necessary to provide a suitable number of exits of adequate width and construction, distributed so that if any one is blocked by fire or smoke there is an alternative way out. Providing means of escape is but one aspect of the wider problem of providing means for people to enter, leave and circulate within the building. The designer looks at this problem primarily from the point of view of ease of access and circulation, and economy of space occupied by stairs and corridors. It would be wasteful to provide additional facilities for escape if normal provision for circulation can be shown to be adequate for that purpose. It is evident that means of escape cannot be divorced from general planning considerations and treated by a series of hard and fast rules.

Certain general principles can be laid down relating to the number, position and widths of exits according to the number of people likely to be in the building, but the general planning of stairs and corridors must be left to the designer, whose skill in producing a result that is satisfactory for normal circulation will go far towards meeting requirements for escape.

In addition to planning the means of escape, the construction of the walls and floors enclosing them must receive special attention; these must prevent spread of smoke and fire into the stairs and corridors, at least until occupants have escaped.

## ECONOMICS OF FIRE PROTECTION

The economics of fire protection for the contents and structure of buildings is a complex matter involving the costs of structural protection, of the installation and maintenance of fire-fighting and alarm equipment in the building, of fire-insurance premiums and of fire-brigade services as a charge on local taxation, all considered in relation to fire losses. Personal safety must be ensured regardless of cost, though wasteful standards must be avoided.

It might be thought that since the subject is covered by building regulations with which the designer must comply, there is no need to do more than ensure compliance with them. But the regulations are concerned primarily with public safety; they are not directly concerned with the safety of the contents, though they contribute to it. To the direct loss of contents and structural damage caused by the fire there must be added the less well defined losses of production and goodwill. The cost of providing protection additional to that required by regulations, especially in commercial and industrial buildings, may be offset by a reduction in insurance premiums. All these are matters which the designer should consider in conjunction with his client, insurance company and local fire services.

*Chapter* 9

# DURABILITY, COMPOSITION AND MAINTENANCE

## THE PROBLEMS OF DURABILITY AND MAINTENANCE

THE durability of building materials and the maintenance of buildings give rise to important technical and economic questions.

The technical problems involve the physical and chemical properties of particular materials, as well as the design features required to use the materials in buildings in such a way that the fullest advantage is taken of their potentialities.

Some materials can be expected to last the whole life of the building and, indeed, any failure of such materials is likely to be serious, both functionally and economically.

There are other materials which will not last for the whole life of the building, and the periodic renewal, for instance, of paintwork or some heavy-duty industrial floors is unavoidable. It is, however, often within the control of the designer to use, say, a more expensive finish which has a longer anticipated life and so may lead to reduction of the cost of periodic maintenance. An economic balance has to be struck to determine the amount of increase of first cost that may be justified by a reduction of the maintenance costs. This aspect is dealt with subsequently and the present chapter is mainly concerned with the more technical problems.

When the composition of a material is fairly definite and constant, the destructive agencies to which it is exposed are familiar and its behaviour in use has been observed over a period of years, durability presents no great problem; experience or test generally provides all the information that is needed. Often, however—and particularly with new materials—there may be variability in quality of workmanship, or the conditions of exposure or use may be uncertain, and short-term or accelerated tests may give misleading indications. A tentative judgment only may be possible, based on technical knowledge and subject to confirmation in due course by observation.

*Exposure as affecting durability*

The durability of any material or method of construction depends firstly upon the conditions of exposure. External weathering, with rapid changes of temperature and moisture content, may cause deterioration of structures and materials that would be unaffected over very long periods if used inside. It is quite unnecessary to apply the same standards to materials to be used under cover as to those for external use.

Exposure conditions are determined by climate, environment, site, aspect, and height of building. For thousands of years these factors have been allowed for in the design of buildings, largely unconsciously through tradition; today, with so many new materials, and with many buildings being designed by those with a less intimate knowledge of local conditions, they more often need to be taken consciously into account.

### Design as affecting durability

The vulnerability of materials to conditions of exposure depends also on the design of the building as a whole. The shelter provided by properly designed projecting eaves, copings, cornices, sills and similar features very much simplifies the problems of rain exclusion and deterioration of surface finishes generally, and in abandoning these features it is necessary to take account of the increased severity of exposure to the weather.

### Estimating durability

In selecting materials in the past the practice was for the architect or builder to choose a material he knew, or was able to find by observation and enquiry, to be durable. This is a valuable method and should on no account be abandoned, subject to two conditions. First, that the material chosen can be identified as being precisely the same as the material shown by experience to be good, and, secondly, that the material chosen is used in exactly the same way as it has been used previously. Experience of previous behaviour can be a most unreliable guide when a material is used in a novel manner; many disastrous failures have resulted from the supposition that an unfamiliar combination of familiar materials can be used with complete freedom.

As a supplement to the teachings of experience there is now accumulating a technique of scientific testing as a basis for standardization. The whole field of building materials and systems of construction is gradually being covered by British Standards and British Standard Codes of Practice. To enable intelligent use to be made of the scientific testing of materials, however, particularly as regards their durability, it is important to have in mind the limitations, as well as the advantages, of these methods.

It is rarely possible in laboratory tests, or in any tests short of full-scale long-term trials in buildings, to reproduce *all* the factors influencing the durability of a material, or to simulate their action in their order of relative significance. It is worth considering each of these factors and the way in which it may influence durability, in some detail.

## FACTORS INFLUENCING DURABILITY

### Frost action

Deterioration of materials by frost action is caused by the expansion on freezing of water contained in pores or other interstices. It might be thought a simple matter to test the resistance of a material to frost action, by subjecting a sample to a number of cycles of freezing and thawing in the laboratory. The results of such tests, however, have often been found seriously at variance with the behaviour of materials exposed in buildings. This problem is still under investigation, but there are so many factors operating—moisture content and moisture gradient, rate of freezing, temperature gradient, pore structure of the material, and probably others still unidentified—that the interpretation of laboratory test results is never likely to be reduced to simple terms.

Materials vary in the extent to which their pores will be filled with water on immersion or on exposure in a building. In some materials nearly the whole of the pore space may be filled, in others only 70 per cent or less of the pore space. The ratio of the volume of the pore space filled on immersion in cold water to the total volume of pore space (which may be determined by prolonged soaking in boiling water and allowing the specimen to cool while submerged or by saturation under vacuum) is known as the saturation coefficient.

If only a part of the total pore space is occupied by water, there may be room for expansion, when the water freezes, without disruption of the material. For this reason, the saturation coefficient often gives some indication of frost resistance; it is not always a reliable index, however, and the only certain guide remains the behaviour of a material over a number of years in actual buildings. A few general notes are given in Table 9.1.

TABLE 9.1

*Susceptibility of materials to deterioration as the result of frost action*

| Class of material | How affected |
|---|---|
| Natural stone . . . | Variable. Best stones unaffected. Some stones with pronounced cleavage along bedding planes are unsuitable for copings or cornices. |
| Clay products . . . | Variable. Best bricks and tiles unaffected. Some products, insufficiently fired, or with flaws of structure originating in the machine, may deteriorate, especially bricks in copings, and tiles on flat-pitched roofs. |
| Cast stone, concrete, asbestos cement. | Material of good quality is rarely affected. |

NOTE: A laminar structure usually makes a material more liable to deterioration.

Frost attack is mostly confined to those parts of a building where materials may be saturated with water when exposed to frost. Thus parapets, the parts of a wall below the damp-proof course, retaining walls and, especially, horizontal surfaces such as copings, cornices and string courses, are the most vulnerable and call for the greatest care in the selection of materials. Among climatic factors, besides the actual incidence of frosts, the likelihood of frosts following immediately on a rainy spell needs to be taken into consideration.

*Crystallization of salts*

Soluble salts may be present initially in certain building materials, or may be conveyed into them by the movement of moisture from the ground or from adjacent materials. They may also be formed by the action of acid gases in the atmosphere on constituents of the building materials. Where the moisture evaporates at the surface the concentration of the salt in solution increases until finally it crystallizes out. If this occurs within the pores of the surface layer—not on the surface—it may cause gradual erosion or flaking (Table 9.2).

TABLE 9.2

*Susceptibility of materials to deterioration due to crystallization of soluble salts*

| Class of material | How affected |
|---|---|
| Clay bricks . . . | Good bricks rarely affected. Some underfired bricks may be badly attacked (see p. 235). |
| Clay tiles . . . . | Good tiles rarely affected. Some tiles suffer erosion at upper end. |
| Terra-cotta . . . | Rarely affected unless underfired. |
| Sand-lime bricks . . | Good bricks rarely affected. |
| Cast stone and Portland cement concrete. | Rarely affected. |
| Sandstones . . . | Vary greatly in resistance. The best stones are excellent. |
| Limestones . . . | Vary greatly in resistance. This is the property which is most important in distinguishing a durable stone. |

NOTE: Decay of a moderate or poor brick or stone may be accelerated by the use of impervious mortar for pointing. Salts may be washed from a limestone or concrete on to sandstone or brick and lead to decay.

Surfaces protected from rainfall are the most vulnerable. This type of deterioration may need to be taken particularly into account with buildings near enough to the sea to be contaminated by wind-borne salt spray.

Apart from causing functional deterioration, efflorescence may mar the appearance of a building; this aspect is discussed in detail later (p. 234).

*Solution by rainwater*

The majority of building materials are obviously sufficiently insoluble in water to render them immune from failure on this account. It must be realized, however, that there are important types of material, which are normally used internally, whose solubility is high enough for them to fail if exposed to rain. Examples of these are the gypsum plasters and magnesium oxychloride cements; these are in fact used externally, with certain design precautions, in very dry climates.

The aggressive power of rainwater is increased by acidity due to atmospheric pollution (Table 9.3). Limestones, calcareous sandstones and, to a less extent, cement products may suffer gradual surface erosion in industrial atmospheres. Some slates may suffer more serious decay in these circumstances.

*Sunlight*

Thermal effects apart, sunlight has a direct influence on the durability of only a few organic materials, such as paints, rubber, asphalt and some plastics.

TABLE 9.3

*Susceptibility of materials to attack by acid gases in polluted atmospheres*

| Class of material | How affected |
|---|---|
| Clay products . . . | Rarely affected, but may retain soot. |
| Siliceous sandstones . . | Rarely affected, but retain soot. |
| Cast stone and cement products generally. | Good quality products only slightly affected. Dense mixes desirable for high degree of pollution. |
| Sand-lime bricks . . | Very slightly affected. |
| Limestones . . . | All attacked to some extent. The more durable stones have a long life in the worst environment. Care needed in selection. |
| Calcareous sandstones . . | Liable to be badly attacked. |
| Slates . . . . | Generally highly resistant, but some suffer rapid decay. See B.S. 680. |

*Biological agencies*

Rodents, insects, bacteria, fungi and plants may all, in one way or another, cause deterioration in a building. In temperate climates, however, it is only the possibility of fungal attack that needs to be taken into account in the design of a building. Timber and other cellulosic materials present the chief risk, but organic decorative finishes may also be affected by mould growths.

Fungal attack occurs only in the presence of sufficient persistent moisture. Attention to the problem of moisture exclusion will take care of this cause of deterioration as a general rule. When the risk cannot be eliminated by design precautions, there remains the second line of defence: pre-treatment of the vulnerable materials with a fungicide.

Climbing plants on buildings should always receive regular inspection to ensure that there is no interference with the rainwater drainage system. Occasionally, also, there is a risk of damage to weak mortar joints, slating, tiling, etc.

*Atmospheric pollution*

Aggressive gases from industrial plants are diluted very rapidly in the atmosphere. It is only in the immediate neighbourhood of their point of ejection that they may call for special protective measures, but they increase the erosive effect of rainwater over a much larger area.

*Abrasion and impact*

Resistance to abrasion and impact will be discussed in the appropriate contexts when considering walls (Part II) and floors (Part III).

*Chemical action*

A chemical change usually involves two or more substances interacting to form other substances, and is accompanied by changes in properties, such as volume, strength and appearance. Many different types of chemical change may occur in a building. The most important general statement that can be made about them applies also to the other processes of deterioration mentioned already in this chapter: nearly all of them occur only in the presence of water.

Water may itself enter into the chemical change, or it may act simply as a vehicle bringing together the substances that interact.

Chemical changes accompanied by expansion occur with building materials described as 'unsound'. When an unsound lime has been used in building, chemical interaction with water may occur—perhaps within a few hours if water is present in the liquid state, perhaps extending over many years of slower action with atmospheric moisture; the process is accompanied by expansion, which may lead to disruption of surrounding material, as when 'popping and pitting' occurs in plasterwork. The use of clinker aggregates containing an excessive amount of unburnt or partially burnt coal may lead to gross expansion of the concrete, or to local disruption, as the unburnt material oxidizes.

Chemical action on metals and on cement products is particularly important in relation to the durability of buildings, and needs to be considered in greater detail.

## CORROSION OF METALS

The use of metals in building calls for special care in design, in choice of materials and in protection, if serious corrosion problems are not, sooner or later, to arise. Not only is the cost of corrosion alone extremely high, but what is perhaps even more serious is the consequent trouble and expense resulting from it. Thus the steel frame of a building may rust and in so doing crack the external cladding. If the reinforcement in concrete rusts, the surface spalls and disintegration becomes progressive. A galvanized hot-water cylinder or a cold-water cistern is perforated and has to be replaced, while incidental damage is probably caused by water leaking from the cylinder or cistern. Metal piping and sheeting may corrode to failure in various ways and this may result in serious interruption to services.

Apart from steel, the metals commonly used in buildings are aluminium, copper, lead, zinc and their alloys.

*General considerations*

Corrosion occurs only under damp conditions.

The corrosion of a metal component in a building may have four important effects:

(1) The structural soundness of the component may be affected.

(2) Where metal is embedded in other building material, growth of corrosion products may cause distortion or cracking of the other material. Trouble may also arise when the metal is in contact with another building material, although not embedded.

(3) Failure of the component may lead to entry of water into the building.

(4) Unsightly surfaces may be produced.

The degree to which any metal will corrode under a given set of conditions depends on its physical and chemical properties. Quite apart from the inherent properties of the metal, stress introduced in its manufacture or application may play some part in bringing about corrosion. Physical structure, including porosity, may also be significant.

Broadly speaking, the following types of exposure may arise:

*Exposure to external atmospheres.* Here the amount of corrosion will depend on the kind of metal or alloy, the rainfall and temperature conditions, the degree of atmospheric pollution, the slope of the exposed surface and the extent to which the metal or alloy is exposed to the prevailing wind and rain.

*Exposure to internal atmospheres.* Again the kind of metal will be important. But here, atmospheric pollution will be modified by internal conditions in a building. Thus, in dwelling houses, exposure will be much more severe in a kitchen or bathroom than in a sitting-room. Another corrosive condition may also arise if condensation occurs in roof spaces or cavity walls. One particularly corrosive 'atmosphere', created within the building but having its effect on flue terminals, is that of the flue gases from the combustion of various types of fuel, which may severely affect chimney cappings in metal.

*Embedment in or contact with various other building materials.* Metal components may be embedded in various building mortars, plasters, concrete or floor compositions, or may be in contact with these. Again they may be in contact with other materials, such as other metals, wood, glass, etc.

*Contact with water or water containing dissolved acids, alkalis or salts.* Many details in building construction may permit rainwater to enter and be retained in crevices between metal surfaces or between a metallic and some other surface. Again, water may drip on to metal surfaces. All these conditions involve a greater risk of corrosion than where a metal is exposed to the normal action of the weather. The risk of corrosion is increased where water contains dissolved acids, alkalis or salts derived from the atmosphere or material with which the metal comes into contact. In some districts the mains water supply may also constitute an increased corrosion risk to metals.

*Contact between dissimilar metals under damp conditions.* It is well known that galvanic action can occur between two different unprotected metals in contact in the presence of moisture, causing preferential corrosion of one of the metals. The degree to which corrosion occurs depends on the kinds of metals involved, the efficiency of the metallic contact, and the conductivity of the water or solutions. It will be accentuated if the area of corroded metal (the anode of the electrolytic cell) is relatively small compared with that of the other metal.

The above considerations serve also to emphasize that in using metals in building, it is important to consider *all* types of exposure and not merely exposure to the external atmosphere. If a building is to be durable and of good appearance, special attention must be paid to the design of *details* involving metals and to essential precautions against corrosion. Failure nearly always occurs in some detail and not in general exposure to the external atmosphere. The resistance to atmospheric corrosion is therefore less important than is commonly thought.

*Building materials*

It is important to consider what corrosive agents may be contained in building materials; Portland cement on mixing with water releases free sodium and potassium hydroxides, which, while protective to ferrous metals, are harmful to lead, zinc and aluminium. Copper is unaffected. High-alumina cement is much less alkaline and the effects either way are therefore much less marked. High-calcium lime provides a solution of lime; this is protective to iron so long as it remains uncarbonated, but has a slight corrosive effect on lead and zinc; aluminium may be more severely attacked; copper is unaffected. Magnesian lime, consisting essentially of a mixture of calcium and magnesium hydroxides, behaves similarly. Retarded hemi-hydrate plasters yield a solution of calcium sulphate, occasionally with lime from a special addition. Keene's plaster will not only give calcium sulphate, but also contains small amounts of alum or potassium sulphate or both; it will sometimes have an acid reaction and may yield a solution with a relatively high salt content. Magnesium oxychloride cement contains magnesium chloride and gives a highly corrosive condition. Wood is sometimes acid and provides soluble salts; particularly troublesome may be Western red cedar and sometimes Douglas fir among the softwoods, oak and sweet chestnut among the hardwoods. Bricks and (to a less extent) tiles may contain sulphates of calcium, magnesium, sodium and potassium. These may lead to intensification of corrosion where a metal is in contact with a brick or tile face.

*Ferrous metals*

The protection of steelwork is particularly important. Except where it is encased in concrete, structural steel may be exposed to a variety of conditions externally and internally, and precautions against corrosion must be suitably increased in the more severe exposures. Experience indicates that the standard of protection often given is too low. Structural steel should be freed from all mill-scale and rust and at the very least protected with suitable paints over a corrosion-inhibiting primer. Better, for more severe exposures, a good metallic coating of zinc or aluminium should be applied first, before phosphating and painting.

Steel in concrete is normally protected by the alkali released from Portland cement, but it is essential that the concrete should be dense, with at least $1\frac{1}{2}$ in. cover to the steel for all external work. Coal residues such as clinker should never be used in reinforced concrete. Additions of calcium chloride up to 2 per cent by weight of cement are permissible in reinforced concrete.

Embedment in or contact with other building materials generally calls for some protection.

Steel sheets (B.S. 798) are galvanized but need additional protection by painting where a long life is required. Ungalvanized sheets need special care in painting; 'paint harling', (paint-coated granite chippings thrown on to a thick coating of a special lead paint), has been used with success. Steel windows and doors (B.S. 990: 1945, Amendment No. 7, 1953) require a zinc coating at least as heavy as the 1·5 oz/sq. ft. required by the Standard for hot-dipped or metal-sprayed windows and doors. Similar considerations apply to other steel components.

Cast iron is usually painted, but again the standard of protection could sometimes be increased with advantage. For example, internal protection of cast-iron rainwater goods may be inadequate and this may lead eventually to cracking resulting from corrosion; a higher standard of protection can be obtained by coating with a composition that has a tar or a bituminous base, or by galvanizing.

*Non-ferrous metals*

Only lead, copper, zinc and aluminium will be considered here. Lead and copper have been in use for a very long time and zinc for about 100 years. Aluminium is a relative newcomer, and a variety of alloys is available; the correct choice of alloy is important.

On simple exposure to the atmosphere the resistance of lead, copper and aluminium, including certain aluminium alloys not containing copper, is high. That of zinc is appreciably lower.

Lead, copper, zinc and probably aluminium also, are attacked by water dripping from roofs, in particular by water made more acid by vegetable growth (algae, moss, lichen) on the roof or by washing over cedar wood shingles. Holes may develop in the metal under the water drip, or the metal may be completely perforated along a line coincident with the edge of a wood shingle. Channelling of lead is typical of the effect of water drip, with eventual perforation. A coating of bitumen, of heavy painting consistency, should be applied to metals exposed to this type of corrosion risk.

Lead is strongly affected by acetic acid (vinegar) fumes and by contact with wood. Lead pipe and sheet can be corroded very severely when in contact with concrete or mortar containing Portland cement, and should be protected by a coat of bitumen paint; aluminium and several of its alloys are also affected to some extent; copper seems to be relatively immune; the behaviour of zinc is not yet clear. In resistance to soil corrosion, lead and copper behave relatively well, as compared with zinc and aluminium.

In the use of copper pipes for water services, trouble has been experienced owing to the presence on the internal walls of carbonaceous or copper oxide films formed during making, with consequent pitting from the inside. The remedy here is in the hands of the makers and, in fact, the relevant British Standard now requires copper pipe to be free from such internal film. Stress-corrosion cracking has occurred where traces of ammonia are present in insulation surrounding pipes made from 'phosphorus de-oxidized copper', and also in a state of stress; avoidance of phosphorus and stress is called for where ammonia may be present.

Aluminium alloys have now been extensively used as structural materials and some troubles experienced have been traced to the use of a copper-containing high-strength alloy susceptible to a laminar form of corrosion. Aluminium rainwater goods should carry rainwater only, since their resistance to normal supply waters and to kitchen and bathroom wastes is uncertain and their use for such exposures cannot therefore be recommended at present.

*Summary*

The need for care in design, in choice of materials and in protection is to be emphasized.

In design it is important to ensure that water cannot enter a structure or lie on horizontal surfaces. Crevices should be avoided, since water or solution may be retained, leading to attack within the crevice; the treatment of joints is discussed in a later section (p. 128). It is also dangerous to place any unprotected metal in contact with a porous material that may contain soluble salts, acids or alkalis, for this will accelerate corrosion; such a contact will ordinarily include a crevice condition as well. It is important also to ensure, as far as possible, uniform embedment of metal in any environment. For example, steel reinforcement or steel piping should not be partly in concrete and partly touching a plaster finish or some other material.

Correct choice of metal or alloy is also important, especially with aluminium and its alloys. It is safest at present to avoid alloys containing copper. Generally, the stronger alloys will need greater care in protection. It is also important to avoid contacts between dissimilar metals.

Protection is often vital to ensure the durability of metals, especially in those details where the chance of corrosion is high. It is false economy to skimp protection. Ferrous metals generally, except where uniformly and properly embedded in an alkaline material like concrete or mortar containing Portland cement, should be adequately protected. All non-ferrous metals usually need protection where in contact with other materials; with zinc and aluminium it is often desirable also to paint generally. Crevices, especially perhaps with aluminium, should be packed with a suitable filling, preferably one containing a corrosion inhibitor. Water systems or pipe lines can also be given additional protection, internally or externally, by cathodic protection devices, in conjunction with suitable protective coatings.

Finally, avoidance of corrosion is a matter for co-operation between manufacturers, architect, builder and user. Many manufacturing details are at fault, not least in domestic plumbing. The architect can help in design of details on his building, choice of materials and protective schemes, the builder by strict care in the execution of the work, and the user by adequate care and maintenance.

## CHEMICAL ACTION ON CEMENT PRODUCTS

Before considering the various substances that can interact chemically with cements and aggregates, it is worth drawing an important distinction. Metals are generally impermeable to fluids, and concretes are not. With metals, therefore, chemical action is restricted to the surface and can progress only as fast as fresh surfaces are exposed; with cement products chemical action may proceed in depth, depending on the permeability of the product to the aggressive fluid. It is necessary to bear this in mind when assessing the suitability of concretes, mortars, asbestos cement, etc., for use in certain situations. In a given aggressive environment, a carefully proportioned dense material may have an adequate life because erosion can proceed only very slowly inwards from the surface; a permeable material made of the same cement and the same aggregate may deteriorate rapidly because of chemical action proceeding simultaneously throughout the mass. Thus, in practice, resistance to chemical attack is not an 'all-or-nothing' affair: much depends on permeability (which may, in turn, depend on mix design and the control of quality on site or in factory) and on whether hydrostatic pressure on one side will tend to force aggressive fluids into the material.

For cement products in the general run of domestic, office and public buildings, there is only one type of chemical attack that need concern the designer: that of sulphate salts in solution. Sulphates may be present in clay products, soils and groundwaters. Other types of chemical attack, liable to occur only in certain industrial buildings, in marine structures or when cement products are exposed in very close proximity to a source of acid fumes, require only brief mention here; in such circumstances the selection of resistant materials is usually a matter for the specialist.

*Sulphate salts*

The sulphates of sodium, potassium, magnesium and calcium occur widely in clays and other soils; they are also liable to occur in burnt-clay products.

In solution, sulphates interact with Portland cement, causing considerable expansion and loss of strength. The rate of attack depends on the persistence of damp conditions, the permeability of the material, the concentration of the sulphates in solution and on whether pressure differences tend to force the solution through the material.

With brickwork, as will be described in detail later (p. 234), it is a sufficient defence against attack on the mortar to design so that the work is not damp for long periods. Where continuous dampness cannot be avoided, either the bricks should be selected for low content of sulphates or the mortar should be based on a less vulnerable cement, such as high-alumina or sulphate-resisting cement.

With foundations in sulphate-bearing soils there can be no question of keeping the concrete dry. The precautions to be taken will depend on the amount of sulphate (generally expressed as the amount of sulphur trioxide) present, on the thickness of the concrete section and on whether there is one-sided water pressure: they are outlined in Table 9.4.

*Acids*

Acids generally are destructive to cement, and ordinary cement products should be avoided wherever there may be prolonged exposure to acid solutions.

There are several organic acids that may come into contact with concrete, particularly where foodstuffs are being processed. Vinegar and fruit juices contain acid, and various acids are formed when milk and other foods go sour or decay. The suitability of concrete floors for food-processing factories depends very much on whether spillage can be avoided or cleaned away before it can cause trouble, and also on whether there is much abrasion. Dairy floors, where the rate of attack on concrete by lactic acid may be increased by the abrasive action of milk churns being rolled around, generally call for special forms of construction.

In referring to foodstuffs, it should be mentioned that sugar solutions, especially when hot, also attack cement.

*Alkalis*

Alkalis offer no serious threat to Portland cement products, but do gradually reduce the strength of high-alumina cement.

## TABLE 9.4

*Precautions recommended when concrete is exposed to sulphate soil conditions*

| Soil conditions | | Precast concrete products | Concrete cast *in situ* | |
|---|---|---|---|---|
| Sulphur trioxide in ground water (parts per 100 000) | Sulphur trioxide in clay (per cent) | | Buried concrete surrounded by clay | Concrete exposed to one-sided water pressure, or concrete of thin section |
| Less than 30 | Less than 0·2 | No special measures. | No special measures, except that the use of lean concretes (e.g. 1:7, or leaner, ballast concrete) inadvisable if sulphur trioxide in water exceeds about 20 parts per 100 000; Portland cement mixes not leaner than 1:2:4, or, if special precautions are desired, pozzolanic cement, or sulphate-resisting Portland cement mixes not leaner than 1:2:4 should then be used. | No special measures, except that when sulphur trioxide in water is above 20 parts per 100 000, special care should be taken to ensure the use of high-quality Portland cement concrete, if necessary 1:1½:3 mixes, alternatively, pozzolanic cements or sulphate-resisting Portland cement may be used in mixes not leaner than 1:2:4. |

| | | | | |
|---|---|---|---|---|
| 30 to 100 | 0·2 to 0·5 | Rich Portland cement concretes, e.g. 1:1½:3 are not likely to suffer seriously except over a very long period of years. Alternatively either pozzolanic, sulphate-resisting Portland cement, high-alumina or super-sulphate cement should be used. | Rich Portland cement concretes, e.g. 1:1½:3 are not likely to suffer seriously over a short period of years, provided that care is taken to ensure that a very dense and homogeneous mass is obtained. For most work, and particularly if the predominant salts are magnesium or sodium sulphates, concrete made with either pozzolanic cement, sulphate-resisting Portland cement, high-alumina cement or super-sulphate cement (1:2:4) is advisable (see NOTE). | The use of Portland cement concrete is not advisable. Pozzolanic cement or sulphate-resisting Portland cement or preferably either high-alumina cement or super-sulphate cement is recommended. |
| Above 100 | Above 0·5 | The densest Portland cement concrete is not likely to suffer seriously over periods up to, say, 10-20 years, unless conditions are very severe. Alternatively sulphate-resisting, high-alumina or super-sulphate cement concretes should be used. | The use of high alumina or super-sulphate cement concrete is recommended. | The use of high-alumina or super-sulphate cement concrete is recommended. |

NOTE: Where 1:2:4 concrete is mentioned, other mixes of equivalent weight ratio of cement to total aggregate, but with somewhat increased ratio of sand to coarse aggregates (e.g. 1:2½:3¾ or even 1:2½:3½) may be used, sometimes with advantage. It may be necessary when using super-sulphate cement to employ mixes somewhat richer than 1:2:4 in order to obtain adequate workability.

*Oils*

Mineral oils do not attack concrete once it has hardened. Vegetable and animal oils may do so, in which case deterioration will be hastened by abrasion. If the aggressive effect is only slight, surface treatment of, say, a concrete floor may give adequate protection. Generally, expert advice should be sought when this type of problem arises.

It is worth noting that cutting oils, used in the machining of metals, and some lubricating oils contain vegetable oils.

*Chapter* 10

# BUILDING ECONOMICS

THE economic aspects of building are complicated by the fact that the functions of design and production are generally separated. At the design stage, therefore, the designer will usually not know the methods and equipment available to the contractor who may ultimately build. Nevertheless, the designer has a dominant part to play in achieving economy in building since he is directly responsible for the materials used which, for most buildings, account for about two-thirds of the total costs of materials and labour. This is not to suggest that the contractor has not a very real contribution to make but, since the labour which he controls costs only about half that of the materials, his efforts can easily be nullified by any design which makes excessive or unnecessary use of material.


## COST PLANNING

The need to have cost data available from the earliest stages of the design has encouraged the development of methods of 'cost planning', and the wider application of such techniques is essential if cost is to become, as it should, an integral part of design.

Cost planning of a job requires the analysis of information from other similar completed schemes in such a way that the cost of the various component parts of the building such as walls, floor, roof, electrical services and so on, is available in a form that can be directly applied in design. Although the data contained in priced Bills of Quantities are presented separately for each trade, they can, without difficulty, be broken down into the form required for cost analysis. In some cases a modified form of bill has been used to facilitate the assembly of data for cost planning. In these 'elemental bills' the pricing is shown for each element separately but, although such arrangement simplifies cost analysis, it is by no means essential to it.

The type of information which it is necessary to obtain by cost analysis for use subsequently for cost control purposes is illustrated by Table 10·1. As an example, the breakdown of prices of a number of blocks of flats is taken; the functional elements used being those which can be reasonably easily obtained from priced bills. It is recognized that for this purpose it is preferable to use actual cost data rather than the information obtained from priced bills, but these data are rarely available.

The form in which the information is set out in the analysis, that is, as the cost per sq. ft or per ft cube or per school pupil, depends upon the type of building involved and it is reasonable to relate the figures to the method employed by the client in stating the cost requirements. Consequently, since the acceptable price of flats is usually expressed in terms of the nett floor area

95

within the flat, this basis has been used in Table 10.1. The prices expressed in this way should be combined with a statement of area ratios of certain of the functional elements—i.e., in this case, the ratio of the areas of external walls or partitions to the nett floor area. The ratios relate to typical upper floors rather than to the building as a whole since the upper floors are generally more strictly comparable. In the example given, data are provided for each of three blocks. These show a range of cost for each element and, in fixing the target for cost planning, judgment must be exercised and the actual design of the examples borne in mind. Some allowance for contingencies is also desirable and the targets suggested in the last column would be reasonable in the example given.

TABLE 10.1

Cost analysis of multi-storey flats
Prices per sq. ft nett

| Component | Project A | | Project B | | Project C | | Target for cost planning | |
|---|---|---|---|---|---|---|---|---|
| | s. | d. | s. | d. | s. | d. | s. | d. |
| Substructure . . . . | 3 | 3 | 3 | 6 | 6 | 3 | 3 | 6 |
| Frame and walls, floors, stairs and roof structure . . . | 20 | 4 | 20 | 2 | 15 | 2 | 17 | 6 |
| Partitions . . . . | 0 | 8 | 1 | 0 | 1 | 0 | 1 | 0 |
| Plumbing and heating . . | 6 | 3 | 6 | 3 | 7 | 1 | 6 | 6 |
| Joinery . . . . . | 4 | 3 | 4 | 4 | 4 | 5 | 4 | 3 |
| Plasterwork . . . . | 3 | 2 | 2 | 11 | 1 | 11 | 2 | 6 |
| Floor finishes . . . . | 2 | 2 | 2 | 11 | 2 | 0 | 2 | 0 |
| Painting and glazing . . | 2 | 5 | 1 | 9 | 2 | 3 | 2 | 0 |
| Windows . . . . | 1 | 8 | 1 | 6 | 1 | 2 | 1 | 3 |
| Electrical . . . . | 2 | 2 | 2 | 3 | 2 | 11 | 2 | 3 |
| Steel and ironwork . . . | 2 | 4 | 2 | 0 | 1 | 4 | 1 | 6 |
| Roof finishes . . . . | 0 | 10 | 0 | 7 | 0 | 8 | 0 | 9 |
| Lifts . . . . . | 4 | 2 | 2 | 10 | 2 | 10 | 3 | 0 |
| Total . . . | 53 | 8 | 52 | 0 | 49 | 0 | 48 | 0 |
| Storeys . . . . . | 8 | | 9 | | 10 | | | |
| Nett area . . . . | 35 000 | | 37 000 | | 22 000 | | | |
| Gross area . . . . | 47 000 | | 46 000 | | 28 000 | | | |
| Area ratios of typical upper floor: | | | | | | | | |
| Nett/gross . . . . | 0·81 | | 0·85 | | 0·84 | | 0·84 | |
| External wall/nett . . | 1·12 | | 1·11 | | 1·14 | | 1·12 | |
| Partitions/nett . . . | 0·80 | | 0·96 | | 0·40 | | 0·80 | |

The source of the data for cost planning will in most cases be the earlier projects carried out by the same design office but it is often necessary to supplement this by information from other designers which may be published from time to time. Because of this use of the data it is desirable that cost analyses should be in such a form that they can be easily converted to any required form of presentation. The inclusion of the area ratios facilitates this.

## PLANNING ECONOMY

The area ratios of the elements provide in themselves a useful means of cost control. It was found, for example, in a survey of the cost of high flats that the ratio of nett to gross area for upper floors was from 0·71 to 0·91 while the ratio of external wall area to nett floor area ranged from 0·80 to 1·60. These two ratios are of particular importance. The first is in a sense a measure of planning efficiency while the second governs, among other things, the heat loss of the building, and hence both the initial and the running cost of the heating installation. The figures obtained in the survey of costs of flats suggest that for typical upper floors the access area should not in fact exceed 15 or 16 per cent. The addition of the unnecessary access area, as much as 30 per cent in some instances, means in fact that the overall cost may be increased by as much as 10 per cent.

The wide range of area ratios shows the importance of establishing target figures for these based on well planned examples of other buildings of the same general type.

A notable example of the economic consequence of a close study of planning requirements is provided by experience in school design in recent years. The figures in Table 10.2 show how strict attention to the real functional requirements has enabled the total area per child in primary and secondary schools to be reduced by about 40 per cent. Within this smaller total area, however, the amount of teaching space per child has been maintained or slightly increased. The result of this planning economy, coupled with other reductions in the cost per unit area, has been that school places cost about 20 per cent less in 1956 than in 1949, despite a rise in building costs of around 50 per cent.

TABLE 10.2

*Total area allotted per child in school design, 1949–1956*

| Year | Primary schools (sq. ft per place) | Secondary schools (sq. ft per place) |
|---|---|---|
| 1949 . . | 68 | 110 |
| 1950 . . | 60 | 90 |
| 1951 . . | 48 | 78 |
| 1952 . . | 44 | 76 |
| 1953 . . | 43 | 75 |
| 1954 . . | 43 | 74 |
| 1955 . . | 42 | 74 |
| 1956 (Jan/June) | 42 | 74 |

Similar reduction of unnecessary area has been found possible in hospital design. By a study of functional requirements for nursing and the needs of patients, it was found that the current standard of 250 sq. ft per bed could be cut to 200 sq. ft without sacrificing the real standards of accommodation.

These examples show how attention to planning and the close study of functional requirements can affect substantial financial economies without any real loss of amenity.

## CONSTRUCTION ECONOMY

The main application of cost analysis is to the comparison of alternative forms of construction. In this there are real difficulties. The direct experience of any one architect or quantity surveyor is necessarily limited, and often, for new forms of construction, actual prices are by no means readily available. On the other hand the publication of prices for different forms of construction presents problems, since they can, conveniently, only relate to average conditions and actual tenders may differ widely from them. Furthermore, prices change with time and the continuous revision of prices for a large number of items would be a considerable undertaking. However, the relative costs of different constructions should change less rapidly with time than the absolute values, and the Building Research Station has published data on the average prices of a wide range of different forms of construction for walls, floors and roofs together with the amount of thermal insulation which was provided ('Thermal insulation of buildings', H.M.S.O., 1955). The man-hours for the operations involved and the basic material costs are also given, so that some adjustment is possible as the costs of either change. From these data the likely cost of a construction to provide a specified degree of insulation can easily be found, or alternatively, the best insulation for a given cost can be selected.

A particularly forceful example of the need for economy in the structural design of buildings is provided by an examination of the design of multi-storey flats. The drawings and specification of a number of flats, which had load-bearing concrete walls, revealed a wide range in the amounts of concrete which had been used. In fact nearly three times as much concrete was used in some blocks as in others and, in consequence, the superstructures (excluding finishings and fittings) of the blocks using the larger amounts of concrete were nearly twice as dear as the others.

In seeking ways of reducing costs without loss of quality, attention must be paid to the methods which are to be employed in actual construction. The designer is often content to leave the matter entirely to the contractor, and while the latter will undoubtedly overcome the problems imposed by the design, this often means that the cost is higher than it need be. The type of plant which may be available should properly be considered at the design stage; the increasing use of tower cranes, for instance, opens up possibilities for handling larger units than could hitherto be economically contemplated.

Another example of the same type is provided by the design of shuttering for concrete. Comparatively minor changes in design from one part of the building to another can prevent repeated use of the same shuttering. Furthermore the shuttering required can be rendered very complex by small design details which might easily be modified without detriment to the architectural conception. The importance of this subject can be realized from the fact that the cost of the concrete in a wall is often less than the cost of the shuttering that encloses it until it sets.

## RUNNING COSTS

Consideration of economy in building design is often restricted to the examination of ways of reducing first cost, but this is too narrow an approach and it is important also to include the costs of administration, heating, ventilating, lighting, and maintaining the building over its life. The equivalent capital value of these may well be as much as, or more than, the first cost of the building itself.

To consider running and first costs together, it is necessary to establish a relation between annual expenditure and the equivalent capital cost. This depends not only on the life considered but also on the rate of interest at which money may be borrowed. Table 10.3 gives the equivalent capital value of an annual expenditure of £1 for some typical cases. The significance of this table is that if a sum of, say, £12 is borrowed at 5½ per cent interest, then an annual payment of £1 will repay the loan and the interest on it in a period of twenty years. It is clear that the figures do not differ very greatly with the period taken for the loan. Since these rates of exchange make no allowance for any inflation during the period, which would in fact increase the running costs, there is much to be said for ignoring the actual term of the loan and taking the figures for an infinitely long loan (nominally 999 years). This has a further advantage that it is no longer necessary to have available tables of the equivalent capital value of £1 per annum, since for a long-term loan the equivalent capital value is the sum which will yield £1 per annum at simple interest without repayment of the capital. For example, at 4 per cent the capital value of £1 per annum is £25, at 5 per cent £20, and so on.

TABLE 10.3

*Equivalent capital value of an annual expenditure of £1 per annum*

| Period | Rate of interest | | |
|---|---|---|---|
| | 5 per cent | 5½ per cent | 6 per cent |
| 15 years . . | 10·4 | 10·0 | 9·6 |
| 20 years . . | 12·5 | 12·0 | 11·5 |
| 40 years . . | 17·2 | 16·0 | 15·0 |
| 60 years . . | 18·9 | 17·4 | 16·2 |
| 999 years . . | 20·0 | 18·2 | 16·7 |

For a loan at the rate of 5½ per cent, which is a typical figure, the capital value of a running cost of £1 per annum is, therefore, about £18. In other words, an added capital expenditure of £18 000 would be justifiable if the running cost could be reduced by £1000 a year. An obvious example of the application of such an approach is to the study of the effect of planning on the administrative labour costs. In one case a revision of the designs of a laboratory block enabled the number of laboratory stewards required to be reduced by one. The cost of a laboratory steward was about £800 a year so that an added cost of £800 × 18, or £14 000, would have been justifiable in order to make this change possible. In the event the revised design did not involve any marked increase in cost, but the example clearly emphasizes the importance of considering the functions of the building, and particularly the staff involved in running it, at the design stage. In general it is likely that the saving of one man's labour would justify an added first cost of at least £10 000.

Similar considerations apply, of course, to other items of annual expenditure of which heating is the obvious example. The balance to be struck is between the added cost of better insulation and the reduction it may mean in first cost of the heating installation and in running costs.

Apart from the standard of insulation, the heating costs are very dependent on the plan adopted. It has been shown, for example, that in schools a compact single-storey school with a storey height of about 8 ft could have a heat loss around 30 per cent less than one with a more straggling design with storey height around 11 ft. This means that the running costs of the heating system will be reduced by about this amount and while the first cost of the heating installation will not be reduced pro rata, the reduction in this also is likely to be at least 20 per cent.

Circumstances can arise in which an increase of maintenance or other running costs may be the only way of achieving an essential reduction in first costs. For example, in buildings for which a relatively short life is required, it may well be important to minimize first cost even at the expense of higher running costs. It is unfortunately the case that there are few materials which, providing a short life, are substantially cheaper than more conventional materials which have a long life. In temporary buildings, therefore, the reduction of first cost must usually be sought by some lowering of standards which may lead to higher running costs. The problem, however, needs to be approached with caution, since there are many 'temporary' buildings now in existence long after the period for which they were originally designed.


## MAINTENANCE COSTS

The equivalent values given in Table 10.3 are applicable when the running costs are more or less constant from year to year, which is the case for heating, lighting and labour costs. There is, however, a tendency for maintenance costs to increase with the age of the building and when this occurs the values given would not be applicable; the general effect of running costs increasing with time is to reduce the corresponding capital value as compared with expenditure of the same total amount by equal sums each year. The extent of this reduction depends on the way in which the expenditure increases with time, and on various plausible assumptions the reduction might be from £18 to £10 or £11 in the case of a loan of 5½ per cent.

An examination of the maintenance costs of local authority housing has shown that their total expenditure (which excluded internal decoration, however) over the life of the house was equivalent to only about 18 per cent of the first cost. A further breakdown of this figure into the maintenance costs of specific items has shown that only in the case of 'water service' and 'external painting' was the maintenance cost a substantial percentage of the first cost. The maintenance expenditure on water service was in fact made up of a number of small elements, such as overflows and ball valves, trivial in work content but of frequent occurrence. A more rational design could, however, achieve a better correspondence between initial and maintenance costs among the various components, and the use of somewhat more expensive items which reduce the cost of external painting is clearly justifiable.

It must be borne in mind, however, that a high maintenance cost may well be appropriate for components which are subject to obsolescence—for example, if it is considered desirable to change the colour of the external painting every few years, then a high cost is justifiable; but it is perhaps inappropriate to regard this as maintenance.

Chapter 11

# PRINCIPLES OF USE OF MATERIALS

THE foregoing chapters have discussed design in relation to the various functional requirements of buildings. Valuable as it is as an aid to understanding, such an analytical treatment may be difficult for the designer to interpret, especially as the requirements so identified are by no means independent when it comes to their fulfilment in a building. This chapter, dealing with some groups of materials used in building, aims at providing helpful cross-linkages, relating the ideas presented in the earlier chapters with examples of how requirements can be met in new ways. Natural stone and clay brick do not receive separate discussion here, as they are dealt with in considerable detail in Part II (pp. 234–46).

## CONCRETE

Many types of concrete are used in modern building construction, ranging widely in density and strength according to their particular use, whether, for example, for thermal insulation, strength and durability, fire protection or appearance. They range from lightweight concrete at one extreme, with a density of perhaps only 25 lb/cu. ft, to the especially heavy concrete, weighing well over 300 lb/cu. ft, required for biological shielding from radio-activity. Strength may range from a few pounds per square inch to well over 10 000 pounds per square inch.

To produce this range of concretes, use is made of aggregates which vary enormously in type and structure, and which may range in maximum size from a small fraction of an inch to well over six inches. The cement can be chosen from a number of different kinds, as will be shown later, to meet the particular conditions under which the concrete is to be used. A classification of the main types of concrete used in building construction is given in Table 11.1. They divide broadly into four functional groups:

(1) for thermal insulation;
(2) for fire protection;
(3) for strength and durability;
(4) for biological radiation shielding.

Generally the lighter and more open-textured concretes are best for thermal insulation, and the subject of lightweight concrete is dealt with later in this chapter.

The fire protection afforded by concrete largely depends upon the type of aggregate used. Flint gravel and, to a lesser degree, other natural stones expand greatly on heating to high temperature and disrupt the concrete, causing it to spall. The spalling generally extends inwards to the nearest plane of weakness in the concrete, usually the plane of the reinforcement

## TABLE 11.1

### Range of concretes used in building construction

| Aggregate | Density of aggregate* (lb/cu. ft) | Concrete density (lb/cu. ft) | Compressive strength (lb/cu. ft) | Thermal conductivity (B.t.u. in./h sq. ft °F) | Particular use |
|---|---|---|---|---|---|
| Expanded vermiculite | 4– 15 | 25– 70 | 70– 1 100 | 0·75–2·0 | for thermal insulation / Fire resistance: Class 1 (a) aggregate |
| Aerated concrete | — | 20– 90 | 500– 1 500 | 0·75–2·5 | |
| Pumice and foamed slag | 30– 55 | 45– 95 | 200– 2 000 | 1·50–3·0 | |
| Expanded clay and clinker | 35– 65 | 45– 95 | 200– 2 000 | 1·50–4·0 | for fire protection — Class 1 (b) |
| Crushed brick | 70– 85 | 105–135 | 2 000– 4 000 | — | for load carrying and durability |
| Crushed limestone | 85–100 | 135–140 | 3 500– 5 000 | — | |
| Flint gravel, granite and crushed natural stone | 85–100 | 140–155 | (i) 2 000– 6 000 (ii) 6 000–10 000 (special-purpose) | — | |
| Barytes | 155–185 | 215 | 3 000 } heavyweight | — | for radiation shielding / Class 2 aggregate |
| Iron shot | — | — | up to 10 000 | — | |

* The density range is influenced by the grading of the aggregate.

nearest the exposed surface, and sometimes even beyond. Certain aggregates such as clean crushed clay brick and slag do not cause spalling, and any weakening of concrete with these aggregates is due principally to the dehydration of the cement. If the concrete does not spall, the process of disintegration of the concrete is very slow. Additional protection can be given by thickening the cover to the reinforcement, but if the concrete has a tendency to spall owing to the type of aggregate used, little benefit is obtained from this because the whole of the cover, whatever its thickness (within the limits commonly used in practice), may spall and fall away. Disintegration of the concrete beyond the plane of the reinforcement is usually much slower if the disintegrated concrete is held in position by the steel, since this will delay the rise in temperature of the material in the interior of the structural member. The accepted classifications of aggregate in descending order of merit for fire resistance of the concrete made from them, is as follows:

CLASS 1 (a) Pumice and foamed slag.
    (b) Blastfurnace slag, crushed brick and burnt clay products, well-burnt clinker and crushed limestone.

CLASS 2 Siliceous aggregates generally, e.g. flint gravel, granite and all crushed natural stones other than limestone.

To provide adequate strength and durability, concrete must be carefully proportioned, preferably batched by weight, with materials consistently uniform throughout the work. Provided this is done, the amount of mixing water will determine the workability of the mix. An experienced concretor can control the workability sufficiently closely by eye, and can adjust the amount of water entering the mixer accordingly. The workability required depends on the type of work and the care with which the concrete can be placed. Sometimes it is the method of transporting and the means of placing the concrete, that control the workability. For example, when placing concrete by pumping it along a pipeline the workability has to be carefully controlled, and this helps to produce concrete of good and uniform quality. It is usual to check the uniformity of the concrete by making sample cubes which can be tested at specified dates. With reasonably good control it has been found quite easily possible to produce concrete whose crushing strength, as measured by cube tests, shows a coefficient of variation (see Appendix I) of between 5 per cent and 10 per cent.

*Choice of aggregate*

The quality of the concrete will depend on the quality of the ingredients, on the type of cement, and the types of aggregates, particularly the sand or fine aggregate, as well as on the quantity of cement and water in the mix. The grading of the sand and the size distribution of its particles are important, also its surface area and the shape and texture of its particles. All these influence the strength and durability of the concrete. Some sands are unsuitable for concrete, particularly those contaminated by impurities. There has been a long-standing prejudice against fine sands for concrete, but recent research at the Building Research Station has shown that many that might previously have been discarded as being too fine can in fact be utilized for concrete, by careful adjustment of the ratio of the fine material to the coarse. In order to examine the gradings of the sands available in England

TABLE 11.2

*Grades of concreting sands, and suggested proportions of sand and coarse aggregate in concrete mixes*

| British Standard type of sand | Sand — Percentage by weight passing British Standard sieves: | | | | | | | Suitable proportions of sand to coarse aggregate for normal concrete work. Parts of coarse aggregate to one part of sand (by weight). Maximum size of coarse aggregate: | | |
|---|---|---|---|---|---|---|---|---|---|---|
| | $\frac{3}{8}$ in. | $\frac{3}{16}$ in. | No. 7 | No. 14 | No. 25 | No. 52 | No. 100 | $\frac{3}{8}$ in. | $\frac{3}{4}$ in. | $1\frac{1}{2}$ in. |
| Zone 1 . . . . | 100 | 90–100 | 60–95 | 30–70 | 15–34 | 5–20 | 0–10* | 1 | $1\frac{1}{2}$ | 2 |
| Zone 2 . . . . | 100 | 90–100 | 75–100 | 55–90 | 35–59 | 10–30 | 0–10* | $1\frac{1}{2}$ | 2 | 3 |
| Zone 3 . . . . | 100 | 90–100 | 85–100 | 75–100 | 60–79 | 15–40 | 0–10* | 2 | 3 | $3\frac{1}{2}$ |
| Zone 4 . . . . | 100 | 95–100 | 95–100 | 90–100 | 80–100 | 15–50 | 0–15* | 3† | $3\frac{1}{2}$† | — |

* For crushed stone sands the permissible limit is increased to 20 per cent.
† Suitability for concrete in reinforced concrete structures should be ascertained before use.

and Wales a survey was made by the Station, in collaboration with the Ballast, Sand and Allied Trades' Association and, in view of the predominance of fine sands, a programme of research was undertaken on the use of fine sands in concrete. This research has resulted in a reclassification of sands into four zones, given in Table 11.2, according to their fineness of grading, and this new classification is now embodied in B.S. 882, for concrete aggregates from natural sources. The sands in each of these grading zones are suitable for making concrete, but to ensure concrete of high strength and good durability the mix proportions should be chosen according to the grading characteristics of the sand used, the ratio of sand to coarse aggregate being reduced as the sand becomes finer. In particular, the correct design of the mix becomes increasingly important as the grading of the sand approaches the coarser outer limit of Zone 1, or the fine outer limit of Zone 4, and the suitability of a given sand grading may, in some circumstances, depend on the grading and shape of the coarse aggregate. As a general guide, however, for normal structural concrete, suggested ratios of sand to coarse aggregate as the sand gets finer are given on the right-hand side of Table 11.2. It will be seen, for example, that when using $\frac{3}{4}$-in. coarse aggregate the ratio of sand to coarse aggregate will vary from $1:1\frac{1}{2}$ for Zone 1 sand, to $1:2$ and $1:3$ and $1:3\frac{1}{2}$ for Zone 2, 3 and 4 sands respectively.

The fine sands in Zone 4 tend to produce 'gap-graded' mixes (deficient in intermediate sizes of particle) but again, with careful adjustments to the ratio of fine to coarse material, good concrete can be produced, particularly if the mix is compacted by vibration.

The survey referred to above showed that, although it may often be difficult to obtain sand of a particular grading zone in some parts of the country, there are usually sands that fall in the other grading zones. It is sometimes found that a particular sand may not lie consistently in any one grading zone and it may therefore be desirable to vary the ratio of sand to coarse aggregate in accord with the fluctuation of the grading zone of the sand.

Concrete for biological shielding should be as heavy and as dense as possible, and in some circumstances specially heavy aggregates such as barium sulphate (barytes), iron and lead are used. In large constructions, such as the protecting walls of a nuclear reactor, the use of these special aggregates would be prohibitive in cost, and the necessary protection is obtained by using the more conventional types of concrete, but of much greater thickness. Uniformity is of the utmost importance. Segregation of the concrete should be avoided, since porous pockets might allow leakage of radiation. Shrinkage should be minimized by using as stiff a mix as possible, as cracking of the concrete might be dangerous.

### Durability

A recent survey, by the Building Research Station and the Cement and Concrete Association, of reinforced concrete buildings showed that, whereas some of the oldest showed no sign of deterioration after 50 years, others in a much shorter time had suffered seriously from corrosion of reinforcement. It was clear that in many instances the requirements for good durability had not been fulfilled. The vulnerable element in reinforced concrete is the steel reinforcement: if moisture and air can penetrate to it through concrete of poor quality or of inadequate thickness, corrosion of the steel is inevitable, and this will crack and spall the concrete. Repair can be very costly and difficult.

In many of the buildings examined that were built twenty-five years or more ago, the cover to the reinforcement was in places ½ in. or less. This, in general, proved inadequate to ensure good durability. The Recommendations for a Code of Practice for the Use of Reinforced Concrete in Building (published in 1933) suggested 1 in. as the minimum cover to the main steel reinforcement. Even this is now considered inadequate for good protection, and the new Code of Practice (CP.114) 'The Structural Use of Normal Reinforced Concrete in Buildings' recommends that for all external work the cover should not be less than 1½ in., for all steel, including stirrups, links, etc., except where the face of the concrete is adequately protected by a suitable cladding or by a protective coating necessitated by unduly severe corrosive conditions. The increase in recommended minimum cover from 1 in. to 1½ in. in a matter of thirty years is most striking and significant. Many precast facing slabs have been made in recent years with cover to the reinforcement of less than ½ in. and in a matter of only a few years are in process of decay; careful thought is needed in the design of such slabs to ensure adequate cover to the steel on the exposed face.

*Appearance and finish*

Whatever type of surface finish is adopted, the appearance can be completely ruined by improperly made construction joints and joints between successive lifts; not only will bad joints disfigure the surface of the concrete, they will also allow the penetration of moisture. The position of construction joints should be carefully considered and concreting should be carried continuously up to them. When work has to be resumed on a surface that has hardened, the surface should be removed by hacking. It should then be swept clean, wetted and covered with a layer of mortar composed of cement and sand in the same ratio as the cement and sand in the concrete mixture. This mortar should be freshly mixed and placed immediately before the placing of the concrete. Special attention should also be paid to the design of proper weatherings and flashings on all projecting features, sills, ledges, etc., so that rainwater is thrown clear of the walls. Many otherwise attractive buildings and structures have been disfigured by lack of attention to this matter. If rainwater is allowed to find its own path down a wall instead of being thrown clear it will flow in conspicuous runnels, carrying grime and perhaps corrosive agents with it in doing so.

The types of finish that can be used fall broadly into the following groups:

(1) Smooth surfaces coming direct from forms or linings, or from a light dressing of the concrete by grinding or sandblasting.

(2) Rough surfaces produced by chipping away the surface of the concrete to reveal the aggregate, or by sand moulding.

(3) Applied finishes, which are more expensive, particularly insofar as they may entail periodic maintenance such as painting or rendering.

The general conclusions from an extensive study made by the Building Research Station of the effectiveness of various methods and treatment was that exposed-aggregate finishes are quite satisfactory if the concrete is homogenous and of good quality. In industrial or town environments the rough surfaces do, however, tend to darken as a result of the deposition of soot from the atmosphere, but as the darkening is uniform over the whole surface, and not streaky as it tends to be with smooth surfaces (as distinct from matt surfaces), this defect does not appear to be a serious one.

*Choice of cement*

The number of types of cement available has increased during recent years. Although ordinary and rapid-hardening Portland cements are by far the most commonly used for normal construction work, in special circumstances some other types may give much better results. Different types of cement should not be mixed together. The general characteristics of the various cements may be summarized as follows:

*Ordinary Portland cement* (B.S. 12: 1957). The rate of development of strength is variable, depending on differences in raw materials used in the manufacture. The rate of hardening is accelerated by warmth and retarded by cold. Its resistance to attack by acid and sulphate water is variable, again depending on the chemical composition of the raw materials, but is generally low.

*Rapid-hardening Portland cement* (B.S. 12: 1957). As its name implies, this cement generally hardens more rapidly than the ordinary grade. Some special types also contain accelerators such as calcium chloride. The final strength is, however, much the same as that of ordinary Portland cement. Its rate of hardening is less affected by cold, owing partly to its more rapid evolution of heat on hydrating.

*Low-heat Portland cement* (B.S. 1370: 1957). This cement is intended for use in large masses of concrete as it generates less heat during setting and hardening. The effects of heat and cold upon its strength development are the same as for the other Portland cements. It usually offers better resistance to sulphate waters.

*Sulphate-resisting Portland cement.* This cement offers a higher resistance to sulphate attack. Its hardening is retarded by cold and accelerated by warmth in the same way as Portland cement; its heat of hydration, however, is usually lower.

*High-alumina cement* (B.S. 915: 1957). This cement is valuable for emergency work, for resistance to chemical attack, and for making refractory concrete, but should not be used in rich mixes or in large masses. The cement develops a very high early strength and is particularly useful in cold weather. It offers a high resistance to sulphate waters and to very weak acids. The concrete should be kept very cool after placing. If its temperature is allowed to rise too much, as it may in hot climates or from the heat evolved from its hydration, its strength will be adversely affected.

*Portland blastfurnace cement* (B.S. 146: 1957). This cement, which contains a proportion of granulated blastfurnace slag, develops strength a little more slowly than ordinary Portland cement, but in general has the same characteristics. The heat of hydration is lower. Within recent years there have been developments abroad in the use of granulated slag; one of them is the 'super-sulphate cement' mentioned below, and another is the process developed by Trief in Belgium in which a cream of wet-ground granulated slag is mixed with cement and aggregate at the mixer. Apart from saving the slag-drying operation, the wet grinding produces ground slag, which is inert until the Portland cement is added.

*Super-sulphate cement.* This cement is variable in its behaviour but usually develops a high early strength. It offers a high resistance to attack by sulphate waters and by weak acids. It is particularly useful for sewers, tunnel linings and in contaminated ground. Its heat of hydration is lower than that of Portland cements.

## Lightweight concrete

Lightweight concrete can be produced either by using porous aggregates such as furnace clinker or foamed slag, which are much lighter than the usual rock or gravel, or by forming gas-bubbles in the plastic cement mix, so as to give the concrete a sponge-like structure. The latter type is usually known as 'aerated concrete' or sometimes as 'cellular concrete'.

## Aerated concrete

Three methods may be used for producing the aeration of the concrete mix:

(1) gas is produced by a chemical reaction taking place within the mix before it sets;

(2) a foam-producing substance is added to the mix in order to introduce and stabilize air-bubbles;

(3) a stable pre-formed foam is added to the ingredients during mixing.

Portland cement is normally used as the cementing agent, but lime can be used if a high-pressure steam-curing process is employed. Aerated concretes may be made with or without aggregates, and by suitable adjustment of the mode and details of manufacture it is possible to make a range of concretes of widely differing properties. The lightest material (weighing about 12 lb/cu. ft) is obtained when cement is used without sand or other aggregate: this type has no structural strength and is used only for heat insulation. For denser concretes, mixes of cement and sand up to about 1:4 may be used; for products of medium density (40-65 lb/cu. ft) a 1:2 mix would be used, in which part of the sand must be very fine. Pulverized-fuel ash may be used instead of sand.

When Portland cement is used as the cementing agent, normal curing is likely to lead to a product showing high drying shrinkage. High-pressure steam-curing can be used with great advantage, particularly with respect to development of early strength and a material reduction in drying shrinkage. Much precast aerated concrete is thus treated.

Compressive strengths between 500 and 800 lb/sq. in., can be obtained in the density range between 35 and 50 lb/cu. ft; strengths up to 2000 lb/sq. in. may be expected in the heavier qualities (70–90 lb/cu. ft).

The thermal conductivity of aerated concrete is roughly proportional to the density. Material weighing 30 lb/cu. ft has a conductivity of about 0·75 B.t.u./ft² h °F per inch thickness, while for material of 90 lb/cu. ft the value is about 2·8. These figures compare with 10·0 for normal dense concrete and 8·4 for ordinary clay brick.

The rate of water penetration through aerated concrete is usually low, although total water absorption may be high. Some types, made with certain foaming agents, have a water-repellent character which may prevent deep penetration of water, even after several months of immersion. It is not known, however, how long such water-repellent qualities persist. The larger pores, particularly in the foam-aerated materials, will not fill with water in any conditions likely to be met in practice. This may well account for the resistance of aerated concretes to frost action being greater than would be expected from their porosity.

*Lightweight-aggregate concrete*

These concretes are generally known by the names of the aggregates used in them.

*Clinker.* For the purpose of definition as a concrete aggregate the term 'clinker' applies only to well-burnt furnace residues that have been fused or sintered into lumps, and therefore excludes coke breeze and grate-ashes, with which it is frequently identified in the industry. Even so, certain clinker aggregates have been found to cause expansion of the concrete in which they have been used, owing to the presence of a proportion of unburnt or partially burnt coal of certain types. This undesirable property is termed 'unsoundness'.

Clinker should conform to the prevailing British Standard (B.S. 1165: 1957), which gives limits for the combustible content of clinkers intended for different grades of concrete, as well as a limit for the sulphate content. The Standard also includes a test for soundness.

Some clinkers have been found to contain particles of materials that expand slowly when wetted, thereby causing damage to applied plaster coatings. These particles usually consist of hard-burnt lime, which hydrates slowly with consequent expansion. If the presence of quicklime is suspected, the clinker should be wetted and allowed to stand for some weeks before being used as an aggregate.

Occasionally small pieces of iron or pyrites occur in the clinker, and these may cause rust-staining of the concrete. Much of the iron can be removed by magnets at the crushing stage.

*Foamed slag.* Foamed blastfurnace slag is produced by allowing a limited amount of water to come into contact with the molten slag. The steam generated expands the slag while it is still plastic, to yield a porous material resembling natural pumice. The density of the material may range from 20 to 55 lb/cu. ft, depending in some measure on the size grading. Foamed slag has been used in Britain for many years and is covered by a British Standard (B.S. 877).

*Expanded clay, shale and slate.* When certain clays, shales or slates are heated nearly to melting point, they expand or 'bloat' owing to the generation of gases within the material. The porous structure so created is retained on cooling, giving a lightweight material suitable as an aggregate. In general these products furnish high-quality aggregates. Expanded clays and shales have been used in the United States for many years.

*Pulverized-fuel ash.* This ash is the finely divided residue from the combustion of powdered coal in modern boiler-plants, particularly of power stations. It can be made into pellets and then sintered in a suitable furnace; the small amount of unburnt fuel invariably present in the ash will usually maintain this process without the help of additional fuel. The sintered nodules so produced provide a very satisfactory lightweight aggregate.

*Pumice.* This is the only naturally occurring lightweight aggregate in common use. It is found in many countries, but not in the British Isles: the material used in this country has usually been obtained from Germany or Sicily. The weight of the aggregate varies from 30 to 55 lb/cu. ft.

*Exfoliated vermiculite.* This product and expanded perlite have densities of a very low order. Exfoliated vermiculite weighs 4 to 12 lb/cu. ft and, although the concrete produced from it has virtually no structural strength in the mixes usually employed, it has a very high resistance to heat flow and has been widely used for roof insulation. The mineral resembles mica and is mined principally in America and Africa. When heated to 650°–1000°C, depending on the particular material, it expands to many times its original size by the exfoliation of the thin plates from which it is constituted.

*Expanded perlite.* Perlite is a glassy volcanic rock occurring in America, Italy, Northern Ireland and elsewhere. When it is heated rapidly to the point of incipient fusion it expands to form a very light cellular material having a density of 5 to 15 lb/cu. ft. Like exfoliated vermiculite, it provides a concrete of high thermal insulation.

The relative merits of the various lightweight aggregates must be judged by the character of the concrete they produce. Workability in the plastic state, the strength of the matured concrete, the magnitude of the drying shrinkage and moisture movement, the thermal conductivity and the cost will dictate the choice of aggregate for any given purpose. With appropriate selection of aggregate and mix proportions, concretes can be obtained having densities ranging from 20 to 115 lb/cu. ft, and compressive strengths from 50 to 5000 lb/sq. in.

Many of the lightweight aggregates give concretes of poor workability, owing to the angularity and rough surface of the particles of aggregate. When lightweight concrete is cast *in situ*, a workable mix is required in order to obtain a sufficiently compact concrete. Improvement in workability can be obtained by employing a high proportion of fine aggregate (with some increase in the density and the thermal conductivity) or by using an air-entraining agent.

The porosity of lightweight aggregates leads, in general, to a large amount of water being absorbed during mixing. This may be a disadvantage with concrete cast *in situ*, and particularly with roof screeds, where it is important to ensure that water is not trapped under an impervious finish. A process has been developed for waterproofing lightweight aggregate by coating the particles with bitumen so as to reduce the amount of water needed in the mix. The water content of lightweight concrete is also important because the good thermal insulation associated with this product is exhibited only by dry concrete.

There has been some uncertainty in the past as to the likelihood of corrosion occurring in reinforcement or in structural steel encased in lightweight concrete. Corrosion depends on two factors:

(1) the degree of protection afforded to the metal by the concrete against the access of oxygen and moisture;

(2) the presence in the aggregate of constituents that corrode metals.

Porous lightweight concretes, by their very nature, cannot be expected to afford any high degree of protection to embedded steel, and if there is in addition any risk of corrosive constituents being present, such concretes should not be used where reinforcement is necessary. The heavier grades of lightweight concretes containing sand as fine aggregate can be made sufficiently impermeable if a rich enough mix is used. Of the lightweight aggregates available, clinker is the only one that introduces any serious corrosion risk on its own account.

The properties of lightweight concretes are summarized in Table 11.3. Except where otherwise stated, the results have been obtained from test specimens.

For all types of lightweight concrete the dimensional changes due to changes in moisture content are considerably higher than those in normal dense concrete. Of particular importance is the drying shrinkage displayed when the concrete is dried out for the first time. This initial drying shrinkage together with the lower tensile strength associated with lightweight concrete leads to a greater tendency to shrinkage cracking than exists with normal concrete. Even after initial drying, the relatively high moisture absorption makes for a relatively higher reversible wetting and drying movement. However, lightweight concrete has a wide field of application and the observance of certain precautions much reduces the risk of cracking. Such precautions, including the provision of relief joints, are discussed elsewhere (pp. 128 and 187).

## MORTARS

The term 'mortar' is used in the building industry to denote a mixture of sand or other fine aggregate and some binding agent, used as a jointing or as a surfacing material.

To function as a jointing material for bricks or other masonry units, it might be imagined that a mortar should be as strong and rigid as the units it joins, but this is not so. Some strength is necessary, of course, but the mortar must be sufficiently yielding to accommodate the various differential moisture or thermal movements within the structure. If these movements are small, the stresses set up are within the elastic limits of the materials concerned. Beyond these limits the stresses are relieved by yielding along lines of relative weakness in the structure. In a composite construction of bricks and mortar this yielding will take the form of cracks; these will penetrate the bricks themselves if the mortar is stronger than the bricks, and the effect produced will be unsightly. In a mortar that is weaker than the bricks it is binding together, the relief of stresses will result in a series of fine cracks distributed inconspicuously among the vertical joints in the brickwork, with relative movement between the bricks and the mortar in the horizontal joints.

Mortar must have sufficient strength to be durable, particularly in resisting the effects of frost, but only for special jobs where brickwork of extreme strength is required will a very strong mortar be necessary. Furthermore a strong mortar will be of little value unless it also adheres strongly to the bricks.

Certain properties are required of a freshly mixed mortar during the actual building operations, before it sets. It must be easily workable, to facilitate application and spreading, and to ensure that all the joints are completely

TABLE 11.3

*Lightweight concretes*

| Type | Bulk density of aggregate (lb/cu. ft) | Mix proportions by volume cement: aggregate | Dry density of concrete (lb/cu. ft) | Compressive strength (lb/sq. in.) | Drying shrinkage (per cent) | Thermal conductivity (B.t.u. in./h ft² °F) | Remarks |
|---|---|---|---|---|---|---|---|
| Aerated . . . | — <br> 60 (p.f.a.)—100 (ground sand) | Neat cement <br> 1 : 3–1:1 | 22–52 <br> 38 <br> 45–76 <br> 45–76 | 70– 510 <br> — <br> 300– 750 <br> 900–1100 | 0·33–0·44 <br> 0·12 <br> 0·18–0·36 <br> 0·06–0·11 | 0·60–1·31 <br> — <br> 1·40–2·8 <br> — | Normal curing <br> Autoclaved <br> Normal curing <br> Autoclaved |
| Clinker . . . | 60 <br> 60 | 1:6 <br> 1:9 | 86 <br> 78 | 850 <br> 400 | 0·065 <br> 0·055 | 2·3 –2·8 <br> — | Typical example |
| Foamed slag . . | 30–50 <br> 'Feather-weight' | 1:6 <br> 1:12 <br> 1:8 <br> 1:6 | 80–95 <br> 60–95 <br> 40 <br> 80 | 300–2000 <br> 200– 500 <br> 100 <br> 350– 550 | 0·04–0·06 <br> 0·03–0·05 <br> 0·12 <br> 0·08–0·065 | — <br> — <br> 0·85 <br> — | Machine-made blocks |
| Expanded clay . . | 35–65 | 1:6 <br> 1:12 | 75 <br> 60 | 2000 <br> 850 | 0·055 <br> 0·05 | 2·3 –3·2 | |
| Expanded shale . . | 51 | 1:6 <br> 1:9 | 81 <br> 73 | 1400 <br> 800 | 0·045 <br> 0·04 | — <br> — | |
| Pulverized-fuel ash . | 60 | 1:6 <br> 1:9 <br> 1:6 <br> 1:4 | 75–80 <br> 70–75 <br> 92 <br> 96 | 1100 <br> 750 <br> 1500 <br> 2750 | 0·045 <br> 0·045 <br> — <br> — | 2·3 <br> — <br> — <br> — | Machine-made blocks <br> Machine-made blocks <br> Vibrated concrete <br> Vibrated concrete |
| Pumice . . . | 30–55 | 1:6 | 45–70 | 200– 550 | 0·04–0·08 | 1·4 –2·1 | |
| Exfoliated vermiculite . | 4–12 | 1:9–1:5 | 26–50 | 95– 160 | 0·30–0·40 | 0·75–1·5 | |

filled; it must also stiffen sufficiently quickly, once the bricks are positioned, so that it is not squeezed out as work continues. The workability of a mortar can only be loosely defined, and no satisfactory method of measuring it yet exists. It includes the ability to flow while being sufficiently cohesive and adhesive, the ability to hold water, against the suction of the bricks, long enough to preserve the flow characteristics and yet to allow some subsequent stiffening to take place, and so on. In practice it is found that no one mortar combines all the desirable properties, so a mortar mix must still be designed to provide those that are most important in any particular circumstance.

Many of the properties considered desirable in a brickwork mortar were possessed by the traditional lime-sand mortar. Lime is produced by burning a fairly pure limestone rock in kilns converting it into calcium oxide. When water is added to this quicklime considerable heat is developed and calcium hydroxide (slaked lime) is produced. If this operation is carefully controlled so that just sufficient water is added to complete the hydration, the lumps break down to give the hydrated lime in the form of a dry powder. If an excess of water is added, a very plastic lime putty is produced and it is this material that was traditionally used in lime-sand mortars. Hydration has to be complete, since any unslaked material in the mortar would be liable to delayed hydration accompanied by expansion. Partly for this reason it was customary to mature the lime putty for some time before use. The well-matured putty repaid the trouble expended in preparing it, by yielding a mortar with admirable working properties which could be stored for use over a considerable period; its major disadvantage lay in its very slow rate of hardening. Such mortars would not in fact set at all if immersed in water and for this reason are described as being 'non-hydraulic'. Their early hardening is produced solely by stiffening resulting from the loss of water by evaporation and by suction into the bricks. The mortar eventually gains strength by slow combination with atmospheric carbon dioxide, which converts the calcium hydroxide once again into calcium carbonate. This carbonation takes place most rapidly on surfaces in contact with the atmosphere, and much more slowly below these surfaces.

Apart from non-hydraulic, or 'fatty' limes as they are sometimes called, there is also a range of limes classed as semi-hydraulic, moderately hydraulic, or eminently hydraulic. The distinction between the several types of hydraulic lime is a rather narrow and arbitrary one, but they all share to a varying extent the ability to harden by combination with water (like cement) rather than by atmospheric action. Magnesian limes (which are produced from a dolomitic limestone) and hydraulic limes still enjoy considerable prestige in their immediate areas of production. The British Standard for building limes (B.S. 890) covers both quicklime and hydrated limes which may be of the non-hydraulic or of the semi-hydraulic type; magnesian quicklimes and magnesian hydrated limes are also included. Hydraulic limes are not covered by a British Standard.

The substitution of cement-sand mortars for lime-sand mortars has several disadvantages. To obtain the plasticity that the lime-sand mortars afforded, it is necessary to use similar proportions of cement and sand. While the resulting mortars are appropriate for laying bricks of engineering quality to secure the maximum compressive strength for the brickwork, they are quite unsuited to the majority of applications. Thus sand-lime bricks, concrete bricks, and lightweight concrete units are unable to withstand the restraints imposed on their moisture movement by the strength of the mortar (see p. 194), and cracking is frequent in cement renderings (p. 252).

A satisfactory compromise is achieved by using a mixture of cement and lime for the binder in the mortar. In this way plasticity is retained, there is less tendency for the plastic mortar to shrink away from the brick, and the strength can be controlled over a wide range. A limit to the amount of cement that can be replaced by lime is imposed by the need to maintain an adequate rate of hardening in cold weather and to secure the mortar against damage by frost. Suitable mixes for the general run of brickwork and clay and concrete block constructions are shown in Table 11.4. Mixes for natural stone masonry are given on p. 245, and mixes for rendering are given in Table 18.3 (p. 254). As the mixes recommended here are specified by dry volume, it is likely that site-made mixes will always err on the rich side because of the increased bulk of wet sand for which no allowance is normally made. For brickwork the general rule is that the mortar should match but not exceed the strength of the bricks, and for renderings strong finishing coats should never be applied over weaker backgrounds. Where walling is designed primarily for strength, the strength of the mortar has to be taken into account as discussed later (p. 160).

In cement-lime-sand mortars, the lime functions to all intents and purposes only as a plasticizer, and other materials can be used for this purpose. Quite satisfactory mortars can be produced by substituting finely-ground sand or limestone for the lime. Some cement manufacturers have introduced 'masonry cement', a cement ready-mixed with inert plasticizer, thus providing the builder with a single material in place of the two he had required previously to mix with his sand.

A further method of plasticizing a cement-sand mix has recently been developed. Certain chemical agents added in very small proportions to a cement-sand mortar during the mixing operation cause air to be entrained as a large number of minute bubbles uniformly dispersed. Such air entrainment can plasticize very lean cement-sand mixes that would otherwise be quite unworkable. Although it is less easy to control the workability of the mortar by this means than by using lime, there are economies in transport and storage. Some masonry cements contain air-entraining agents as well as solid inert plasticizers. There is little doubt that air-entrained cement-sand mortars fulfil all the requirements as regards workability. As far as their functional aspect in the building is concerned more time will be required before a final judgment can be pronounced. Studies so far made show that the aerated mortars are somewhat superior to the lime-plasticized mortars in resistance to frost, and slightly inferior in strength. As the overall strength of the brickwork is a more important factor than the strength of the mortar itself, the differences noted may not be important. Within the limited time that observations have been made on external renderings in both types of mortar, it has not been possible to form definite conclusions on how they compare as regards resistance to cracking and rain penetration.

## TABLE 11.4
### Mortars for brickwork and clay or concrete block masonry

| Type of construction | Position in building | Degree of exposure to wind and rain | Time of construction | Recommended mixes (parts by volume) |
|---|---|---|---|---|
| External walls Clay bricks Clay blocks Sand-lime bricks Concrete bricks Concrete blocks Cast stone — Normal construction, not designed to withstand heavy loading | Above damp-proof course | Sheltered and moderate conditions | Spring and summer | Cement:lime:sand, 1:2:8–9, or Hydraulic lime:sand, 1:3 |
| | | Sheltered and moderate conditions | Autumn and winter | Cement:lime:sand, 1:1:5–6, or Hydraulic lime:sand, 1:2 |
| | | Severe conditions | All seasons | Cement:lime:sand, 1:1:5–6, or Hydraulic lime:sand, 1:2 |
| | Parapets, free-standing walls or below damp-proof course | All conditions | All seasons | Cement:lime:sand, 1:1:5–6, or Cement:lime:sand, 1:¼:3* |
| Clay bricks, over 5000 lb/sq. in. crushing strength — Engineering construction | All positions | All conditions | All seasons | Cement:lime:sand, 1:¼:3* |
| Internal walls including partitions — Normal | — | — | Spring and summer | Cement:lime:sand, 1:2:8–9, Cement:lime:sand, 1:3:10–12, or Hydraulic lime:sand, 1:3 |
| | | | Autumn and winter | Cement:lime:sand, 1:1:5–6, Cement:lime:sand, 1:2:8–9, or Hydraulic lime:sand, 1:2 |

| | | All conditions | All seasons | Hydraulic lime:sand, 1:2–3, or Cement:lime:sand, 1:2:8–9 |
|---|---|---|---|---|
| Tall chimneys | — | — | — | |
| Pointing | — | — | — | The best mix for repointing old work is that given in this table for the conditions in question; this mix should also be used for pointing new work if the pointing mortar differs from the bedding mortar. |

\* The small proportion of lime is added to improve workability; it has negligible effect on the strength of the mortar.

NOTES

'Sheltered conditions' are where the construction is protected by overhanging eaves or by nearby buildings. Typical examples of these conditions occur with ground and first storeys of buildings in the middle of towns.

'Moderate conditions' refer to those in which the construction gets some protection from overhanging eaves or from nearby buildings.

'Severe conditions' occur when the construction is exposed to the full force of wind and rain. Typical examples are buildings projecting well above the surrounding buildings, and those on elevated and exposed sites and in coastal districts.

'Lime' refers to non-hydraulic or semi-hydraulic lime.

Where alternative sand contents are shown (e.g. 5–6 or 8–9), use the higher figure if the sand is well-graded, and the lower figure if the sand is coarse or uniformly fine.

# TIMBER

The classification of timbers as hardwoods (from deciduous trees) or soft-woods (from conifers) is not very convenient as regards their use in building. Softwoods are generally, but not always, close-grained and easy to work; hardwoods, however, range very widely in their mechanical properties— they include balsa wood, used in model aircraft construction, and greenheart, which sinks in water.

Hardwoods may be sub-divided into three classes, based mainly on weight and working properties:

(1) Light hardwoods, mostly within the range 30–40 lb per cu. ft (and generally suitable for most purposes for which softwoods are commonly used).

(2) Medium hardwoods, such as oak and beech, mostly within the range 40–50 lb per cu. ft.

(3) Heavy hardwoods, mostly weighing more than 50 lb per cu. ft and including timbers generally suitable for heavy construction and for special purposes, such as sills, heavy-duty flooring and work benches where high resistance to wear or certain other destructive agencies is required.

*Structure and conversion*

The general structure of wood is a complex arrangement of cells. It is to this cellular structure that timber owes most of its general characteristics, and to differences in the sizes, shapes and arrangement of the cells that different timbers owe their individual characteristics.

While the structure and manner of growth of wood account for the main features common to all timbers, many influences, natural and accidental, contribute to the variations that can be seen between different timbers and between different pieces of the same timber. Some of these variations, although they may reduce the strength, are much prized for the enhanced figure they give; some are defects in every way. The commonest, and among the more serious of the natural defects of timber, are knots. When branches are shed by the tree at an early stage, cut off close to the trunk by the forester, or broken off, the wood of the trunk grows over the stumps, which then appear in the converted timber as knots. Small knots, if the end of the branch has not died off or become infected by fungus, and if they are not too numerous, are not always serious defects, but large or loose or fungus-infected knots are.

Conversion is the process of sawing the felled log into sizes convenient for seasoning, marketing and use; timber once converted and again sawn into smaller sizes is said to be 're-converted' or 're-sawn'. The way in which timber is sawn from the log has an important bearing on its appearance and subsequent behaviour. The operation calls for much skill on the part of the sawyer if he is to get the best out of a log, eliminating the many irregularities and defects likely to be met with, and avoiding undue waste.

Various ways of converting a softwood log are shown in Fig. 11.1.

*Moisture content*

Moisture content is defined in B.S. 565 as the amount of moisture in timber expressed as a percentage of its oven-dry weight. If the moisture content of timber is either above or below that of the environment, moisture

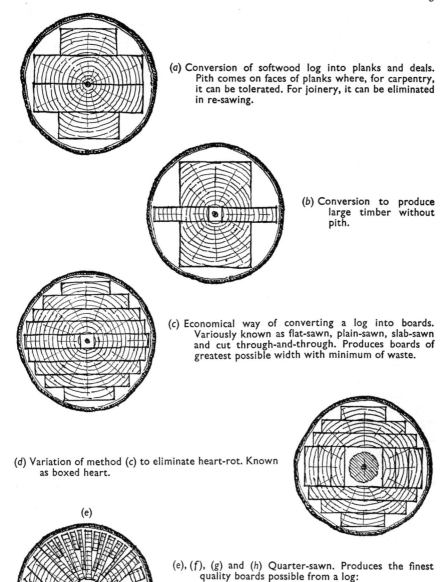

(a) Conversion of softwood log into planks and deals. Pith comes on faces of planks where, for carpentry, it can be tolerated. For joinery, it can be eliminated in re-sawing.

(b) Conversion to produce large timber without pith.

(c) Economical way of converting a log into boards. Variously known as flat-sawn, plain-sawn, slab-sawn and cut through-and-through. Produces boards of greatest possible width with minimum of waste.

(d) Variation of method (c) to eliminate heart-rot. Known as boxed heart.

(e)

(h)

(f)

(g)

(e), (f), (g) and (h) Quarter-sawn. Produces the finest quality boards possible from a log:

(e) The true radial cut, with every board parallel to the rays. It is wasteful and is only used where a pronounced ray figure is wanted, as in true wainscot oak.

(f) Less wasteful than (e); produces pieces of good figure.

(g) and (h) produce, respectively, thin and thick boards, mostly without ray figure.

FIG. 11.1

*Conversion of softwood log*

will be either lost or absorbed until a balance is reached. The timber is then said to have reached 'equilibrium moisture content'. This will rarely be a stable condition because of continual fluctuations of atmospheric humidity, but these fluctuations are to a great extent compensated for by the slowness of the timber to react to them. The ideal condition for timber for any purpose is at equilibrium moisture content, and values for moisture content to which timber should be seasoned for various purposes, deduced from average conditions, are given in the chart prepared by the Forest Products Research Laboratory, Fig. 11.2.

Shrinkage on drying does not occur equally in all directions. It is greatest tangentially, in the direction of the annual rings, less in the radial direction (along the medullary rays), and so little in the direction of the length of the log (along the grain) that it can be neglected. Its magnitudes differ in different timbers, but they can be taken as averaging respectively, in drying from green to oven-dry, 5 to 15 per cent, 3 to 5 per cent and 0·001 per cent of the original dimensions. Thus, if an unconverted log is allowed to dry out, the stresses set up by a reduction in diameter will cause the log to split along the rays. Fig. 11.3 shows the effects of these differential shrinkages on timbers cut from the log in different ways and how it is that flat-sawn timber will warp more than quarter-sawn timber. Irregularities of grain, the presence of knots and other imperfections, as well as faulty seasoning, can lead to irregular distortion.

Not only is it important that timber be at the proper moisture content in the first place, but it is desirable that it should remain so until normal conditions have been established in the building in which it is installed. This is a counsel of perfection rarely attainable in practice, but all possible precautions should be taken, by careful storing after manufacture and on the site, and by delaying the delivery (of joinery in particular) to the site until it is needed, to avoid exposure to conditions materially different from the conditions expected in service. Lack of care in this respect is responsible for much trouble with timber in buildings. The priming of joinery immediately after manufacture, before it leaves the shop, will delay absorption of moisture by the wood; it will not, however, prevent absorption if the timber is exposed to moist conditions for long.

*Strength*

The strength of timber lies mainly in the denser and harder summer wood. The rate of growth, controlling the relative proportions of spring wood and summer wood, has an important bearing upon strength. A rapidly growing softwood tree will form more spring wood, while a rapidly growing hardwood tree will form more summer wood. Thus, fast-grown softwoods are the weaker and fast-grown hardwoods are the stronger, up to a point. Very slow-grown or very fast-grown woods of either class become deficient in strength progressively as the rate of growth decreases or increases. The key to all this lies in the width of the annual rings, which represents the amount of wood formed in each growing season. The variation in width that can occur without materially impairing strength is wide and variable; as a general rule it can be taken from 30 to 10 rings to the inch for softwoods and 8 to 16 rings in hardwoods. The denser and harder heartwood is always stronger than the sapwood.

Strength is affected by many other factors, amongst them: irregularities of grain; abnormalities of growth; the presence of knots, shakes, wane or decay; the way in which a piece of timber has been cut from the log; faults in seasoning; moisture content; and invasion by insects. B.S. 1860 defines characteristics of softwood timber that affect its strength and prescribes methods for measuring them for the purpose of computing permissible stresses in structural members by the rules given in British Standard Code of Practice CP.112. More elaborate methods for stress grading of softwood timbers have been derived by the Forest Products Research Laboratory, but these necessitate expert inspection of every piece of timber so graded.

In compression, or in tension, a piece of timber is stronger when loaded in the direction of the grain than across it; resistance to flexure, too, is greater in the direction of the grain—with most timbers it is negligible across the grain. Compared with other structural materials, timber that is suitable for structural use (not all timbers are) is strong weight-for-weight but, as it is comparatively light, it is weaker size-for-size.

*Durability*

Timber, in itself a durable material, is subject to deterioration or destruction by many agencies, the more important of which can be considered under the heads:

Fungal growth              Chemical agencies
Insect attack              Mechanical agencies
Physical agencies

Resistance to these agencies varies greatly. Hardwoods are not necessarily more durable than softwoods. The darker woods are often held to be more durable than the lighter ones, and it is true that, if the darker colour is due to the presence of natural resins or tannins that have a preservative effect, the wood will be more resistant to fungal attack. On the other hand, the darker colour may be due to rot having attacked the wood of the growing tree. The heartwood of a tree is harder and more durable than its sapwood.

*Fungal growth*

Wood is liable to fungal attack at any stage in its existence, given certain conditions. The conditions necessary for fungal growth are an adequate supply of food, moisture and air, and a suitable temperature. Food is available in the wood; moisture is always present in unseasoned, or insufficiently seasoned, timber, and may or may not be present when the timber is in use; air is generally available, unless the timber is buried deep in the ground or is completely and permanently submerged in water; temperatures in buildings are usually suitable for fungi, which can grow in temperatures ranging from about 32°F to about 105°F. It may be assumed that all timber, however sound it may appear, is infected in some degree with fungus, which can lie dormant in the wood awaiting the establishment of the necessary conditions to become active. To prevent this it is necessary to ensure that the four essentials for fungal growth are never available together. Of these, it will be clear that air and temperature cannot, in normal circumstances, be controlled; it is necessary, therefore, to control food or moisture. It is generally easier to control the latter in timber in buildings, and the former in outside timber.

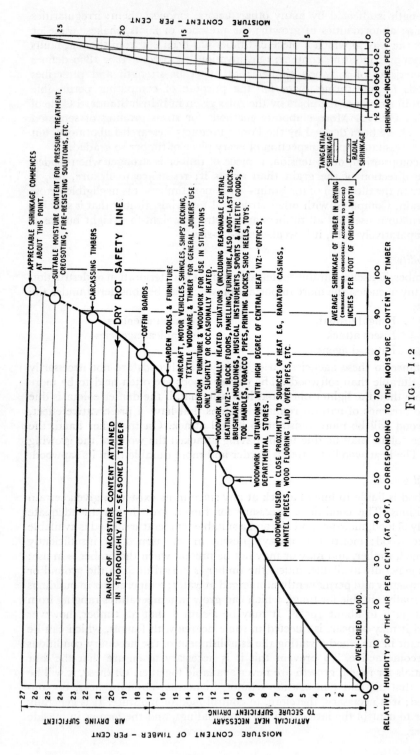

FIG. 11.2

Moisture contents of timber for various purposes

The figures for different species vary, and the chart shows only average values

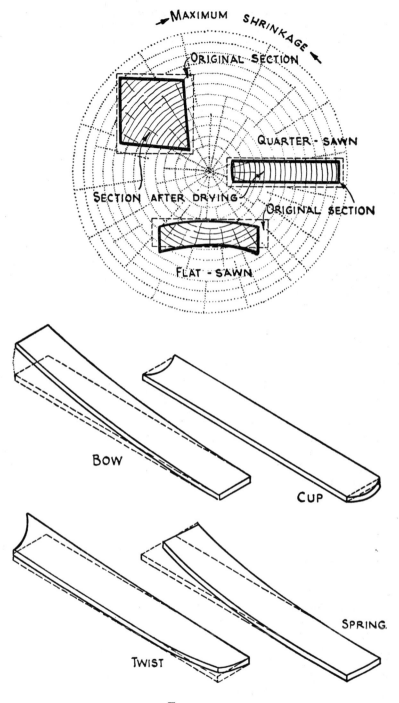

Fig. 11.3

*Forms of warping*

Timber is safe from fungal growth at moisture contents below 20 per cent and these, as shown in Fig. 11.2, can be obtained without difficulty by either air seasoning or kiln seasoning. If fungal growth has already begun at a high moisture content, it will be halted when the timber dries out, with one important exception, which will be discussed later. If the moisture content rises again to above 20 per cent, growth will begin again, unless the fungus has been killed, and even then the danger of re-infection is always present. It is, therefore, always essential, for all purposes where the control of moisture is relied upon as protection against fungal attack, to ensure two things: first, that properly seasoned timber is used; and second, that, throughout the whole service life of the timber its moisture content cannot rise above the danger limit. The latter may be done by keeping the timber away from damp situations and contact with walls, floors and other parts of the building that may be, or may become, damp; or by protecting it with paint or in some other way.

With timber in situations where prolonged dampness is unavoidable, as when built into external walls, set in the ground or exposed unprotected by paint to the weather, it is necessary to control the food supply of fungi. This is done by treating the timber with a preservative which will render the wood toxic to fungi. Cedar shingles, however, need not be so treated; they are able to dry out quickly after rain, and the wood itself is relatively resistant to fungal attack.

Special mention must be made of one particular source of fungal decay of timber in buildings, the so-called 'dry-rot', caused by a small group of fungi, the commonest of which is *Merulius lacrymans*. So prevalent is it and so persistent once it has become established, that special care is necessary to guard against it. These fungi have the peculiar ability to produce the moisture they need for further growth, once they have become established. Thus, the subsequent drying out of infected timber will not stop the growth and spread of the disease. Moreover, the fungus can spread extensively in materials others than timber. Once established in any part of a building, it can eventually spread to timber throughout the whole building. It is a wise precaution, therefore, to treat with preservative all timber used in situations where there is any doubt as to the efficacy of the measures taken to keep it dry.

*Insect attack.* Many kinds of insects will attack the wood of standing trees and timber before and after it is installed in buildings, and if not checked at an early stage the result of attack can be disastrous. The damage is done by the insect larvae boring into the wood. As they do not appear on the surface until they emerge as fully developed insects, attack is rarely suspected until much of the damage has been done. Some woods are more prone to attack than others, sapwood more than heartwood, and some insects will not attack wood until it has been infected with fungus. Signs of insect attack have often led to the discovery of fungal attack.

The first precaution is never to use infested timber. Other precautions include those that should be taken against fungal attack and, where protection is of particular importance, treatment with an insecticidal preservative. Many preservatives in common use are both fungicidal and insecticidal.

*Physical agencies.* All timbers are combustible, hardwoods no less than softwoods; dense hardwoods, however, may be slower to ignite than softwoods.

Continuous exposure to temperatures only moderate compared with that needed for actual ignition can, in time, cause decomposition of the wood. At least one example is on record of severe decomposition of softwood timber after some years of more or less continuous exposure to temperatures in the region of 160°F behind a hot-water radiator. Spontaneous combustion even, especially of loose shavings, has been known to occur at temperatures little higher than this.

It is doubtful if low temperatures in themselves have any adverse effect upon wood, but repeated freezing and thawing of any water contained in the wood will eventually break down its structure. Exposure to light will change the colour of timber, but it is not known to have any destructive effect, although it may contribute to slow deterioration over many years.

*Chemical agencies.* Timber may be decomposed by solutions of acids or alkalis. For use in situations where it is likely to be brought into frequent contact with these, by spilling or otherwise, it is necessary to use a timber known to be resistant to the particular acid or alkali. Apart from such situations, timber may be brought into contact with acid or alkali contained in certain synthetic-resin adhesives or paint strippers. With proper care in using these materials little harm is likely to be done, but careless use can lead to weakening of the wood.

*Mechanical agencies.* Apart from damage resulting from the overloading of structural members (which can be guarded against by proper design, care in the selection of timber and efficient workmanship), mechanical damage will usually take the form of wear and impact shocks. Some timbers have high resistance to wear and, in general, they will be found among the medium and heavy hardwoods. Timbers having high resistance to impact shocks will be found among both the softwoods and the hardwoods of all classes. Much depends on how the grain of the wood is disposed; end-grain wood blocks, for example, have been widely used in road construction and still provide the most economic surfacing for some very heavy-duty industrial floors.

## SHEET CLADDINGS FOR WALLS

The term 'sheet claddings' usually refers to the range of thin sheet coverings developed to form external weatherproof skins on the outside of framed structures, mainly of industrial buildings. The most common materials used are steel and asbestos cement, but aluminium is now quite widely accepted and certain plastics are finding increasing use. All are supplied and fixed as separate sheets, usually two or three feet wide and up to about eight feet long, so that only one, or at most two men, are needed to handle them. They are generally stiffened in the long direction by some form of corrugation, and the joints are commonly formed dry by lapping the sides and ends in such a way as to shed rainwater. The sheets are commonly fixed back to the frame by hook bolts which engage frame members and whose threaded shanks usually come out through holes provided along the ridges of corrugations. Nuts and shaped washers then draw the sheets home securely. Other types of fixings are available.

This type of cladding should not be confused with panel fillings for curtain-wall systems. Curtain walls, although they also are used for cladding framed structures, take the form of panels received into a cladding frame (distinct from the building frame) from which they generally get their main stiffening. Thus the type of fixing, the joint and the stiffening are all characteristically different. Curtain walls are discussed separately in Part II (pp. 183, 185 and 209).

The primary functions of sheet claddings are to exclude water and to provide a wind-barrier. Any corrugation is usually arranged so that adjacent sheets can overlap and nest together along the sides and across the ends. These junctions, even though not sealed, can exclude rainwater satisfactorily and exclude wind fairly successfully. Some air movement can take place through the joints, however; if the inside of the structure is lined and made relatively air-tight, external cladding joints should then do no more than ventilate the cavity. Tapes of various kinds are sometimes used in the joints to avoid noise from wind vibration and to minimize air-flow or to reduce the slight risk of capillary movement of moisture.

It is usual for sheet cladding makers to provide a range of matching corner pieces, ridges, fascias, and frames to receive doors and windows so that the entire wall of a building and in some cases the roof as well, can be formed in the material of the main sheeting.

Sheet claddings cannot offer very much sound or thermal insulation, though heat gain and loss by radiation are affected somewhat according to the surface characteristics of the material.

The most significant characteristics of the various materials for the present purposes can be summarized as follows.

Unprotected steel corrodes rapidly in damp climates or industrial atmospheres. Paint coatings are vulnerable at the edges of sheets, whence corrosion may spread rapidly. Other forms of protection have been or are being developed, the price of sheet steel being usually low enough to enable protective coatings to be added without excluding the material from the range of competitive costs. The toughness of steel and its ability to withstand distortion without cracking are attractions in many circumstances.

Apart from galvanizing, the most usual protective coating hitherto has been some form of bitumen-felt, well bonded to both sides of the sheet under factory conditions. The coating is sometimes applied in two layers to ensure that no minute perforations in either layer will enable corrosive agents to reach the metal. The coating usually incorporates asbestos fibre, and may also be given some kind of external treatment such as a grit finish to protect the bitumen and to reduce solar heat absorption, or an inner finish to give it a lighter colour or to increase its resistance to heat transfer by radiation. Bitumen coatings are combustible and this can be a demerit. Unless carefully maintained, their life is likely to be of the order of fifteen to thirty years in fully exposed situations.

Vitreous enamelling has been used already to some extent on such sheeting and may come into wider use. It resists corrosion well and offers attractive possibilities for colouring. It is slightly vulnerable to chipping but, owing to the formation of an intimate bond between the vitreous base coat and the metal, rusting will not spread rapidly from a chipped spot. The chemicals required for developing this bond restrict the base coat to dark colours but this coat alone offers satisfactory protection; lighter colours, which have to be added over the base, add to the cost. Vitreous coatings should have an unlimited life in any atmosphere, provided chipping does not occur.

Stainless steel is of course a possibility; technically as well as aesthetically it has obvious attractions, but its development for sheet cladding is at an early stage. It should have a long life in ordinary atmospheres.

In the general search for sheet cladding offering a good appearance, reasonable life, and low maintenance costs, aluminium is another metal that has recently begun to attain a competitive position. It is produced in a wide range of alloys, but unfortunately even those most able to retain their initial appearance seem unlikely to do so for a period approaching the normal life of the sheet itself or the building, unless cleaned at quite short intervals. There is insufficient experience of large wall-areas of un-maintained aluminium in this country to enable much to be said about the appearance it develops under various conditions of exposure. Anodizing and other surface treatments can reduce the need for maintenance to preserve initial appearance but they add appreciably to the cost. Anodized aluminium can be coloured by dyes, but quality and life depend on the dye, the colour and the processing, and vary considerably.

Asbestos cement is made from Portland cement and asbestos fibre. It is formed initially as a thin sheet, in a process rather similar to that of paper-making, and the final product is a build-up of a number of these layers. They bond intimately in manufacture, with no tendency to de-laminate subsequently. Before the cement sets, the flat sheet may be corrugated or cut and shaped over moulds to form detail elements. The final product hardens with age and exposure and ultimately becomes brittle. In corrosive atmospheres deterioration is more rapid, and the life of the product may then be of the order of thirty years or so.

The exposed surface etches away in the course of time and then retains dirt increasingly easily, but products of different quality may differ in the rate at which this happens. The result is not always unattractive, and the growth of lichens and algae may improve it, though they are inclined at the same time to shorten the life of the material.

Coloured asbestos-cement products have been developed by incorporating colour in the body of the material or by stoving it on the surface. Asbestos cement can also be painted with special paints, but the maintenance of large areas of external paintwork is expensive and the practice is therefore not widespread.

The material is used in many circumstances where its appearance has not been considered important and the result has often been unattractive; but, with well-designed details and the right approach on the part of the designer, the appearance can be very acceptable.

Although the material incorporates asbestos and is non-combustible, it is liable to shatter when strongly heated.

Sheet claddings made of plastics have come into use and are being developed steadily. There are at present three principal types, clear acrylic sheet, translucent or opaque polyester laminates with glass-fibre reinforcement, and opaque paper/phenol-formaldehyde laminates. All are combustible, though the first two ignite more readily than the others. They are tough and flexible, and these are useful attributes in the circumstances for which sheet claddings are commonly used. They tend to lose surface gloss on prolonged exposure to the weather, but apart from this there is not yet sufficient experience of these products in their present forms to permit reliable forecasts about how appearance may change during their anticipated life. Such experience as is available should therefore be examined by designers when considering what materials to use for particular buildings.

## MOVEMENT JOINTS AND JOINTING COMPOUNDS

It has been pointed out in earlier chapters that building materials change in dimensions under the influence of changes of temperature or of moisture content. To avoid buckling and other troubles, it is often necessary to accommodate such movements at joints between panels or around such components as doors and windows. Weather-proofing such movement joints has long been a problem in building. With the increasing use of unit construction and of light cladding, moreover, the problem is of growing importance, since the efficient functioning of the building may depend on movement joints that are weatherproof and have reasonable expectations of a long life without undue maintenance.

The solution of this problem may be attempted in various ways. A gap may be filled with a building mastic (sometimes called a caulking or joint-sealing compound) or by a gasket, or may be bridged by a metal or rubber strip fixed into the sides of the joint; alternatively, reliance may be placed on the overlap of adjoining members, as in a tile-hung wall, or on coverstrips; or some combination of these methods may be adopted. It is not always safe to rely entirely on joint-sealing to exclude rain and snow; often it is advisable to make provision for draining or ventilating the cavity behind the face, especially if condensation may occur there, much as is done in a brick cavity wall.

*Building mastics*

A building mastic is a joint-sealing or caulking compound intended to maintain a weatherproof seal between the sides of a joint subject to some degree of movement.

This definition also applies to a large extent to putties. These are essentially similar to mastics, but are generally cheaper products which deteriorate more rapidly as they age and weather. For this reason, their use should be confined to places where the putty will be protected by paint throughout its life, as in external glazing.

Building mastics consist of oils, bitumen, tar, natural or synthetic resins or rubbers, or mixtures or emulsions (see Appendix I) of these, combined with fillers in powder or fibre form, and sometimes small amounts of volatile thinners. Sometimes the mastic is provided in two parts, to be mixed immediately before application.

British Standards relating to mastics include B.S. 1737 for jointing materials for pipes and B.S. 2499 which sets out methods of test for certain sealing compounds for concrete pavements. A more general Standard may be evolved in time, but it is unlikely that an accelerated test for the weathering of any type of mastic will be developed.

Mastics may most conveniently be classified by method of application.

*Gun.* The material is soft enough for extrusion from a nozzle, either by squeezing a collapsible tube or by using a 'gun', an appliance actuated by lever or compressed air.

*Hand, knife or trowel.* The material is of such consistency at normal temperatures that it can be dug out of the container and pressed into the recess to be filled or spread over a surface. It must adhere to the sides of the joint; to ensure this, it may be necessary to wet the knife or trowel frequently in a suitable solvent to permit easy working.

*Poured.* These mastics are usually based on bitumen and are heated to make them sufficiently fluid for pouring into a joint.

*Tape or strip.* The mastics prepared in this form are usually stiff and are protected until immediately before use by a wrapping of cellophane or polythene.

### Properties of mastics

*Ease of application.* The mastic should be easy to apply to the particular joint or surface in the site conditions prevailing at the time. For example, a hot-poured mastic is almost always suitable for a joint in a pavement or floor, but when poured into a long vertical joint in very cold weather it may chill too quickly and fail to fill the joint.

*Retention of form.* However soft a mastic may be when placed, there must be no risk that it will flow out of the joint, either immediately after application or later, even after a rise in temperature; it must not creep or slump to any appreciable extent even in a vertical groove. To control the amount of mastic used, as well as to provide support, some joints may first be part-filled with mortar or a joint filler such as rot-proofed fibreboard. Mastics are not generally intended to carry loads, and various load transfer devices are used to prevent mastic squeezing out, e.g. tow in jointing gutters, and mortar in the horizontal joints of slab walling, provided such insertions will not interfere with the degree of movement required in the joint.

*Adhesion.* The mastic should stick well to the sides of the joint; adhesion is generally more easily developed with soft mastics. To assist adhesion the surfaces of the joint must be dry and free from grease, dirt and dust. It always helps, but may not always be necessary, to apply a primer before applying the mastic. If it is not practicable to dry the surfaces, a mastic based on emulsions might be considered. If the panels are of porous material, moisture may find its way through the material to the interface and this could reduce the adhesion of any type of mastic.

*Accommodation of movement.* The movement that the mastic can accommodate without rupture will depend on its stiffness and on the thickness of the mastic in the direction of movement; the greater the thickness, the greater the allowable movement. As a rough rule it may be said that, for soft mastics, the thickness should be at least ten times the maximum movement to be expected. The risk of breakdown depends also on the speed of movement. All mastic materials flow more easily to the new shape if the movement is slow and gradual; the forces that may cause rupture or destroy adhesion to the sides are correspondingly less. Sudden movement may occur, for example, where movement is at first restrained by static frictional forces that are suddenly overcome. Temperature movements may be relatively rapid, e.g. they may take place in a matter of a few hours in hot sunshine.

*Permanence.* It is too often expected that a mastic will remain unchanged indefinitely. Some change is inevitable and it is the probable rate of change

under the particular conditions of use that is important. Some changes occur
fairly early, e.g. volatile solvents evaporate, oil may be absorbed into porous
surrounding material. Others occur more slowly, the result of complex
chemical changes on ageing. Exposure to air and sunlight will hasten the
process. The result of such changes is that the material hardens and shrinks.
Good joint design will slow these processes; thus the mastic will change less
if it is shielded from light and if the surface exposed to air is small in relation
to the general bulk of the material. Priming porous surfaces will prevent
their robbing a mastic of its oil.

*Freedom from bleeding and staining.* If there is a risk that bleeding into, and
staining of, porous materials will occur, priming the surfaces may help.

*Resistance to alkalis.* Concrete and external rendering contain alkalis which
may attack some mastics, particularly those containing drying oils, in damp
conditions. Mastics based wholly on bitumen are resistant to alkali; if a
mastic that is affected by alkali must be used, the surfaces should first be
given two coats of an alkali-resistant primer.

*Ability to take paint.* Most oil mastics can be painted as soon as they are
sufficiently hard. If they are painted when too soft, cracking, flaking or
discolouration will occur. It is difficult to paint bituminous mastics
satisfactorily.

## Gaskets

A gasket is used in very much the same way as a mastic in compression or
sliding joints, but relies on close contact, often under pressure, to make a
joint weatherproof. Gaskets may also be caused to adhere by the use of
adhesives. The gasket may consist of cork, natural or synthetic rubbers or
resins, sometimes filled or foamed, or similar materials.

Unless stuck by adhesives to the surfaces they join, gaskets are less effective
than mastics in excluding water, but they permit a greater degree of movement
in the joint. They are not immune to change with time.

## Intermediate types of jointing material

Mastics are sometimes enclosed in sheaths of cotton, or impregnated into
ropes of natural fibre or of asbestos, in order to limit their extrusion under
pressure.

Sometimes, the one type of material can be used in both ways. Thus
thiokol, a synthetic rubber, can be used as a preformed gasket or obtained as a
mastic in two parts which are mixed immediately before application.
Similarly, some foamed resins sometimes used as gaskets may in due course
be obtainable in mastic form.

## Joint design

The requirements of the type of joint under consideration are that it shall
exclude the weather for a prolonged period, in spite of the continuing
movement of the sides of the joint and of changes in the properties of any
mastics or gaskets with the passage of time.

In designing the joint, it is first necessary to assess the degree of movement
between the sides of the joint. Reference should be made to the chapters on
dimensional stability elsewhere in this work, and to the preceding section
on sheet cladding.

Where the movement is large, it may be advantageous to reduce the movement at each joint by increasing the number of joints. There are however, many factors to be considered, such as appearance, ease of erection, difficulties of inspection and renewal of mastics or gaskets.

Some types of joint are illustrated in Figs. 11.4–6.

In considering the particular type of joint, it has already been pointed out that changes with age in the properties of mastics are reduced if the joint is shaped so that the mastic is shielded from light and if the amount of the mastic exposed to the air is small in relation to its volume. Attempts to economize in mastic by not filling joints completely may lead to a short life. Shielding may also reduce the temperature attained in sunlight and the dangers of scour by the run-off of rain, or damage by window-cleaners or children. The durability of gaskets, also, is greater if they are shielded.

A good mastic-filled joint will exclude rain and snow, even if wind-driven, so long as the mastic is sound and adheres well. Gaskets may permit a slight seepage of rain, but are less affected than mastic joints by ageing; unless used with an adhesive, they may fail to exclude wind-driven snow or rain. With unsealed lap joints the clearance should be of greater than capillary dimensions, to avoid rain being sucked up.

Some examples that have arisen in practice will help to illustrate further these principles of joint design.

*Examples*

1. A wall was to be clad in large precast concrete slabs, of such size that the movement across the joint under the particular conditions of exposure was unlikely to exceed one-tenth of an inch. It would not be possible to drain the cavity behind the slabs.

At the design stage, it was felt that a mastic seal should be used, as shown in Fig. 11.4 (top right). The mastic was shielded to some extent, but could be fairly easily renewed by gun. The horizontal joints were to be filled with a weak mortar during erection, the mortar being such that it would take the weight of the slab if the fixings proved defective, but would crush before the slab spalled. A similar mortar or a joint filler of impregnated fibreboard was to be used in the vertical joints. The mastic was to be a soft bituminous composition, applied by gun, resistant to the alkalis in wet cement and capable of extending at least 50 per cent before rupture, when tested in accordance with B.S. 2499, Appendix F. It was decided that the design depth and width should both be one inch for various reasons: (1) to give a mastic width ten times the maximum movement, (2) to give a depth such that hardening of the mastic throughout would take a considerable time, and (3) to permit reasonable tolerance of slab sizes, and erection tolerances, without reducing the gap unduly. A tolerance of $\pm \frac{1}{4}$ in. on the joint as erected was considered attainable from previous experience with similar constructions.

Manufacturers of suitable mastics were consulted and offered materials, for gun application, which would form a surface skin but would not harden throughout in five years' exposure. They were not prepared, however, to guarantee freedom from slump in joints wider than $\frac{1}{2}$ in. This joint width, being only five times the movement, was not considered acceptable by the architect, as it provided little margin of safety for tolerances in erection and for hardening of the mastic with age. Trials showed that a slightly stiffer

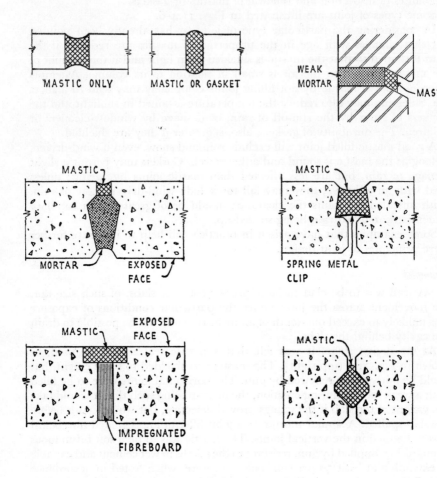

MASTIC ONLY

MASTIC OR GASKET

WEAK MORTAR

MASTIC

MASTIC

MORTAR

EXPOSED FACE

MASTIC

SPRING METAL CLIP

MASTIC

EXPOSED FACE

IMPREGNATED FIBREBOARD

MASTIC

# BUTT JOINTS

Fig. 11.4

*Joint design*

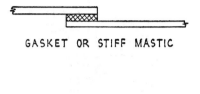

GASKET OR STIFF MASTIC

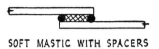

SOFT MASTIC WITH SPACERS

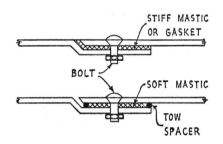

CLADDING JOINT

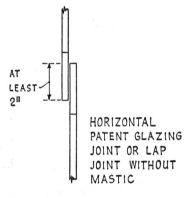

HORIZONTAL PATENT GLAZING JOINT OR LAP JOINT WITHOUT MASTIC

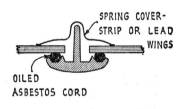

GUTTER JOINTS

VERTICAL PATENT GLAZING JOINT

FIG. 11.5

*Joint design*

mastic of similar composition could be formulated, which would stand in a width of 1 in. and a depth of $\frac{3}{4}$ in., with only slight rippling of the surface. This would have been unsightly in a mastic exposed to view, but did not materially affect the depth of the mastic and did not increase once a skin had been formed.

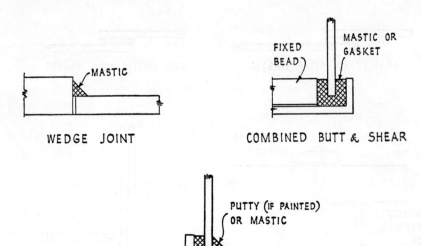

WEDGE JOINT        COMBINED BUTT & SHEAR

COMBINED BUTT, SHEAR & WEDGE

FIG. 11.6

*Joint design*

Provision was made for inspection, and renewal if necessary, at yearly intervals during the life of the building. This would be done from cradles, working from a track on the roof.

2.   In a form of curtain walling, coloured glass panels were to be carried in a light aluminium sub-frame, bolted to the concrete frame of the building. The cavity was to be ventilated and drained and slight seepage of water was not likely to affect the heat-insulating layer, which was separated from the glass by a cavity.

The extent of thermal movement of the glass panels under the condition of exposure was estimated to be not more than $\frac{1}{20}$ in. overall. The connections between the sub-frame and the building would permit sliding, under thermal movement, so buckling was not expected to occur.

To provide adequate tolerances in cutting and erection, a clearance of between $\frac{1}{4}$ in. and $\frac{3}{8}$ in. all round between the frame and the glass was suggested. The two figures represented a working tolerance, and ensured a mastic thickness of at least ten times the expected movement at each joint ($\frac{1}{40}$ in.), as suggested where reasonable durability of soft mastics is required.

Lead spacers were to be inserted to prevent direct contact of the glass with the lower member of the frame. Consideration was, however, given to the relative merits of a gasket instead of a mastic, and it was finally decided to use a neophrene gasket, because:

(1) The drained and ventilated cavity permitted some seepage without damage.

(2) If the glass did not slide evenly on the lead spacers, the whole movement might come at one edge, so that the thickness of the mastic would be only five times the expected movement, and durability would be shortened.

(3) The building was tall and exposed, and provision of spacers to prevent extrusion of the mastic under wind pressure would make erection complicated.

Where clear glass was to be used in windows, however, seepage could not be tolerated, and mastic was to be used. The movement here would be less, since clear glass becomes much less heated than coloured glass.

A simple form of construction is shown in Fig. 11.6 (top right).

*Summary*

In order to enable satisfactory joints to be designed, it is essential to calculate the movement expected between the sides of the joint.

A weathertight joint can be achieved by the use of mastics, but in the absence of a satisfactory accelerated test for mastics, and in view of the variation in conditions of exposure, the durability of such joints is not easy to forecast. Gaskets or simple overlaps can also be used, but do not form so positive a seal against wind-driven rain or snow. The durability of mastics and gaskets is likely to be enhanced if they are shielded from light and if as small an area as possible is exposed to air; priming porous surfaces may also help and will generally improve adhesion.

Because complete exclusion of the weather for prolonged periods cannot always be achieved, even with good workmanship, it is of advantage if the joint is backed by a drained and ventilated cavity. If this is not possible, the jointing material should be accessible for inspection and renewal.

It may, in due course, prove possible to adopt a further method; thin metal or plastic sheets may be corrugated, to prevent distortion as their temperature or moisture content changes, and welded or similarly united at each joint. In the construction of caravans, factory welding is already used for aluminium roofs, and similar methods are used for polyester coachwork; site welding is used for polyvinyl chloride waterbars and rigid bitumen-asbestos sheeting.

## INTERNAL LININGS

Building boards are supplied in sheets of appropriate size, thickness and rigidity for use as coverings for walls, ceilings and framed partitions. Some of them can be used as flooring or as floor coverings and some have special uses as sound absorbents and for thermal insulation.

The main classes of materials of this sort are noted in Table 11.5, which includes reference to the British Standard (if any) appropriate to each. The manufacturers issue leaflets and other literature outlining the varied uses of their materials, with recommendations on procedures; much relevant information will also be found in the British Standard Code of Practice for board, sheet and slab coverings to framed walls and partitions (CP.124).

The sizes obtainable and some features of the boards depend on the way in which they are made.

*Fibre building boards* are made from wood or other vegetable fibre by a continuous process similar to that used for making paper. Insulating board is a low-density product obtained by drying the felted sheet as it comes from the machine. Hardboards in the various grades are formed in the same way and are then compressed and cured in heated presses. Each board is compressed on a gauze screen, which allows the steam to escape, and unless the board is specially prepared one side carries the pattern of the screen. Superhardboard is hardboard that has been treated in the course of manufacture to increase its hardness and resistance to water. Laminated fibre building board is made up from thin layers of felted fibre glued together with an adhesive.

*Insulating board* is used, as its name implies, to provide heat insulation. It is also used as a sound absorbent, either plain or perforated with a pattern of holes to increase its efficiency. It is not strong enough to withstand heavy wear and tear, so it is customary to restrict its use to ceilings and the upper parts of walls.

*Hardboard* is more resistant to wear and tear than insulating board. It has relatively little intrinsic value for thermal insulation, but, in common with all sheet wall coverings, it contributes towards an improvement in the thermal resistance of the wall if it is fixed with an air-space behind it. Hardboard can be used as a floor covering in places where there is no likelihood of its becoming excessively wet and where it will not be subjected to heavy traffic. It is also used as a facing for flush doors.

Hardboard is supplied in a perforated form designed to be fixed over a mat of glass wool or slag wool to serve as a sound absorbent. This perforated board has also found extensive use as a decorative wall-covering and for shop fitting, where it lends itself to the display of light merchandise.

*Superhardboard* is designed to be used out of doors in reasonably sheltered places, under porches and verandahs. Trials have shown that superhardboard and even hardboard offer surprisingly good resistance to weathering. There is scope for use of either of them out of doors in temporary buildings, if some degree of roughening of the surface is not considered objectionable. Regular painting improves the weather-resistance and prevents surface deterioration. The edges of the boards are inclined to be vulnerable, and it is not easy to ensure that they are effectively protected: absorption of water causes the board to swell and may cause cracking of the paint applied to the edges.

*Gypsum plasterboard* is made by a continuous process. It comprises a core of gypsum plaster enclosed between and firmly bonded to two sheets of heavy paper. The paper is chosen to be either of a roughish texture, designed to be finished with a coat of plaster, or of a smoother texture, designed to be

## TABLE 11.5

*Properties of sheet materials for walls and ceilings*

| | British Standard | Density (lb./cu. ft) | Modulus of rupture (lb./sq. in.) | Thermal conductivity (B.t.u. in./sq. ft h °F) | Moisture expansion over range 40–90 per cent relative humidity* (per cent) |
|---|---|---|---|---|---|
| Fibre building boards: | | | | | |
|   Insulating board | B.S. 1142 | 16–25 | 150– 500 | 0·35–0·45 | 0·18–0·33 |
|   Bitumen-bonded insulating board | B.S. 1142 | Not more than 23 | — | — | — |
|   Homogeneous fibre wallboard | B.S. 1142 | Not more than 30 | 300– 350 | — | — |
|   Laminated fibre wallboard | B.S. 1142 | 40– 50 | 1 000– 2 000 | 0·53 | 0·24–0·85 |
|   Medium hardboard | B.S. 1142 | 30– 50 | 800– 2 500 | 0·5 –0·7 | 0·10–0·26 |
|   Standard hardboard | B.S. 1142 | 50– 65 | 3 500– 8 000 | 0·5 –0·7 | 0·10–0·35 |
|   Superhardboard | B.S. 1142 | 50– 65 | 4 000– 8 000 | 0·5 –0·7 | — |
| Plywood | B.S. 1455 (British-made plywood) B.S. 1203 (Adhesives) | 35– 45 | 1 500–20 000 | 1·0 | 0·07–0·34 |
| Gypsum plasterboard | B.S. 1230 | 45– 80 | 200– 1 600 | 1·1–1·4 | 0·01–0·07 |
| Asbestos-cement sheet | B.S. 690 | 110–120 | 2 500– 5 000 | 1·5 –1·9 | 0·02–0·08 |
| Asbestos wallboard | — | 60– 80 | 1 500– 3 000 | — | 0·03–0·04 |
| Asbestos wood | — | 70– 80 | 2 500– 4 000 | — | 0·10–0·78 |
| Synthetic-resin bonded-paper sheet (laminated plastics sheet) | B.S. 1323 | 80– 85 | 15 000–30 000 | 1·4 –2·3 | — |
| Wood chipboard | B.S. 1811 B.S. 2604 | 30– 80 | 400– 1 300 | 0·8 –1·7 | 0·07–0·83 |
| Resin-bonded asbestos board | — | 80–100 | 5 000– 8 000 | — | 0·04–0·05 |
| Asbestos fibre board | — | 40– 50 | 1 000– 1 500 | 0·75 | 0·01–0·12 |
| Wood-wool building slab | B.S. 1105 | 25– 50 | 50– 250 | 0·6 –0·7 | — |

* Test pieces conditioned successively to equilibrium with atmosphere at 40 per cent and 90 per cent relative humidity at 20°C

self-finished or to be decorated with paint or distemper. One variety, described as gypsum wallboard, has a different grade of paper on either side so that it may be used either way, as desired. Gypsum lath, which is intended to be plastered, is supplied in smaller sizes and has a specially designed edge. Insulating plasterboard is faced on one or both sides with a bright metallic surface of low emissivity. Perforated plasterboard is supplied for sound insulation.

*Asbestos-cement sheet and asbestos wood* are made from Portland cement and asbestos fibre. Asbestos wood, having a higher proportion of asbestos fibre, is the less brittle. Asbestos-cement products are normally intended to be used out of doors. There are sundry other varieties of asbestos board, bonded with agents other than Portland cement, which are generally more appropriate for use indoors. Boards containing Portland cement need an alkali-resisting primer if they are to be painted.

*Thermosetting synthetic-resin bonded-paper sheets* (often described as laminated plastics sheets, and commonly known by proprietary names) are made by impregnating paper of a suitable quality with a synthetic resin and subsequently bonding together an appropriate number of sheets to make a board of the required thickness. Phenolic resins yield dark-coloured products. Where a light-coloured finish is required, paper impregnated with either a urea or a melamine resin is used. Usually, but not necessarily, this forms a facing on a phenolic resin-bonded core. The outer sheet of impregnated paper can carry a printed design, which then forms a permanent feature of the decoration. Resin-bonded paper sheet is strong and durable. It is decorative and can easily be kept clean.

*Resin-bonded wood-chip boards* (known in the United States as 'wood-particle boards') are made by coating or impregnating wood chips or sawdust with a synthetic resin and then compressing and curing the mixture in a press. Such boards may be homogeneous or may be faced in the course of manufacture with a selected grade of wood chips. They can also be faced with impregnated paper or with wood veneer. There have been considerable developments in the manufacture of wood-chip boards of recent years. Besides their use as wall linings, some have been used as floor surfacing or as floor tiles, and some are strong enough to be used on joists as suspended flooring, provided that all the edges are adequately supported.

*Plywood* is made from wood veneers glued together with adhesives of various kinds. The water-resistant grades of adhesives have proved to be highly resistant to weathering agencies. Plywood bonded with these can be used out of doors without fear of delamination of the veneers. But the wood itself is still susceptible to the effects of moisture and fungi and needs to be adequately protected by regular painting or by fungicidal treatment.

*Wood-wool building slab* is not strictly a sheet building material. The slabs are made from wood-wool and an inorganic cementing agent (Portland cement or magnesium oxychloride) in 6-ft lengths, 2 ft wide and in thicknesses up to 3 in. Unlike the other materials described, they can be built to form self-supporting walls. They provide good thermal insulation and the coarse texture of the surface forms a good base for plastering or rendering. They may be used for sound absorption if left unplastered. They are dealt with in the British Standard Code of Practice for walls and partitions of blocks and of slabs (CP.122).

Among the various kinds of building board, the size of sheet varies according to the method of manufacture and the custom of the industry. Plywood and some other materials can be supplied to any size required. Boards that are made by continuous processes—insulating board, plasterboard and some kinds of wood-chip boards—can be supplied to order in standard widths and in any reasonable length. Such boards can be fixed horizontally over the full width and length of the room. This procedure simplifies the problem of jointing.

As will have been seen from the foregoing description, some boards are intended to be used as a base for plastering; some are intended to be decorated with paint or distemper; some are self-finished. Some have particular merits in respect of good appearance, resistance to wear, ease of cleaning or thermal insulation. With the aid of a wide range of water-resistant glues, it is possible to build up composite panels to combine the good insulation properties (provided by insulating board or other insulating material) with some other desirable property in the facing sheet, and gain the special advantage of each. Rigid, self-supporting panels can be made in this way. These can be either solid or of hollow construction with a honeycomb or similar type of core.

*Acoustics*

Sheet materials, perforated or otherwise, are used as sound absorbents to secure good acoustic qualities in concert halls and to reduce the level of noise in canteens and offices. Some of the energy of the sound waves is absorbed by the material or by the absorbent placed behind the perforated covering, so that less is reflected back into the room. The decorative finish must be appropriately chosen if the sound-absorbing qualities are to be retained.

As discussed on p. 53, there is apt to be confusion between sound absorption and sound insulation. Sound insulation relates to the reduction in the intensity of sound transmitted from one side of a wall or floor to the other side, and is substantially proportional to the weight per unit area of the separating structure. Insulating board and other sheet materials, being light in weight, have no special merit for reducing sound transmission. If good insulation is required in a framed partition the weight of the partition must be increased by loading the space between the two faces with sand, or else the back and front of the partition must be built as two completely separate and independent units. Even then the sound reduction may not be all that could be desired.

*Fixing*

Building boards can be fixed with nails or screws to timber battens, studs or other suitable supports. They can also be fixed in simple channel members of metal or plastics or in proprietary framing systems designed to accommodate particular makes of board. Boards made in adequate thicknesses, or formed into suitable composite units, can be used with channel members to form partitions. In some circumstances adhesives can be used for fixing, and boards can also be bonded to solid walls with plaster, though these methods are not commonly practised. Some varieties can be used as permanent shuttering. That is to say, the boards are laid in position in the forms so that the concrete poured against them becomes bonded to the boards and holds them in position as a facing when the formwork is struck.

When boards are nailed or screwed to supporting members, all the edges must be supported, using nogging pieces where necessary. The spacing of the supports must be appropriate to the strength and rigidity of the board.

Building boards are subject to varying degrees of moisture expansion and drying shrinkage in response to changes in the relative humidity of the environment. Some respond to these changes more quickly than others. Boards should be conditioned to a normal moisture content before they are fixed, and adjacent boards should be fixed with a small gap between them to accommodate any subsequent expansion. Rigid boards should preferably be drilled with oversize holes and be fixed with screws, since they are more likely to buckle or to pull from their fixings than the softer varieties which can yield, to some extent, at the supports.

*Treatment of joints*

The ultimate appearance of the work depends on how the joints are dealt with. Cover-strips of wood, fibre board, metal or plastics can be used to conceal the joints and the nail beads. Alternatively, the boards can be fixed with panel-pins and the edges can be bevelled to make a decorative feature of the joints. These practices give a panelled effect and the layout of the boards must be such as will produce an acceptable pattern.

When plasterboard or insulating board is used as a base for plaster, the joints are dealt with first by applying metal gauze or hessian scrim set in position in plaster. Plastering then proceeds over this in accordance with the instructions of the board manufacturer. These instructions should be followed implicitly; use of the wrong kind of plaster or the addition of lime to some kinds of plaster may lead to loss of adhesion or other defects. Internal plastering is dealt with in a British Standard Code of Practice (CP.211). Plastering lath is intended to be plastered without need for reinforcement of the joints.

Plasterboard can be supplied with tapered edges. These provide a shallow depression at the joints which can be scrimmed and plastered to bring the surface flush with the faces of the boards, which carry a grade of paper intended to receive the decoration. With careful workmanship such joints can be made to be virtually imperceptible when decorated to a matt or semi-matt finish. A high gloss finish betrays any imperfections there may be in the plastering and is usually too revealing of any deficiencies in that respect.

The practice of reinforcing the joints, which is intended to reduce the tendency for cracks to develop in the plastered finish, is not always effective, particularly on ceilings. Plasterboard shows relatively small moisture expansion and drying shrinkage. Hence, cracking of the joints in plasterboard ceilings is more likely to be caused by shrinkage of the timber or by deflection of the joists than by moisture movement in the boards. For that reason, a painted or distempered finish on fair-faced plasterboard, with thick paper cover-strips to conceal the joints, may be considered preferable to a plastered finish.

*Durability*

Organic building materials—fibre building boards, plywood, the paper facing of plasterboard, wood chipboards and the like—are prone to decay if they are used in damp and unventilated situations without adequate protective treatment. Dampness may be caused by leakage of rain through roof and walls, by lack of adequate damp-proof courses or by excessive condensation. Under conditions of high humidity, boards used for the insulation of flat roofs may become saturated with condensed moisture, unless an effective vapour barrier is provided to prevent the diffusion of water vapour through the board to the cold undersurface of the structural roof.

In a wet condition the board loses a substantial proportion of the insulation value and may in time become rotten; boards used as permanent shuttering in the construction of concrete roofs will be prone to lose their adhesion to the concrete and fall from place. Where boards are used to form a suspended ceiling below the roof of a factory or other building in which the air is at a high humidity, condensed moisture dripping from the roof may saturate the boards, causing them to lose their strength and stiffness and to fall out of the supporting framework. In these circumstances, if high humidity in the room is unavoidable, the aim should be to reduce the relative humidity of the air in the roof space by providing ample ventilation and by sealing the surfaces of the boards and the joints between them, so far as practicable.

Board linings on battens provide a simple way of dealing with damp walls to improve appearance and comfort in places where it would be difficult or too costly to remedy the defects, as for instance in old property where there is no damp-proof course, or in places where rain penetration occurs and cannot be cured. In these circumstances the battens used should be impregnated under pressure with an inodorous, non-staining preservative and should be fastened to plugs of rot-proof material. The face of the wall and the back of the boards should be treated with a colourless toxic wash, and openings should be provided at the top and bottom of the panels to allow reasonable ventilation of the interspace.

*Fire hazard*

The fire hazards associated with the use of sheet materials as wall and ceiling linings need special consideration. The relevant tests are described in the British Standard for Fire Tests on Building Materials and Structures (B.S. 476).

Plasterboard and some of the boards incorporating asbestos fibre can be used to assist in securing the requisite degree of fire-resistance in structural steelwork, and these and others can be used to improve the fire-resistance of timber floors or other elements of structure. Examples, with relevant data, are illustrated in 'Investigations on Building Fires. Part V: Fire Tests on Structural Elements' (H.M. Stationery Office 1953). As explained on p. 77, fire-resistance is not a property of a material, but of the element of structure in which it is used.

Asbestos-cement sheet is non-combustible, but, because it is liable to shatter explosively when it is strongly heated in a building fire, it does not contribute to the fire-resistance of an element of structure and is not suitable for that purpose.

Among combustible sheet materials, it is the 'spread of flame' properties that determine where and how a board may safely be used. An internal lining that allows the flame to spread rapidly over the surface may be the cause of a widespread extension of the fire, and may prevent the escape of the occupants. The danger lies not only in the rapid spread of the fire but also in the sudden flash-over that occurs when the temperature of a combustible material exposed to radiant heat reaches the ignition point.

Building materials used as linings for walls and ceilings are classified by the 'surface spread of flame' test described in the British Standard (B.S. 476). This test measures the rate of spread of flame under standardized conditions of radiation, and groups materials in four classes of very low (Class 1), low (Class 2), medium (Class 3) and rapid (Class 4) flame spread respectively. The classification of a particular material may be influenced by the decorative treatment applied to it and there are flame-retardant treatments that are designed to be applied to improve the classification of the less satisfactory materials.

The classification of the spread-of-flame test was intended to provide a simple means for deciding whether a board or sheet material would be safe to use as a wall or ceiling lining in particular circumstances. But experience has shown that those combustible materials that achieve a classification in Class 1 only by reason of a treatment applied to them, may still constitute a fire-hazard. Such treatment may delay but does not prevent the absorption of radiant heat and the consequent rise in the temperature; a flash-over may still occur. At the time of writing (1958) efforts are being made to find a better method of evaluation. Meanwhile it is recommended that only non-combustible materials or materials that are inherently Class 1 should be used as linings for walls and ceilings of rooms and passages that afford means of escape for the occupants of the building.

In addition to freedom from fire risks, internal linings must be strong enough to withstand the severity of usage to which they may be subjected. Beyond these considerations, the special requirements may be decisive. Insulating qualities, sound absorption, appearance or smoothness of surface, ease of cleaning, ease of decoration, working qualities, may each assume predominant importance and the choice must be made accordingly.

## APPEARANCE OF BUILDINGS, CLEANING AND RESTORATION

No building retains its pristine appearance for very long. Time and weather begin to have their effects on the colour, texture and condition of the materials as soon as the work is completed. Exposure to the weather may bring out natural variations in colour and texture of the materials employed, when it is said to 'develop their character'. Such changes are usually regarded with favour. But there are others that are considered by common consent to be unsightly, and there are some on which opinion is divided. Some changes in appearance take place quickly, others develop slowly. Some of the effects are temporary; others are permanent in the sense that they persist until the owner of the building thinks it worth while to remedy them.

It would not be appropriate here to consider questions of taste, but it is proper to consider those technical aspects of the use of building materials that may make or mar the aesthetic effect that the architect aims to create.

It is not the intention in this chapter to enlarge upon those matters affecting the appearance of buildings that are dealt with under appropriate headings elsewhere, but only to refer to them in general terms to establish principles that apply to the choice of materials and the way they are used and maintained. Some changes that have an adverse effect on appearance are unavoidable; some may occur by mischance, despite every care. Some can easily be eliminated. Recognition of their causes is the first step towards knowing how to avoid them and how to deal with them when they have occurred.

*Air pollution*

Under present conditions in the United Kingdom the air is heavily polluted with smoke and sulphur dioxide derived from the burning of fuel. At least half of this pollution comes from domestic sources. Buildings in large cities become overlaid with grime. Those in rural areas are less disfigured by soot. Sulphur dioxide is widely distributed and its effects can be seen in towns and cities and even in country districts where the buildings are reasonably clean.

The passing of the Clean Air Act (1956) represents a first step towards a reduction in the emission of smoke. Its effect on the level of air pollution will depend upon the extent to which adequate supplies of smokeless fuel can be provided to replace coal. Unfortunately there is no prospect yet of preventing the emission of sulphur dioxide derived from the combustion of the sulphur compounds that are present not only in bituminous coal, but also in anthracite, coke and other smokeless fuels and in fuel oil. There is no known way of extracting these compounds from the fuel, and it is only in large installations that the flue gases can be purified—at some considerable cost. Present concern with the smoke nuisance gives hope for the future. Meanwhile the effects of smoke and fumes on buildings have still to be reckoned with.

Soot deposition affects building materials in different ways. Buildings in the more durable kinds of sandstone tend to become blackened all over— and are difficult to clean. The rain-washed surfaces are the first to darken in colour. Granites which become similarly discoloured can be kept in a reasonably clean condition if the surfaces are polished and are cleaned regularly. Rough-textured bricks become more or less uniformly blackened. Those of a smoother texture take longer to acquire a uniformly darkened appearance and in the meantime the building may have a variegated appearance. With any kind of brickwork erosion of the mortar may produce a strong contrast in colour between the bricks and the joints.

The surfaces of limestone, cast stone, concrete blocks and cement renderings, being slightly soluble in water, tend to retain a cleaner appearance where they are washed by rain, and to present a more or less striking contrast between the exposed and sheltered parts. Black incrustations accumulate beneath projecting features and irregular downwash produces light-coloured streaks on a dark background. Where crazing occurs in cement and concrete products, differential deposition of soot and dirt makes the pattern more conspicuous. From all these materials the deposits can be removed by washing with water and they can be kept looking clean if they are washed at appropriate intervals.

Pollution of the air with sulphur dioxide accelerates the rate of erosion of rain-washed surfaces but this is seldom of any moment except where it detracts from the appearance of statuary and carving; even then it may be a long time before the effects become obtrusive. Sulphur dioxide also causes decay of some types of limestone, in the form of unsightly blistering and scaling, but this does not imply that limestone is unsuitable for use in towns and cities, for there are other types that withstand the effects admirably. Limestone is often preferred to the more resistant varieties of sandstone because it does not assume a uniformly black appearance and it has the further advantage of being more easily cleaned. Cast stone and sandstones containing carbonates are also susceptible to the deleterious effects of air pollution. Roofing slates containing a high proportion of carbonate are affected, but, because the deterioration takes place on the undersurfaces, the effects may escape notice until the slates begin to slip out of position. Bricks are not directly affected by sulphur fumes, but bricks of the softer kinds may be damaged where they can absorb sulphates derived from neighbouring limestone. Sandstones of otherwise durable quality may be similarly affected; some are less tolerant of contamination in this way than others.

In choosing materials for use in polluted atmospheres it is more than usually necessary to choose with care. Observation of their behaviour in buildings affords the best guide.

*Frost*

Frost can cause spectacular damage to susceptible materials if they are used in circumstances in which they can become highly saturated with water (see p. 82).

There are other materials that are virtually immune to damage by frost. All risk can be averted by making a suitable choice and taking such precautions as may be necessary to prevent undue saturation with water. Free-standing walls, plinths, and unprotected copings, cornices, sills and string courses are the most vulnerable features.

*Soluble salts*

Soluble salts may disfigure buildings by obscuring the surfaces with efflorescence and may cause damage by crystallization within the pores of brick or stone (p. 83). Some materials are more susceptible than others.

Salts are brought to the surface in solution in water, which evaporates from the face, leaving the salts behind. Some, like the sulphates of sodium and magnesium, appear as efflorescences; others, like calcium sulphate and sodium chloride, seldom effloresce. Potassium sulphate tends to form a hard, glassy film on the surface.

Evaporation of the water used in construction often leads to the appearance of efflorescence on new brickwork. As a rule this is gradually removed by wind and rain until it finally disappears leaving the bricks none the worse. The risk of an unsightly appearance in a newly-completed building offers a temptation to prevent the development of efflorescence by applying a water-repellent treatment to the brickwork. The effect of this is to break the capillary path at the surface. Evaporation still proceeds slowly and the salts, instead of reaching the surface, are forced to crystallize within the pores and in doing so they may cause spalling of the bricks. Efflorescence cannot be suppressed without risk of causing harm. The better course is to assist its removal by rinsing with water after removing as much of the salts as possible with a stiff brush. As the wall dries more salts will be brought to the surface and several repetitions of this procedure may be necessary.

If there is a continuing entry of moisture, through an unprotected coping or cornice, for example, or rising damp from the foundations, there will be a continuous movement of salts to the faces of the wall which will cause a continuous or intermittent appearance of efflorescence outside and damage to the decorative finish inside. In walls with ill-constructed parapets it is not uncommon for a fresh crop of salts to make an appearance each spring after the walls have been saturated by the winter's rain. Similar considerations apply to stone facings backed with brickwork or concrete and to renderings. Movement of water brings salts to the face of the wall where they cause disfigurement and damage. Water that seeps through the fabric picking up salts on its way is a serious threat to durability and to appearance.

Bricks and concrete products inevitably contain or produce a small proportion of soluble salts. Building stone is usually substantially free from soluble salts when it is quarried but there are many ways in which it can become contaminated before or after it is placed in the building. It should be axiomatic that all reasonable precautions should be taken to avoid contamination in the handling and transport of worked and unworked blocks and in the detailing of the design, particularly of plinths, copings, cornices, and the like.

In principle, the subsequent maintenance of the building should avoid all procedures that involve the risk of introducing a soluble salt. But this is not always possible when obstinate stains have to be removed. Chemical treatment may have to be adopted as a last resort. In that event the stained area should first be soaked with water to reduce absorption to a minimum and should be thoroughly washed afterwards.

Another general rule is that any surface treatment that tends to trap moisture and salts behind the face is unlikely to be effective and may do more harm than good. This is illustrated by the preference for absorptive rather than dense impervious renderings and by the comments made above about the risks attaching to the use of water-repellent liquids to prevent the appearance of salts as an efflorescence.

The introduction of salts by rising damp has its own problems. Moisture absorbed through the foundations rises to a height at which there is a balance between the rate of evaporation from the surfaces of the wall and the rate at which it can be drawn up from the soil by capillary forces. This height may vary somewhat with the time of year and the level of the water table in the soil. Any procedure that restricts evaporation from the surfaces, such as the application of paint or a dense rendering, will tend to drive the moisture to a higher level. In remedial work on buildings without damp-proof courses the aim should be to increase the evaporation and it is sometimes helpful to excavate the soil to expose as much of the base of the wall as possible.

In new buildings attempts are often made to hide the damp-proof course, with the intention of improving the appearance. This practice commonly defeats the purpose for which the damp-proof course is provided. It is much better that the damp-proof course should be visible than that the plinth should be disfigured by the stains and efflorescent salts that all too frequently follow attempts to conceal it.

*Staining*

There are various causes of staining other than those that are obviously associated with air pollution, rain penetration, or rising damp. Some of these are easily avoidable. The pattern-staining of ceilings, for example, is indicative of differences in thermal conduction and can be prevented by an appropriate disposition of insulating material to equalize the conduction. The staining of stone pedestals supporting bronze statuary can be eliminated if the bronze is designed with provision for collecting and draining the run-off through the pedestal. Galvanized wire screens used to protect windows cause iron staining if they are not renewed before rusting occurs. Light-coloured granite may show iron staining if the acid used to remove the particles of iron left by the saws is not thoroughly washed off afterwards, or if wood blocks used to space the blocks of stone in the stack become contaminated with this acid.

There are other kinds of staining which might be averted if it were practicable to take elaborate precautions in the selection of the materials. These are not of such common occurrence that precautions would generally be worth while.

The brownish stains that sometimes develop on newly-built limestone are attributable to the action of alkaline constituents absorbed from the cement grout on organic matter present in the stone. Portland cement contains small and variable amounts of alkali. The staining potentialities of any batch can be ascertained by test if the need arises.

Sporadic stains sometimes appear on newly-plastered walls or on the plastered soffits of hollow clay tile floors. Paint and distemper fail to adhere properly to the stained patches. These are attributed to the deposition of a glassy film of potassium sulphate and are associated with, for example, the use of black-cored bricks or tiles, which it may or may not be possible to eliminate by sorting.

Dark brown stains on brickwork facings can be induced by reaction between lime in the mortar and iron compounds extracted from the bricks by acid rain water. Such staining seems to be largely restricted to walls built in unusually wet weather.

The brownish stains that sometimes appear after soot-discoloured limestone has been cleaned are referred to in a later paragraph.

*Vegetation*

The polluted state of the air in towns and cities prevents the growth of algae, lichens and mosses on the external surfaces of buildings. In consequence, the appearance of stone, bricks, slates and tiles used in towns may be very different from their appearance in rural surroundings, quite apart from the other differences induced by air pollution.

Algae, lichens and mosses flourish on walls and roofs in country districts, sometimes to the extent of obscuring the surfaces on which they grow. They are usually regarded as contributing to the picturesque character of the buildings concerned. It is only rarely that they cause any material harm. They obscure the form of carving and inscriptions, however, and if need be, they can be killed by treatment with a fungicidal solution.

Acids derived from the metabolism of vegetation growing on a roof are liable to cause channelling and eventual perforation of lead, zinc, copper and aluminium valleys, gutters and weatherings. The metal can be protected by applying an occasional coat of bituminous paint.

Serious disfigurement of stone and brickwork by the extensive growth of black organisms has been met with. Renderings and cement paints often show a greenish tint because of the growth of algae, and there are black or coloured organisms that can grow on painted surfaces in bakeries and the like where the conditions are favourable. All these can be suitably dealt with by the use of toxic washes (p. 258).

*Cleaning*

The appearance of buildings in towns can be much improved by periodic cleaning. External cleaning in rural areas is seldom necessary.

There was at one time a school of thought that contended that soot deposition on buildings is admirable in its effects and should not be interfered with by cleaning. Some may still hold that opinion. Nevertheless, the comments that have been made following the cleaning of particular buildings —whether modern, commercial buildings or old buildings of historic interest—have demonstrated that cleanliness is now generally preferred. Where buildings have been cleaned results have been received with general favour and the example has soon been followed by other owners.

The harmful practice of using alkaline detergents to facilitate the cleaning process, which was common some thirty years ago, and which caused the steam cleaning process to fall into unmerited disrepute, has now been abandoned by all responsible cleaning firms. It would be hardly necessary to reiterate the point that alkaline detergents should be avoided, were it not that proprietary preparations are sometimes offered in ignorance of, or without regard to, their potentially harmful effects.

Limestone, cast stone and renderings can all be cleaned with ease after the deposits have been softened by water applied in the form of a fine spray for a suitable period. This method has largely displaced the steam-cleaning process, although steam still has its uses for cleaning more difficult materials —sandstone, granite and brickwork.

Operators of the spray method often use far more water than is needed. This, besides causing inconvenience, enhances the risk of penetration of water to the interior surfaces with consequent damage to the decorations. The principle of the method is to keep the surfaces wet for long enough to soften the deposits and ease the labour. No more than a minimum amount of water is necessary to achieve this object. Eminently successful results have been obtained on old, soot-blackened limestone, using jets that delivered no more than $2\frac{1}{2}$ gallons per hour under the pressure of the mains. Where there are massive incrustations, time can be saved by the judicious use of a wooden scraper to remove the deposits as they become progressively softened.

Before the water spray method is used, open joints should be pointed and all vulnerable points that might permit access of water to the inner face of the wall should be suitably protected. This applies particularly to old buildings, where the walls may not be as well constructed as they might be and where the penetration of large amounts of water might lead to outbreaks of dry rot.

Limestone and similar surfaces need no detergent or other chemical aid to assist the cleaning. Sandstone and granite are more difficult to deal with but, again, alkaline detergents should on no account be used. In the hands of experienced firms, acid solutions can be used without risk of causing immediate or subsequent damage. In some circumstances abrasion with carborundum wheels to remove the blackened surface, which is only skin-deep, achieves the purpose satisfactorily.

Occasionally the development of brownish stains on newly-cleaned lime-stone has caused disappointment. These are no fault of the operator. They are attributed to soluble matter that has been absorbed into the stone from the soot deposits and is brought to the surface as the stone dries. They occur fortuitously and it is conceivable that their development depends in some measure on the prevailing weather conditions: slow drying would encourage staining; rapid drying would discourage it. The stains often disappear quite quickly, but sometimes they persist for some considerable time. Repeated rinsing with water is helpful but is not always fully effective.

While it is important to bear these occasional difficulties in mind, they should not be allowed to outweigh the advantage of cleanliness. Cleaning removes unsightly soot deposits. It also helps to combat the effects of sulphur fumes, but it is an academic question to ask if this will prolong the life of a stone building which, in any event, may be expected to last for some hundreds of years. Regular cleaning maintains a continuously good appearance and allows the stone to give the best service of which it is capable. Where circum-stances permit, hosing limestone at half-yearly or yearly intervals will keep it in a surprisingly clean state, even in a heavily polluted atmosphere.

Brickwork varies in ease of cleaning and it is best to place the work in the hands of an experienced firm. Some bricks can be cleaned with water; others respond better if steam is used.

## Restoration

The restoration of old buildings demands a sympathetic regard for the work of past centuries and is not a task to be undertaken lightly. The first aim should be to remedy all defects that permit entry of water and lead to deterioration of the fabric, deferring the replacement of the work of the original craftsmen for as long as possible, until such time as it becomes necessary to restore an acceptable appearance or to obviate the risk of injury from falling fragments. Decisions on the extent of replacement in old stone buildings are often difficult to reach. Some blocks may be extensively decayed, while others may appear to be reasonably sound. It is better to reface the whole façade than to leave no more than a few of the older blocks here and there, because these will be liable to deteriorate before the newer stone, and in that event will spoil the ultimate effect of the restoration.

Any new stone introduced should be compatible with the old. Limestone should be repaired with limestone, sandstone with sandstone and so on. There is still a fair range of sandstones to choose from in matching the colour and texture of the stonework to be repaired, but it is becoming increasingly difficult to find limestones that suitably match existing buildings dating from times when the limestone formations were more extensively worked for building stone than they are now.

The alternative method of restoration in a plastic composition has its uses but is not always successful. The method should never be used except by experienced operatives under skilled supervision. Success demands time, patience and enthusiasm. In inexperienced hands the result can be disas-trous. One difficulty is that the material used for repair and the original material may weather differently, with the consequence that repairs initially matching the old work may become unpleasantly obvious in course of time. The finish of the jointing has a predominant influence on the final appearance. If the work cannot be dealt with block by block, it is better to choose a mix of suitable composition and to use it frankly as a rendering, taking care to secure a good key to the background. Simulating the joints by scoring the face of the work betrays the method of repair to the most casual observer and entirely fails to convey the impression intended.

In some circumstances plain ashlar has been redressed to remove an unsightly and badly weathered face, exposing a new surface of reasonably sound stone, and has already postponed the need for a replacement for some forty years. Such experience demonstrates that there is no need to be deterred by the common belief that stone deteriorates rapidly if the weathered face is removed. Redressing involves difficulties at door and window openings, but these are not insuperable.

PART II

# The Wall and its Functions

# Preamble to Part II

I T will be convenient to consider the whole range of wall functions together, even though any given wall, external or internal, loadbearing or non-load-bearing, may not have to perform all of them.

The predominating factor in the design of a wall is whether it has to carry an imposed load. If it has, then choice is restricted to materials that are economic when used in the thickness required. Thus, merely satisfying the strength requirement provides a wall of fair thickness, which is already some way towards satisfying other requirements as a barrier to wind, water, heat, sound and fire. If there is no imposed load, then there is greater freedom in designing to meet the requirements that remain.

Strength and stability requirements of loadbearing walls will therefore be discussed first.

## Chapter 12

# STRENGTH AND STABILITY

It was not until comparatively recently that any detailed consideration was given to the strength characteristics of walls. For all but small buildings, the thickness of walls was determined from well-established empirical rules relating thickness to height and length of wall. In small buildings of one or two storeys it has been found that provision for other functions gives a wall of more than adequate strength: for example, the thickness of brickwork necessary for effective protection from the weather, mainly by excluding rain, gives a wall strength many times greater than that required to carry the loads.

When a wall is to be designed for strength, there are certain factors that apply whatever the system of construction, such as conditions of loading, conditions of vertical and lateral support, and permissible stresses (or load factor).

## LOADING

For convenience in estimation, the loading of a structural element is considered to be made up of two separate components. The first is the 'dead load', being an estimate, as accurate as possible, of the weight of all parts of the structure itself that come upon the member. Thus, at the base of the wall of a building the dead load will comprise the weight of the wall itself above the part under consideration, together with that proportion of the weight of floors, roofs, etc., that may reasonably be considered to be supported by the wall. Since, however, it is not possible in practice to weigh each component of the dead load, it has been found necessary to find some conventional basis for estimation of weights of building materials, and one is given in British Standard 648: 1949.

The second component of the load on a structural member of a building is termed the 'imposed load'. It consists of the weight of the people, furnishings and materials that may reasonably be expected to be present in the building when it is normally occupied, together with wind pressures. It is impossible to make any precise estimate of the actual imposed load in a building, and it has been necessary to formulate conventional tables of loading for buildings with different kinds of occupancy. It must be realized that these are conventions only, not real loads, and that they represent values which, when inserted in design formulae, have been proved by experience to give safe structures. The conventional values for imposed loads are satisfactory for calculating the strength of various components of the structure, but should not be followed blindly in calculations of the loads imposed on the soil by foundations: in considering the settlement of foundations on the soil it is

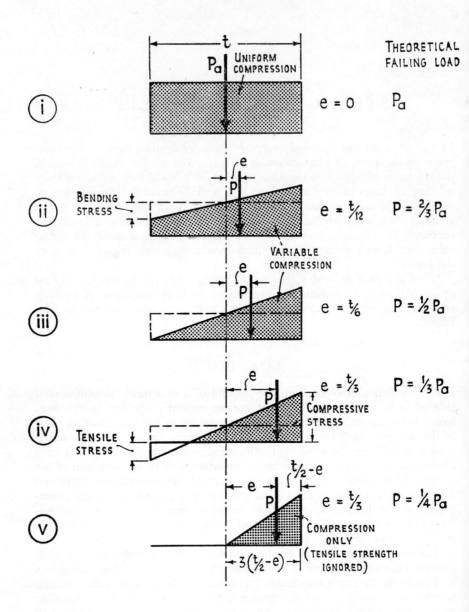

$t$ = Thickness of column
$e$ = Eccentricity of load

Fig. 12.1

*Effect of eccentricity on the strength of masonry columns*

important to arrive at the nearest possible approximation to the actual load, whereas the conventional table of imposed loads may be said to represent a 'probable worst' condition of loading.

The tables of imposed loads in current use have been discussed in Part I, pp. 7–9.

*Eccentric and concentrated loading*

In practice, it is difficult to avoid eccentricity of the applied loading. If a wall carries a floor, for example, deflection of the floor tends to concentrate the load on the inner edge of the wall: this effect will be greater for relatively flexible flooring systems, such as the ordinary timber floor, than for a stiffer floor of reinforced concrete. Eccentricity of loading has a very marked effect on the strength of the wall and should be minimized.

The theoretical reduction in strength of a masonry column as the eccentricity of load is increased is shown in Fig. 12.1 relative to the strength of an axially loaded column of the same height. In the case of loading (ii) where the eccentricity is one-twelfth of the thickness, the maximum bending stress is less than the direct stress and there is compression all over the cross-section of the column. In case (iii) where the eccentricity is one-sixth of the thickness there is zero stress on that side of the column remote from that on which the load is carried: any greater eccentricity, as in case (iv), leads to the development of tensile forces on this side.

Masonry is capable of resisting some tension, but the tensile strength is small and very variable. A figure of 20 to 30 lb. per sq. in. is sometimes used by designers, but usually there is a preference for working on a basis of experience rather than on a calculation based on tensile strength, particularly if that strength is an important factor in the design. In design recommendations, the tensile strength of masonry is usually ignored, and it is assumed

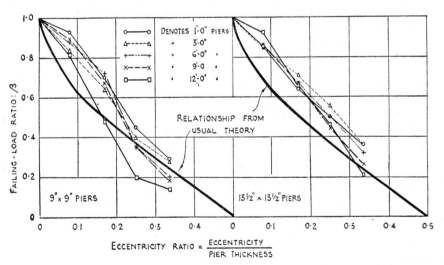

FIG. 12.2

*Reduction of load-carrying capacity of brick columns as eccentricity of loading is increased*

that when the eccentricity is greater than one-sixth of the thickness cracking will occur and part of the section will become inactive. The working portion may be found by assuming that the distribution of the compressive stress is linear so that the resultant passes through the centroid of the triangular stress block, as shown in (v). It will be seen that the useful thickness is therefore reduced to three times the distance of the load from the compressive face of the column.

The theoretical reduction in strength of brick columns with increasing eccentricity is compared in Fig. 12.2 with actual experimental data. It will be noted that for eccentricities of less than about one-quarter of the thickness of the column the actual failing load is not reduced by the eccentric loading as much as the conventional theory would indicate. This fact may be partial justification for the 25 per cent increase in calculated stress allowed in design by existing building regulations when this increase is due solely to eccentricity of loading (see pp. 178–9).

Examples of loading conditions in practice are shown in Fig. 12.3. The floor load on an external wall is distributed over a width of bearing of four inches or so from the inner face of the wall and the centre of the load is eccentric in relation to the axis of the wall. With a timber floor the eccentricity of load is often about one-third of the wall thickness: with the stiffer concrete floor the eccentricity may be only about one-sixth of the wall thickness. Floor loads on partitions usually come from flooring on both sides of the partition and although these loads do not balance exactly, it may usually be assumed that the total load on the partition is central, not tending to cause bending. Party walls may also be considered to be centrally loaded if carrying floors from both sides; if, however, the plan is such that floor joists come on to the wall from one side only, the wall will be eccentrically loaded as is an external wall.

Concentrated loads may set up high local stresses, and it is necessary to spread the load on to a sufficient area so that local crushing does not occur. Examples include loads from a spine beam carrying a heavy load from floor joists; roof trusses; lintels over brick openings; and sometimes even from floor joists themselves. However, the strength of a small element of the wall, especially when restrained by surrounding construction, is much greater than that of the wall as a whole, and the local bearing pressures may be greater than the average values permissible for loading that is continuous over the full area of the wall section. Code of Practice CP.111, for example, allows an increase of 50 per cent in the stress in brickwork or plain concrete due to concentration of the load.

*Lateral support and effective height*

It is well known that a structural member loaded in compression fails at decreasing loads as its height increases. This is taken into account by limiting the 'slenderness ratio', a value defined as the ratio of the 'effective height' to the 'effective thickness'. Where a wall is laterally supported top and bottom, the effective height is taken as three-fourths of the height between such supports; if unsupported laterally at the top, the effective height is taken as doubled—i.e. as one-and-a-half times the actual height.

Where the slenderness ratio is greater than unity, and of course this is usually the case, the permissible working stresses are reduced. The maximum

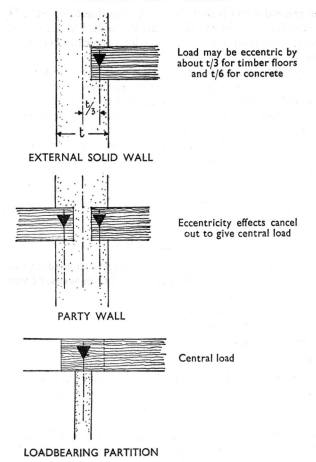

EXTERNAL SOLID WALL

Load may be eccentric by
about t/3 for timber floors
and t/6 for concrete

PARTY WALL

Eccentricity effects cancel
out to give central load

LOADBEARING PARTITION

Central load

FIG. 12.3

*Eccentric and central loading on solid walls*

value of the ratio is set usually at 18; it may be increased to 24 for reinforced concrete walls and for dwelling houses, and should never exceed 12 for masonry jointed with lime mortar.

Concrete floor or roof slabs bearing on walls are regarded as providing adequate lateral support, but with timber floors special attention should be paid to anchorage (see vol. 2).

Piers built integrally with a wall are provided either to carry local loading, e.g. from roof trusses in single-storey buildings, or to stiffen the wall, so that the wall can carry load without buckling.

When only the pier carries the vertical load it receives some assistance from the adjoining wall panels if it is properly bonded to them. Tests have shown that this helpful interaction between pier and panel is most important when the load is applied eccentrically to the pier so that it tends to bend slightly out of the plane of the wall. When the load is applied to the centre of the pier there is, however, very little strength increase due to help from the wall. The general effect is that the weakening due to eccentricity of load on the pier is reduced by interaction with the wall, but since such weakening is still present, it is desirable to apply the load centrally to the pier and ignore help from the wall.

When piers are used merely to stiffen a wall, the increased strength of the wall to carry vertical loading is not accurately known, but may be estimated on the basis of a reduced slenderness ratio. Code of Practice CP.111 gives a table for the 'effective thickness' of a wall stiffened by piers at various spacings, and the use of this increased value for the thickness leads in turn to a reduced slenderness ratio and to increased working stresses of perhaps 25 or 50 per cent beyond those for a similar wall without piers.

The stiffening effect of an intersecting wall may be regarded as equivalent to that of a pier of width equal to that of the intersecting wall, and of thickness equal to three times the thickness of the stiffened wall.


## MASONRY

Assuming for the time being that height is constant and the loading axial, the strength of masonry walls depends upon a number of factors, of which the following are the most important:
(1) Strength of the individual unit
(2) Strength of the mortar
(3) Workmanship.

*Strength of the unit*

The purchaser of wall units will often have data put before him regarding the strength of the material he is asked to buy. It is most desirable that manufacturer's data should be obtained by uniform and reliable methods of testing. The interpretation and, particularly, the comparison of strength test data has pitfalls, and discrimination is called for. First and foremost it cannot be too strongly urged that a strength test result alone, with no mention of the method by which the test was performed and no indication of the number of samples tested, is usually worthless. Any value for the 'strength' of a material can only mean the strength of the material when tested in some specific manner. Assuming that due allowance has been made for the method of test, the next factor to consider is whether the sample actually tested is fairly representative of the article in bulk. In common with many other building materials, bricks and blocks are liable to vary considerably within any one batch or consignment. There may also be variation between batches from the same works on different occasions; examples of this are shown in Table 12.1.

There are several reasons for this. Clay deposits may not be uniform. Firing temperatures may not be the same throughout the kiln. There is often some kind of selection of the product at a brickworks, thus hardest fired units may be picked and sold as superior grades; but even within the limits of the ordinary commercial grading there are wide variations in strength. It is important, therefore, to test a sufficient number of specimens of any batch in order to obtain a representative average value for strength. A sample of twelve bricks or blocks should be regarded as the minimum on which to form a reliable opinion.

TABLE 12.1

*Variations in mean strength of batches of wirecut bricks from seven works*

| Type of clay and works | No. of batches | Mean* strength (lb/sq. in.) | Range of strength (lb/sq. in.) | Range as percentage of mean |
|---|---|---|---|---|
| *Glacial clay* | | | | |
| Works A . | 16 | 4590 | 6620–3140 | 144–68 |
| *Triassic clay* | | | | |
| Works H . | 17 | 3020 | 4360–2340 | 145–77 |
| Works J . | 14 | 2590 | 4000–1480 | 154–57 |
| Works O . | 10 | 3540 | 4220–2720 | 119–77 |
| *Carboniferous clay* | | | | |
| Works K . | 22 | 3080 | 4310–2540 | 140–82 |
| Works L . | 22 | 3210 | 5340–1890 | 166–59 |
| Works M . | 11 | 5680 | 8200–4320 | 144–76 |

*Tested according to B.S. 1257

Since, ultimately, it is the strength of the wall and not the strength of the individual unit with which the user is concerned, the test chosen for the unit should be the one which affords the most reliable index of the strength of the wall. This subject has been investigated at the Building Research Station and other laboratories, and the crushing test now standardized in Great Britain is carried out on a whole brick or block tested as laid in the wall, the frogs of bricks being filled with mortar. The specimens are tested after immersion in water. This is important, since many bricks and other building materials show a marked reduction in strength when wet, so that a strength test result in which the water content of the bricks is not controlled or stated is of doubtful value.

An exception to the usual test method exists at present in B.S. 187, 'Sand-lime (calcium silicate) bricks'. The Standard provides for compressive or transverse strength tests as alternatives, and in the compression test the bricks are tested flat, without frog filling, between sheets of plywood. The compressive strengths (tested wet) required are as follows:

| | | |
|---|---|---|
| Bricks for special purposes | . | 3000 lb/sq. in. |
| Class A building bricks | . . | 2000 lb/sq. in. |
| Class B building bricks | . . | 1000 lb/sq. in. |

The following figures are intended to give merely a general idea of the range of compressive strength values attained by various walling units:

| | | |
|---|---|---|
| Engineering bricks, defined by B.S. 1301 as having a minimum average strength of 7000 lb/sq. in. (Class A minimum 10 000, Class B minimum 7000) | . | 7000–16 000 lb/sq. in. |
| Common bricks | . . . . | 1000–10 000 lb/sq. in. |
| Limestone blocks | . . . . | 1000–10 000 lb/sq. in. |
| Sandstone blocks | . . . . | 7000–15 000 lb/sq. in. |
| Granite blocks . | . . . . | 5000–20 000 lb/sq. in. |
| Hollow clay walling blocks (to B.S. 1190) | | |
| laid with perforations horizontal | . | 500–1500 lb/sq. in. |
| laid with perforations vertical . | . | 500–3000 lb/sq. in. |

In addition to these, concrete blocks can be designed to give any strength up to about 8000 lb/sq. in. Hollow and perforated clay bricks and blocks are capable of higher strengths than is usual with blocks to B.S. 1190, and development of improved types in Britain is beginning.

*Strength of mortar*

Most of the studies of the influence of mortar strength on the strength of masonry have related to brickwork; other tests have shown that with larger units relatively higher wall strengths are developed, i.e. the fewer the mortar joints the stronger the wall. The effect of variations in the strengths of the bricks and of the mortar on strength of brickwork can be illustrated by some results of tests on short square columns loaded axially.

Some typical results for a particular type of brick are given in Table 12.2 for the following conditions:

(i) Brick strength—about 3000 lb/sq. in.
(ii) Cementitious material for mortar—ordinary Portland cement and dry hydrated lime (non-hydraulic).
(iii) Sand for mortar—a pit sand of rounded grains.
(iv) Age at test—three months.

The amount of cement plus lime in the mortar was varied from all cement to all lime, with intermediate combinations of 50:50, 60:40, 70:30, 80:20 and 90:10 per cent lime:cement by volume. The crushing strengths of the columns are expressed in Table 12.2 as a percentage of the strength of the strongest column, built in 1:3 Portland cement mortar.

TABLE 12.2

*Effect of mortar proportions on strength of brickwork*

| Proportion of cement and lime to sand (by volume) | Strength of brickwork, expressed as percentage of strength of brickwork built in 1:3 cement mortar, for the following ratios of lime:cement by volume | | | | | | |
|---|---|---|---|---|---|---|---|
| | All cement | 50:50 | 60:40 | 70:30 | 80:20 | 90:10 | All lime |
| 1:1 . . | — | 72 | 70 | 66 | 58 | 47 | — |
| 1:1½ . . | — | 87 | 84 | 77 | 68 | 56 | — |
| 1:2 . . | 96 | 94 | 90 | 84 | 74 | 60 | — |
| 1:3 . . | 100 | 96 | 92 | 87 | 79 | 65 | 48 |
| 1:4 . . | — | 92 | 87 | 81 | 71 | 59 | — |

These results illustrate a very important feature of brickwork strength, i.e. that there is usually no advantage in using a very strong mortar; for the bricks used in these tests, the optimum strengths were obtained for proportions of (cement + lime): sand of 1:3. With a greater or lesser amount of cementitious material the brickwork is weaker. It will be observed also that there is very little effect on the strength of the column if 50 to 60 per cent

of the cement is replaced by lime. With a 50 per cent replacement, corresponding to a 1 cement: : 1 lime : 6 sand mix instead of 1 cement : 3 sand,
the mortar strength was reduced by over 40 per cent, but the strength of the
brickwork was lowered by only 4 per cent.

The same characteristic was shown in columns built with stronger and
with weaker bricks. With the higher-strength bricks, a stronger mortar can
be used to advantage and for certain engineering structures, using a brick of
10 000 lb/sq. in. strength, a 1 : 3 cement : sand mortar is necessary to
develop the full possible strength of the brickwork. Some lime is almost
always of value, however, even for high-strength construction, because it
improves the working qualities of the mortar. With weaker bricks the maximum strength was developed with weaker mortars.

In general, there is, for any particular strength of brick, a corresponding
mortar strength which gives maximum strength to the brickwork. Hence
for a given ratio of cement + lime to sand (say 1 : 3 as commonly used),
there is no gain in strength if more cement is used than is needed to give this
maximum. The mortars giving this maximum are roughly:

(1) for a low-strength brick (1500 lb/sq. in.)—1 cement: 2 lime: 9 sand,

(2) for a medium-strength brick (3000–5000 lb/sq. in.)—1 cement:
1 lime : 6 sand,

(3) for a high-strength brick (7000 lb/sq. in. or more)—1 cement:
3 sand, to which lime, up to one-quarter of the volume of the cement,
may be added to improve workability.

Cement-lime mortars are valuable for other reasons, e.g. improved resistance of brickwork to cracking, less risk of efflorescence on the bricks.
Cracking of brickwork in practice is rarely due to directly applied loads:
usually it is a result of differential movements between the various parts of
the structure caused by foundation settlement or by thermal or shrinkage
movement. With a strong mortar, cracks develop between the mortar and
the brick and may pass also through the bricks themselves. With a weaker
mortar, however, the mortar can 'give' a little to take up differential movements, and so cracking is often avoided; should movements be so great that
cracking still occurs, it will tend to be distributed throughout the brickwork
in the joints rather than through the bricks (see p. 115).

As a general rule, therefore, it is advisable not to use a mortar stronger
than is just necessary to give the optimum brickwork strength. This rule
may, however, need to be varied for some work in winter, for which a
1 : 2 : 9 or weaker mortar may not always have sufficient frost resistance
during construction.

Most of the tests described above were carried out on columns with all
joints filled solid with mortar, and where single-frog bricks were used the
bricks were laid frog up. The individual brick strengths referred to were
determined according to the method prescribed by B.S. 1257, i.e. with the
frogs filled with mortar. Recently tests have been carried out on similar
columns, in which single-frog bricks were laid frog down and unfilled: the
brick strengths were obtained by testing the brick between plywood, i.e.
with frogs unfilled. The results of these tests confirm that, when brickwork
designed according to B.S. Code of Practice CP.111 is to be laid frog down,
the brick strength to be used in design should be that obtained when bricks

are tested with unfilled frogs (as described in Note 1 on page 6 of B.S. 1257). For brickwork built to the thicknesses set out in the Third Schedule of the Model Byelaws 1952 the position of the frog is usually of no consequence.

*Strength of wall and strength of the unit*

Here again, most of the available information relates to brickwork. Fig. 12.4, based on tests made at the Building Research Station, shows the relationship between brick strength and the strength of brickwork piers.

It will be seen that the strength of brickwork increases with the strength of the individual bricks, but not in direct proportion to the latter: the full value of the stronger units is not developed. It will also be noted that, with a weak mortar, the strength of brickwork generally exceeds the strength of the mortar itself.

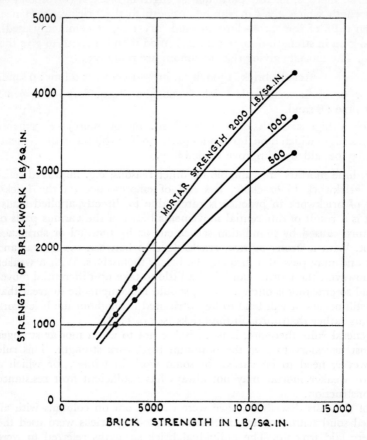

FIG. 12.4

*Relation between strength of brick and strength of brickwork*
*piers, for three different mortars*

It has been found that the difference between good and bad workmanship can make a difference of 25–35 per cent in the strength of brickwork. This should be borne in mind in interpreting test data, as usually masonry test

## TABLE 12.3

*Maximum permissible uniformly distributed compressive stresses (at and after the stated times) on masonry members with slenderness ratio of unity*

| Description or mortar | Mix (parts by volume) not weaker than | | | Hardening time after completion of work (days)† | Maximum uniformly distributed stress in lb/sq. in. corresponding to units whose crushing strength (in lb/sq. in.) is:‡ | | | | | | | | |
|---|---|---|---|---|---|---|---|---|---|---|---|---|---|
| | Cement | Lime | Sand | | 400 | 1000 | 1500 | 3000 | 4000 | 5000 | 7500 | 10 000 | 10 000+x |
| (i) Cement . . . | 1 | 0–¼* | 3 | 7 | 40 | 100 | 150 | 210 | 250 | 360 | 510 | 660 | 600+0·042x but not more than 900 |
| (ii) Cement-lime . . | 1 | 1 | 6 | 14 | 40 | 100 | 140 | 190 | 230 | 260 | 350 | 350 | 350 |
| (iii) Cement-lime . . | 1 | 2 | 9 | 14 | 40 | 80 | 120 | 170 | 210 | 250 | 350 | 350 | 350 |
| (iv) Cement-lime . . | 1 | 3 | 12 | 14 | 30 | 70 | 100 | 130 | 170 | 200 | 200 | 200 | 200 |
| (v) Hydraulic lime . | — | 1 | 2 | 14 | 30 | 70 | 100 | 130 | 170 | 200 | 200 | 200 | 200 |
| (vi) Non-hydraulic . | — | 1 | 3 | 28§ | 30 | 60 | 80 | 100 | 100 | 100 | 100 | 100 | 100 |

*This proportion of lime may be included in what is nominally a cement mortar, to improve workability.

†The period should be increased by the full amount of any time during which the air temperature remains below 40°F, plus half the amount of any time during which the temperature is between 40° and 50°F.

‡Linear interpolation is permissible for units whose crushing strengths are intermediate between those given in the table.

§A longer period should ensue where hardening conditions are not very favourable.

G

specimens will be built with rather more care than would be employed on a building site. The normal factors of safety may be regarded as including an allowance for variations in workmanship. There is as yet no way under British By-laws and Codes of taking advantage, in the design of masonry, of good workmanship and careful supervision.

*Permissible stresses*

In designing a masonry wall or column permissible stresses are laid down according to the materials employed and the slenderness ratio of the structural member. The greatest value allowed is when the slenderness ratio is unity and Table 12.3, taken from the British Standard Code of Practice (CP.111.101), gives these basic stresses, as they may be called, for bricks and blocks of average strengths ranging from 400 lb/sq. in. to over 10 000 lb/sq. in. and for a wide range of mortars.

When the slenderness ratio of the wall or column is greater than unity the basic stresses of Table 12.3 are multiplied by a reduction factor for slenderness as given in Table 12.4.

The permissible stresses derived in this way are based on an overall value of about 0·40 for the ratio of the strength of the wall to that of the building unit for bricks of low or medium strength. For stronger bricks the permissible stresses are based on a ratio which decreases, with increasing brick strength, to about 0·25 for very strong bricks. These ratios fitted in best with experimental data from numerous tests on walls and columns built with bricks or blocks of similar proportions, i.e. with a ratio of block height to thickness of about two-thirds. Other and more recent test data, such as those given in Table 12.5, have indicated that this ratio may be unduly low for building units whose ratio of height to thickness is greater than that of the standard brick. Code of Practice CP.111.101 allows for this effect by recommending that the basic stresses of Table 12.3 be doubled for blocks with a height not less than twice the thickness. As regards blocks with a height-to-thickness ratio between $\frac{2}{3}$ and 2 the Code is not explicit, but it seems reasonable to assume that for these intermediately shaped units the permissible stress should be obtained by interpolation. It may be noted that this increase in permissible stress is not justified for the single high-strength perforated clay block included in Table 12.5.

TABLE 12.4

*Reduction factors for slenderness ratio*

| Slenderness ratio | Factor | Slenderness ratio | Factor |
|---|---|---|---|
| 1 | 1·00 | 12 | 0·50 |
| 2 | 0·96 | 14 | 0·40 |
| 4 | 0·88 | 16 | 0·35 |
| 6 | 0·80 | 18 | 0·30 |
| 8 | 0·70 | 21 | 0·25 |
| 10 | 0·60 | 24 | 0·20 |

## TABLE 12.5

*Strength of storey-height walls (axial loading) built with various types of block*

| Particulars of block | | Height/ thickness ratio of block | Mortar mix (cement: lime: sand) | Strength (lb/sq. in.) | | Ratio: Strength of wall / Strength of block |
|---|---|---|---|---|---|---|
| Type | Dimensions l″ × h″ × t″ | | | Block* | Wall | |
| Foamed-slag concrete blocks | 10 × 8 × 8 | 1·0 | 1 : 2 : 9 | 370 | 310 | 0·83 |
| | 8 × 8 × 8 | 1·0 | 1 : 2 : 9 | 370 | 340 | 0·93 |
| | 18 × 9 × 9 | 1·0 | 1 : 4 : 9 | 560 | 370 | 0·66 |
| Lightweight concrete blocks | 18 × 9 × 9 | 1·0 | 1 : 4 : 9 | 410 | 440 | 1·08 |
| | 18 × 9 × 9 | 1·0 | 1 : 4 : 9 | 270 | 240 | 0·89 |
| Hollow clay blocks | 9 × 9 × 9 | 1·0 | 1 : 1 : 6 | 560 | 380 | 0·68 |
| | 8 × 6 × 6 | 1·0 | 1 : 1 : 6 | 1430 | 650 | 0·46 |
| | 9 × 8½ × 8½ | 1·0 | 1 : 0 : 3 | 920 | 520 | 0·57 |
| | 9 × 9 × 9 | 1·0 | 1 : 0 : 3 | 640 | 520 | 0·81 |
| | 12 × 9 × 6 | 1·5 | 1 : 0 : 3 | 430 | 370 | 0·86 |
| | 9 × 6 × 4 | 1·5 | 1 : 0 : 3 | 1430 | 1200 | 0·84 |
| | 9 × 9 × 4 | 2·25 | 1 : 0 : 3 | 550 | 450 | 0·81 |
| | 9 × 9 × 4 | 2·25 | 1 : 0 : 3 | 940 | 1040 | 1·10 |
| | 12 × 9 × 4 | 2·25 | 1 : 0 : 3 | 250 | 360 | 1·44 |
| | 12 × 9 × 3 | 3·0 | 1 : 0 : 3 | 360 | 410 | 1·14 |
| | 12 × 9 × 3 | 3·0 | 1 : 0 : 3 | 1320 | 1600 | 1·20 |
| | 12 × 9 × 3 | 3·0 | 1 : 0 : 3 | 810 | 870 | 1·06 |
| | 12 × 9 × 2½ | 3·6 | 1 : 0 : 3 | 350 | 440 | 1·25 |
| Perforated clay block | 9 × 9 × 4¼ | 2·1 | 1 : 4 : 3 | 4280 | 1610 | 0·38 |
| Cored clinker block | 18 × 9 × 9 | 1·0 | 1 : 2 : 9 | 460 | 350 | 0·76 |
| | 18 × 9 × 4½ | 2·0 | 1 : 1 : 6 | 500 | 440 | 0·88 |
| Cellular clinker block | 18 × 9 × 4½ | 2·0 | 1 : 1 : 6 | 590 | 460 | 0·78 |
| | 18 × 9 × 4½ | 2·0 | 1 : 1 : 6 | 720 | 530 | 0·73 |
| | 18 × 9 × 3 | 3·0 | 1 : 1 : 6 | 860 | 540 | 0·63 |

*Crushing strength calculated on gross area of block.

### Lateral strength of masonry walls

All walls, whether designed to support vertical load or not, are liable to be subjected to lateral loading. Exterior walls of buildings must resist wind pressures, exterior basement walls have to resist bending caused by earth pressure, material may be piled against a panel wall in a warehouse, and walls may be called upon to resist earthquake or explosive effects.

With any particular wall, critical conditions may exist for which its bending strength will be the criterion of failure. For example, in domestic buildings with walls built with units of crushing strength of 2000 lb/sq. in. or more the actual vertical loads will seldom reach the permissible working values, and if insufficient support is given to the perimeter of the wall its resistance to lateral loading may well be the governing factor.

It is generally agreed that the lateral strength of walls is closely related to the quality of the bond between the mortar and the building units, since in transverse tests on normal walls initial cracking almost invariably results from a breakdown of the brick-mortar bond, rather than from tensile failure of the mortar or the bricks. If the cement content of the mortar is increased the tensile strength of the mortar is also increased, but the increase in wall strength is not proportional and cement-lime mortars for instance are likely to give a relatively better performance under lateral loading than the stronger cement mortars.

What test data are available have indicated that storey-height walls $4\frac{1}{2}$ in., 9 in. and $13\frac{1}{2}$ in. thick, built in cement-lime mortar, when supported at top and bottom and subjected to lateral loading only, may fail under lateral pressures of about 10, 50 and 100 lb/sq. ft respectively.

The behaviour of a masonry wall simply supported on all four sides is, however, markedly different, and transverse loading tests carried out at the Building Research Station on walls 10 ft square without openings have shown that such walls can, before collapse, support lateral pressures in excess of 70, 350 and 700 lb/sq. ft for wall thicknesses of $4\frac{1}{2}$ in., 9 in. and $13\frac{1}{2}$ in. respectively.

Mention may be made of some tests carried out at the Building Research Station, in which some slender walls were subjected to both vertical and horizontal loading. The results given in Table 12.6 indicate that hollow clay blocks may bond better with mortar than do bricks and that a mechanical key is of advantage. The wall built with a type of block provided with undercut grooves along the horizontal bed joints was very much stronger than the other walls, and the increase was not entirely attributable to the higher strength of the mortar in this wall. The tests showed that the vertical load increased the resistance of the wall to lateral pressure, particularly for the walls with relatively low modulus of rupture.

TABLE 12.6

*The transverse strength of walls built with various building units*

(Direct end load = 1 ton/sq. ft)

| | Thickness of wall (in.) | Mortar | | Modulus of rupture at cracking (lb/sq. in.) |
|---|---|---|---|---|
| | | Mix (cement: lime: sand) | Tensile strength (lb/sq. in.) | |
| Fletton bricks    .    .    .    . | $4\frac{1}{2}$ | 1:2:9<br>1:1:4<br>1:0:3 | 60<br>205<br>240 | 35<br>38<br>43 |
| Engineering bricks   .    .    .    . | $4\frac{1}{2}$ | 1:2:9<br>1:1:4<br>1:0:3 | 65<br>170<br>270 | 37<br>56<br>76 |
| Hollow clay blocks  .    .    .    . | 3 | 1:2:9<br>1:1:4<br>1:0:3 | 50<br>225<br>230 | 67<br>100<br>100 |
| Hollow clay blocks with undercut grooves on bed faces | 4 | 1:0:3 | 310 | 148 |

If a wall is built into a stiff framework, considerable lateral pressure may be sustained, even after cracking of the wall, by its acting as a flat dome. Tests at the Building Research Station have shown that walls of this type could sustain even higher pressures than those mentioned for walls simply supported on all four sides.

The foregoing data for the transverse strength of walls have been considered in terms of walls of normal shape but without openings. It is obvious, however, that cracking in a wall as a result of lateral loading will be largely controlled by the extent and location of openings in it and that the transverse strength will be reduced by them.

*Strength of rubble masonry*

Very little work is now done in rubble masonry, and its strength properties do not appear to have been investigated systematically. Probably the simplest way of regarding it would be as a concrete with a very large aggregate, in which case the strength of the mortar will be very important. The flint wall cannot be regarded as a simple masonry structure. In one case the walls of a large building were erected of flints set in a moderately hydraulic mortar, and after a period of twenty to thirty years the walls cracked and begun to bulge so badly that the building had to be demolished. The mortar had failed to develop any appreciable strength owing to the use of a very fine sand and, possibly, to unsuitable handling of the lime in the first instance.

The British Standard Code of Practice (CP.111.101) calls for a reduction of 25 per cent in the permissible stress for walls in rubble masonry, and this appears to be a sufficient guide; it is doubtful whether there is any practical need for a 'design' basis.

*Strength of composite walls*

By a composite wall is meant a form of construction in which two or more different types of wall unit are used together. The importance of this form of walling as a loadbearing structure is not now so great, as the present tendency is to use a thin skin of the ornamental material, backed up with brickwork. This can be observed even in localities where stone is the traditional walling material. The facing becomes more of a veneer, and, consequently, less useful as a loadbearing component of the wall.

Nevertheless, even if such a facing is neglected in designing for strength, the possibility of differential movement may need to be taken into account. If the loadbearing material deforms under load, or shrinks on drying, more than the facing, a proportion of the load may be transferred to the facing, which may then be spalled off or otherwise damaged.

A certain amount of experimental work has been done in the United States of America on composite walls made up of hollow concrete blocks faced with strong facing bricks and on walls of medium-strength bricks incorporating piers of hollow clay blocks. These experiments are more applicable to conditions there than to any form of construction commonly used in Great Britain, since here it is not often that hollow-block walling faced with brick is used. Some of the conclusions, however, are of general interest, and the following in particular may be mentioned: (1) A facing of medium-strength brick to walls with piers in hollow clay block produced no noticeable effect on the ultimate strength, the modulus of elasticity or the lateral deflection of the piers; in fact the combined wall-pier unit behaved just as though it were in hollow-block construction. (2) Composite walls of strong facing bricks and hollow concrete blocks developed high strengths and showed satisfactory interaction of the two materials, though, as might be expected, there were large differences in deformations of the two faces of the wall in some cases.

The general conclusion reached from these results was that composite forms of wall construction might be relied upon to act in a satisfactory manner as loadbearing members when the quality of workmanship and mortar was approximately the same for the facing and backing, and that for a strong facing material with a weaker backing a wall designed on the basis of the strength of the weaker material should be safe.

The case of a weak facing over a strong backing is one which often arises—e.g. a hand-made, sand-faced brick facing to a massive wall in a brick of medium or high strength. The safest treatment in such cases would be to design on the basis of the strength of the weaker brick for thinner walls, and for thick walls to regard the facing brick as non-loadbearing.

*Strength of cavity walls*

The cavity wall may be regarded as a special type of composite wall, even if both leaves are of the same material, in that it is difficult to be sure how an applied load will be shared between the leaves; moreover, there may be differential movement between the leaves.

The lateral stiffness of a cavity wall is much less than that of a solid wall which has a thickness equal to the sum of the thicknesses of the two leaves, and for this reason the effective thickness (for the purpose of calculating the slenderness ratio) should be taken at only two-thirds of this sum. This holds, however, even if the load is carried by one leaf only, as the other leaf may then be regarded as a stiffener. If the ties are fully effective, the sideways movements of the leaves will be identical, and bending is shared by the two leaves; it is desirable, therefore, to have an adequate number of sufficiently strong ties to obtain this condition. Tests made at the Building Research Station have shown that ties conforming to B.S. 1243 (1945) are satisfactory in this respect.

Where external brick cavity-walls are used for large expanses of brickwork, as in multi-storey blocks of flats, important differential movements may occur between the two leaves as a result of temperature changes. A light metal tie allows such movements to take place, but in doing so, the tie loses some of its effectiveness for its normal function. Its resistance to compression is reduced and heavy wind pressure on the outer leaf may not be properly shared by the inner leaf: continued relative movements between the leaves may also lead to a breakdown of the bond of the tie in the mortar joint, particularly when a mortar of high lime content is used. Because of these effects it is desirable to limit the thermal movements by dividing the wall into separate panels of length not greater than 40–50 ft and carried up not more than three storeys (Fig. 12.5). For such conditions, it is desirable to use strip ties rather than the lighter wire ties.

Metal hangers have been used to carry the floor joists on one leaf of a cavity wall; this arrangements leads to considerable eccentricity of load on the wall and should be avoided whenever possible.

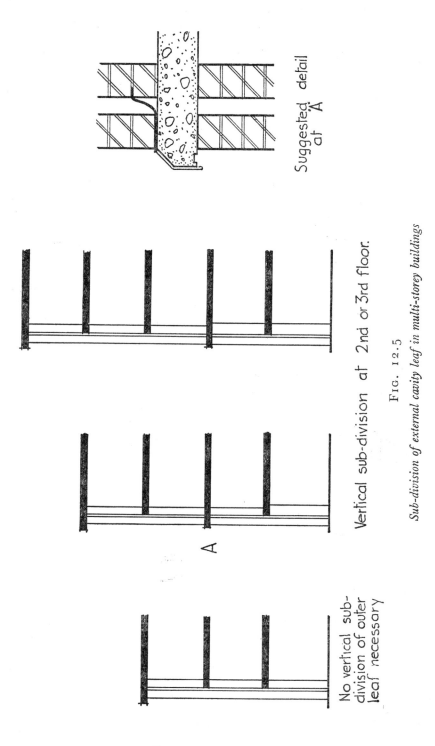

Suggested detail at 'A'

Vertical sub-division at 2nd or 3rd floor.

A

No vertical sub-division of outer leaf necessary

FIG. 12.5

*Sub-division of external cavity leaf in multi-storey buildings*

It has been usual in 11-in. brick cavity-wall construction to put the wall plate, for receiving roof rafters, on the inner leaf of the wall. It is preferable, however, to allow some of the roof load to be carried by the outer leaf, which is thereby made more stable (as in (*b*), Fig. 12.6).

Where lightweight or medium-weight concrete blocks of a strength of at least 400 lb per sq. in. are used for the loadbearing inner leaf of the cavity walls of a two-storey house, this leaf is not likely to require a thickness of more than 4 in. in the lower storey, with ties at the usual spacing of 3 ft apart horizontally and 18 in. vertically. For the inner leaf of the upper-storey walls, if part of the roof load is taken by the outer leaf, a thickness of 3 in. is usually sufficient with double the number of ties, i.e. four per square yard. These thicknesses would apply to the inner leaves of the walls of the two top storeys of a three-storey building, but from ground floor to first floor the thickness of the inner leaf is not likely to be adequate if it is less than 6 in.

The use of cavity-wall construction with lightweight concrete blocks for the inner leaf may also be adopted for blocks of flats, either for a part or the whole of the height, subject to proper consideration, based on the Code of Practice CP.111, of the loads to be carried. In the lower storeys of non-framed construction, brick walling may be necessary, but in some cases the use of a thicker block for the inner leaf may provide sufficient strength. In frame construction the use of lightweight blocks in place of bricks offers the advantage of a reduction in the loading on the framework, and may, therefore, effect some economy.

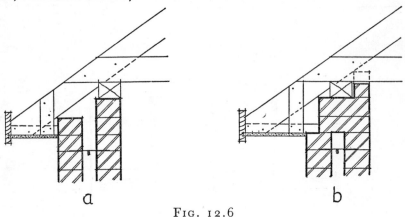

FIG. 12.6

*Methods of carrying roof load on cavity wall*

*Reinforced walls*

The use of horizontal and vertical reinforcement in loadbearing masonry walls has, over the past thirty years, increased considerably in countries such as India and Japan, which are subject to earthquakes. Experience and tests have shown that the addition of such steel provides valuable tensile properties which will help the wall material to hold together in the event of any abnormal lateral loading. Even small amounts of steel reinforcement will hold a brick wall together and enable it to deform sideways, without collapse, to an extent far beyond any deformation a similar but unreinforced brick wall could attain.

In this country masonry walls are rarely reinforced in both directions and it is more usual for the steel to be employed in the horizontal direction only. Used in this way it can help to reduce the effects of uneven settlement, such as is sometimes experienced in mining areas; also it can minimize the risk of serious cracking near the edges and corners of openings in walls.

Some interesting tests have been carried out at the Building Research Station on brick cavity walls as panel fillings, in which the outer leaf was bedded against the stanchions of a steel framework and the inner leaf was built into the frame. In some of the walls, reinforcement, consisting of the usual two-wire type often employed in 4½-in. brick walls, was placed in alternate horizontal courses of each leaf of the brickwork. The walls were all subjected to lateral loading simulating uniform wind pressure and the results indicated that the use of light reinforcement in this way led to an increase of some 30 per cent in the maximum load carried as compared with unreinforced walls.


## MONOLITHIC CONCRETE

There has been a marked increase in the use of monolithic concrete walls in building since 1945, particularly in housing. They are now used in a wide variety of dwellings, ranging from small detached houses to large blocks of flats. Improvements in design and methods of construction have made it possible to use the walls more economically, particularly for high flats and maisonettes, while concretes of lighter weight now compete with other wall materials for non-loadbearing walls and walls that are not required to withstand high intensities of loading.

The choice of monolithic concrete walls in preference to other types of loadbearing wall or a framework of columns and beams is mainly governed by the required function and architectural treatment of the building. The type of accommodation to be provided and the type of floor plan required are of first importance. They are usually the over-riding considerations, because monolithic concrete walls are most economic when used for both enclosure (or division) and support. If the building is to consist of a single accommodation unit, or a number of separate units, with small spacings between permanent dividing walls, loadbearing monolithic concrete walls are likely to be economic. On the contrary, if the spacings must be great to provide large open floor areas, or if provision must be made for this in the event of a change of occupancy, the walls will be uneconomic unless they can be combined cheaply with columns and beams. They are therefore used mainly in housing, where permanent dividing walls can usually be arranged at spacings not greater than about 15 ft, rather than in offices and factories requiring greater spacings. There is still much scope for using them with columns and beams, however, and they can be used economically in multi-storey framed buildings to resist wind forces.

The walls are used in housing as external and internal loadbearing walls, but not always both externally and internally. The type of floor plan and requirements as to external appearance and finish generally decide this matter. When used in detached, semi-detached and terraced houses the walls usually serve as external walls, party walls and major divisions between rooms. They may also be used in this fashion instead of loadbearing brickwork in flats and maisonettes up to about six storeys in height, and in higher blocks up to ten storeys, which might otherwise be of framed construction. In high blocks they are often used externally only at the ends of the block, however, and not as external walls lying parallel to the main axis. In these blocks they are used also as party walls, in staircase and lift units, and as spine walls providing lateral stability under wind forces.

Other arrangements of the walls are possible, of course, but in high-flat construction the above alternative arrangements are being used most frequently. No-fines concrete walls have so far been used in high blocks built with the first arrangement, while the second arrangement is often favoured for dense concrete walls and has acquired the name 'cross-wall construction' by reason of the crosswise arrangement of loadbearing walls at right-angles to the main axis of the block.

No-fines concrete walls should be used only when eccentricities of load can be kept down to a minimum, because no-fines concrete is particularly weak in tension and reinforcement is not usually provided in walls of this material. Special attention should be paid, for the same reason, to the design of the foundations of no-fines concrete buildings to prevent cracking of the walls by differential settlement. It is therefore usual in designing high buildings of this material to use a box-foundation of reinforced dense concrete to provide a very stiff support for the no-fines wall system.

There are differences of opinion as to the advantages and disadvantages of monolithic concrete walls in flats and maisonettes. Some designers consider that the walls impose too much restriction on planning, while other acknowledge some restriction, but contend that the advantages outweigh this disadvantage. The planning restriction arises, first, because the walls should be as far as possible free from openings if they are to be used economically as loadbearing components, and secondly, because they should be spaced at intervals of not more than about 18 ft for an economic combination of walls and floors. It is not possible to be precise in regard to economic wall spacings, because factors apart from the relative cost of walls and floors are involved. The most economic spacing depends not only on the type of floor used in combination with the walls, but also on the materials used elsewhere in the construction, and especially for the external walls.

Low cost is the most important advantage claimed for the walls in the construction of flats and maisonettes. This advantage is claimed for dense concrete cross-walls in high blocks in particular, and for no-fines concrete construction mainly up to about five storeys. The designers of a recent ten-storey project claim savings by using no-fines concrete walls instead of a frame, but their project is the only one so far completed in the United Kingdom where no-fines concrete loadbearing walls have been used above five storeys. The walls have been used in other European countries in blocks of greater heights with similar claims of economy, however.

Other advantages claimed for cross-wall construction are that it provides greater freedom of choice in regard to the external walling and finish, because the external walls (excepting the end walls) are non-loadbearing, and that beams and columns do not protrude into the rooms of the building. In addition, the system provides repetition through the height of the building and is thus suited to prefabrication of the remainder.

When no-fines concrete is used internally and externally it combines good thermal insulation with loadbearing capacity. Moreover, since the concrete is lighter than dense concrete and exerts much smaller pressures on formwork, the wall forms can be of relatively light construction and savings in their cost are therefore possible. This point is of particular importance in monolithic concrete wall construction, because the cost of formwork is a major proportion of the total cost of the walls.

*Structural design*

B.S. Codes of Practice CP.111: 1948 (for plain concrete) and CP.114: 1957 (for reinforced concrete) contain recommendations for structural design. When these are followed the relevant functional requirements of the Model Byelaws of the Ministry of Housing and Local Government are deemed to be satisfied.

Allowances are made in design for uncertainties that arise in regard to the quality and variability of the concrete, the standard of workmanship and the wall loadings. High variability of the concrete, and curvature and lack of good alignment are particularly important to avoid in thin walls, because they cause accidental eccentricities of load. These eccentricities, and differences between the loads and restraints assumed by the designer and those that may actually occur, are taken into account in design.

Plain concrete walls may be unreinforced or may contain reinforcement to reduce cracking due to shrinkage and thermal movements. The term 'plain' is not, therefore, used simply to mean 'without reinforcement': it is used for walls that do not contain steel for the purpose of resisting forces induced by loading.

No-fines concrete is not specifically mentioned in CP.111, but the recommendations of the code apply in general to walls of this material. However, research has shown that varying the density of no-fines concrete by compaction has a marked effect on the strength. Since the method of compaction recommended in CP.111 for test cubes aims at full compaction in the cube moulds, this method does not apply to no-fines concrete. The concrete should be placed in the moulds to simulate the packing of the aggregate particles in the structure. This is difficult, and so the difference between the concretes in the structure and in test cubes cast with it is particularly uncertain in no-fines concrete construction.

The design recommendations for reinforced walls contained in the 1957 edition of CP.114 take into account experience and research since 1948, when the earlier edition of the code appeared. They provide for more economic design than the recommendations of the 1948 code. They allow greater flexibility in design than CP.111 (for plain walls) and are generally less conservative because they are based on the assumption that the design is entrusted to chartered structural or civil engineers qualified in reinforced concrete and the construction is directed by a qualified supervisor.

*Shrinkage reinforcement*

Shrinkage reinforcement is often desirable in plain concrete walls, depending on the type of concrete and the end restraints on the wall. CP.111 recommends that it should consist of at least 0.2 per cent vertical reinforcement and 0·2 per cent horizontal reinforcement parallel to the wall faces.* This recommendation is based largely on experience of cracking in buildings, for although many laboratory investigations of shrinkage and thermal movements of concrete have been made it is not yet generally practicable to calculate shrinkage reinforcement requirements.

The reinforcement is most effective when the bars are closely spaced and of small diameter. The bars should be arranged equally horizontally and vertically in two layers equidistant from the wall faces, unless the wall is thin and only one layer is practicable. CP.111 recommends a *minimum* cover of ½ in., noting that a greater cover than this may be necessitated by conditions of exposure or risks of corrosion (see p.107). Since shrinkage effects are greatest around openings, extra bars should be specially provided to reduce cracking at these points.

Shrinkage reinforcement is not usually necessary in no-fines concrete. Reinforcement may also be omitted from dense concrete when the concrete is lean and of low shrinkage, provided that end restraints on the walls are small. The end restraints that are likely to occur in some cross-wall construction are small, and shrinkage reinforcement may sometimes be omitted in this type of construction. Generally, however, plain concrete walls should be reinforced against shrinkage unless there is good reason to believe that the effects of shrinkage and thermal movement will be small during construction and in service.

*Axial loads*

In designing plain and reinforced walls to resist axial loads, basic permissible compressive stresses are used with stress reduction factors that depend on the slenderness ratios of the walls. The basic stresses and reduction factors specified in CP.111 and CP.114, for plain and reinforced walls respectively, are not the same and are generally more conservative for plain walls. This is so because greater supervision and control are generally required for reinforced walls, while the inclusion of steel to give added resistance to loading provides a greater margin of safety against accidental eccentricities of load. CP.111 does provide for two standards of construction and workmanship, however, and two grades of concrete with different basic stresses are included accordingly. For both the higher grade of concrete, known as the structural grade, and the lower grade, the same stress reduction factors apply. These factors diminish from unity to just less than one-half as the slenderness ratio increases from unity to 18, i.e. to the allowable maximum slenderness ratio, unless specified quantities of reinforcement are included for shrinkage and at supports and around openings. When these quantities of steel are provided, the allowable maximum slenderness ratio is 24 and the reduction factor is just less than one-third.

*Reinforced walls*

Reinforced walls should be designed generally as reinforced concrete columns, with layers of wall reinforcement well tied together to prevent

---

*This refers to the percentage by volume of the reinforcement or, what is the same thing, the percentage area of reinforcement in a cross-section of the wall. In a 4-in. wall, for example, 0·2 per cent reinforcement amounts to one layer of ¼-in. bars 6 in. apart; in a 6-in. wall, to two layers of ³⁄₁₆-in. bars 4 in. apart. In practice, in walls of about 6-in. thickness two layers of ³⁄₁₆-in. bars at 12-in. centres are often used.

buckling of the vertical bars. Such ties between layers can be a disadvantage in placing and compacting the concrete, however, and lateral ties may be omitted from walls that are not heavily loaded and do not require assistance from the vertical reinforcement to withstand compression. A smaller quantity of horizontal steel parallel to the wall faces can also be used in these circumstances, unless shrinkage steel requirements prevent this, and in thin walls a single layer of steel may be used.

Basic concrete stresses used for reinforced walls of nominal and designed mixes are included in CP.114. Concretes of strengths that differ by ± 25 per cent from the minima normally required may also be used, and for these concretes the basic stresses are ± 25 per cent different from the normal basic stresses. This flexibility in design is particularly applicable to walls that are only lightly loaded, and when the concrete materials and strength are not closely controlled.

The permissible concrete stresses and corresponding design loads for axially-loaded reinforced walls may be increased when the ratio between the storey height and the length of the wall is less than 1·5. A stress increase of 20 per cent is permissible when the ratio is 0·5 or less, and for ratios between 1·5 and 0·5 the permissible increases should be calculated by linear interpolation between values of zero and 20 per cent.

*Unreinforced walls*

Compression tests on unreinforced dense concrete walls have shown that walls of practical slenderness ratios are at least as strong as short concrete

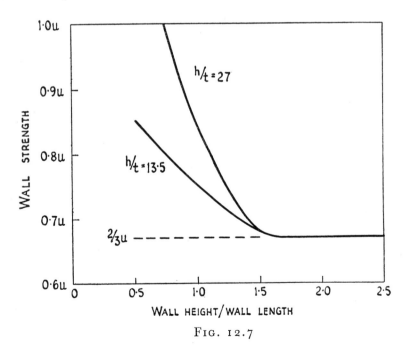

FIG. 12.7

*Effect of height/length and height/thickness ratios on strength of
concrete walls (u = 4-in. cube strength of concrete)*

columns, when loads are applied over the full wall length and are accurately centred. For values of the height/thickness ratio up to about 30, the ultimate mean compressive stresses are not less than two-thirds of the cube strength of the concrete (the short column strength) and the effect of increasing slenderness is small. Typical test data are shown in Table 12.7. Provided that the top and bottom of the wall are restrained against rotation, failure may still occur by crushing of the concrete (rather than buckling) when the height/thickness ratio is as great as 50. Buckling may occur instead, but the ultimate stress with crushing or buckling is still generally as great as for walls of more practical ratios less than 30. There is also an important length effect on strength; the wall strength increases when the wall length is increased and the height/length ratio is reduced below about 1·5. This effect is illustrated in Fig. 12.7 for walls of different height/thickness ($h/t$) ratios. The strength (ultimate mean compressive stress) has been found to be as great as the cube strength of the concrete for height/length ratios of 0·75 or less.

The strengthening effects of shrinkage reinforcement in concrete walls have been examined in tests on walls containing single and double layers of steel. A single layer of 0·8 per cent vertical and 0·4 per cent horizontal reinforcement increases the ultimate load of a wall by not more than the yield load of the vertical reinforcement. This is normally not more than 10 to 15 per cent of the ultimate load, and the strengthening effect of a single layer of reinforcement is therefore generally small under axial loads. Two layers of steel well tied together can provide a marked increase of strength, however. With good workmanship and control, 0·4 per cent vertical and 0·2 per cent horizontal reinforcement in two layers can increase the strength by as much as 50 per cent, although the yield load of the vertical reinforcement may amount to only about 5 per cent of the ultimate load. This phenomenon may be explained by restraint of the concrete by the horizontal reinforcement and is similar in character to the effect on strength of increasing the wall length.

*No-fines concrete*

Most of the available data on the strength of no-fines walls have been obtained from test walls of sizes such as those specified in CP.111; the effects of varying the wall dimensions have not been investigated to the same extent as for dense concrete. Typical test data obtained from axial loading tests at the Building Research Station are included in Table 12.7. The ratio between the wall strength and the cube strength varies in particular with the type of aggregate, and the data of the table were obtained for gravel. The value of 0·50 given by the tests is in agreement with the results of tests on gravel, limestone and crushed-brick no-fines concretes made at the Otto Graf Institute in Stuttgart. Smaller values of the ratio, nearer 0·40, have been observed for other aggregates, however.

*Load factors for axial loads*

The load factors against failure that result when walls are designed for axial loads by CP.111 and CP.114 may be seen from the following examples. The calculations are based on the ultimate loads to be expected when the concrete strength just satisfies the minimum strengths specified in the codes.

## TABLE 12.7

*Strengths of unreinforced monolithic concrete walls*

(Height of walls 9 ft)

| | Wall thickness | Wall length | Mix proportions | Total water/cement ratio | Age at test (days) | Ultimate load (tons) | Wall strength (lb/in.²) | Cube strength (lb/in.²) | Wall/cube strength ratio |
|---|---|---|---|---|---|---|---|---|---|
| Dense concrete (river sand and gravel) | 6 in. | 4 ft 6 in. | 1 : 5·50 (by wt.) | 0·56 | 14 | 350 | 2420 | 3500 | 0·69 |
| | 6 in. | 4 ft 6 in. | 1 : 6·70 (by wt.) | 0·67 | 14 | 311 | 2150 | 3020 | 0·71 |
| | 4 in. | 6 ft 0 in. | 1 : 6·25 (by wt.) | 0·625 | 14 | 308 | 2390 | 3340 | 0·72 |
| | 2 in. | 6 ft 0 in. | 1 : 5·50 (by wt.) | 0·56 | 28 | 204 | 3170 | 4120 | 0·77 |
| No-fines concrete (river gravel) | 10 in. | 4 ft 6 in. | 1 : 8 (by vol.) | 0·40 | 36 | 158 | 655 | 1320 | 0·50 |
| | | | | | 34 | 167 | 690 | 1270 | 0·54 |
| | | | | | 33 | 150 | 620 | 1190 | 0·52 |

Consider, first, a *plain dense concrete* wall of 8-ft storey height, 6 in. thick, 12 ft long and laterally supported at the top and bottom. For a 1:2:4 nominal mix of lower grade concrete CP.111 specifies a minimum works cube strength of 2250 lb/sq. in. at 28 days. Taking the height/length ratio into account, a wall strength of 80 per cent of the cube strength, i.e. 1800 lb/sq. in., might be expected. With lateral support at the top and bottom the effective height would be 6 ft and the slenderness ratio would be 12. A stress reduction factor of 0·67 should therefore be used with a basic maximum permissible stress of 600 lb/sq. in., giving a maximum permissible wall stress of 400 lb/sq. in. With this stress in the wall the load factor against failure would be 1800/400, i.e. 4½. If the wall strength were more conservatively estimated to be two-thirds of the cube strength, the load factor would become 1500/400, i.e. 3¾.

Secondly, if the wall were designed in *structural grade concrete* of the same nominal mix, the corresponding figures would be:

Specified minimum cube strength   .    .    .    3000 lb/sq. in.
Expected wall strength: 0·80 × 3000   .    .    2400 lb/sq. in.
Basic maximum permissible stress   .    .    .    1000 lb/sq. in.
Maximum permissible stress: 0·67 × 1000   .    670 lb/sq. in.
Load factor: 2400/670   .    .    .    3·6

If the wall were of *no-fines gravel concrete* of 1:10 nominal mix, the corresponding figures would be:

Specified minimum cube strength   .    .    .    800 lb/sq. in.
Expected wall strength: 0·50 × 800   .    .    400 lb/sq. in.
Basic maximum permissible stress   .    .    156 lb/sq. in.
Maximum permissible stress: 156 × 0·67 .    .    105 lb/sq. in.
Load factor: 400/105   .    .    .    .    3·8

Finally, if the wall were *reinforced* with 0·4 per cent vertical and 0·2 per cent horizontal reinforcement, consisting of small-diameter mild-steel bars with a yield stress of 40 000 lb/sq. in., the figures for a designed mix of 3000 lb/sq. in. works cube strength would be:

Permissible load:
   760 × 71·7 × 1·17 + 18 000 × 0·29
       lb/ft run                : 31 tons/ft run
Expected ultimate load:
   3000 × 0·80 × 71·7 + 40 000 × 0·29
       lb/ft run                : 82 tons/ft run
Load factor: 82/31                  : 2·6

These examples illustrate that CP.111 provides for load factors between 3 and 5 when the concrete strength just satisfies the specified minimum. The factors tend towards the lower end of this range for walls of structural grade dense concrete, and towards the upper end of this range for lower grade concrete, including no-fines. CP.114 provides for smaller load factors, from 2 to 3, which are appropriate for more stringent supervision and control.

*Eccentric loads*

When plain walls are designed for eccentric loads, or compression with bending, the maximum compressive stresses are permitted to be up to 25 per cent greater than the maximum permissible stresses for the same walls under axial loads. The amounts by which the stresses exceed the maximum permissible stresses for axial loads must be due entirely to eccentricity of the loads, however.

This concession is justified by the results of tests on concrete members failing in compression due to bending alone, or bending with axial compression. The ultimate loads exceed those predicted by the elastic theory when it is assumed that compression failure of the concrete occurs at the ultimate compressive stress of the member in uniform compression without bending. They correspond in general with greater maximum stresses, depending on the slenderness of the member, the actual combination of bending and compression, and the cube strength of the concrete. Tests made at the Building Research Station have shown how the strengths of slender, unreinforced concrete walls are reduced with increasing eccentricity of the load, and how the actual strengths compare with strengths calculated by the elastic theory. Some results of these tests are included in Fig. 12.8. For loads placed at the edge of the middle-third of the wall section (i.e. for an eccentricity of one-sixth of the wall thickness), the wall strengths were about 50 to 70 per cent of the

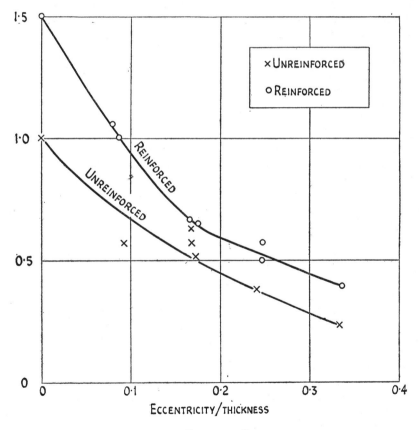

FIG. 12.8

*Relative strengths of plain and reinforced concrete walls under eccentric loading* strengths under axial loads. For this position of the load, and with the assumption that the ultimate maximum compressive stress is the same as the ultimate stress in axial compression, the simple elastic theory (neglecting increasing curvature under load) predicts failure at 50 per cent of the axial strength. If more involved calculations are made by the elastic theory, including the effects of increasing curvature of the wall and eccentricity of the load as the load on the wall is increased, estimated strengths amount to about 40 to 45 per cent of the axial strengths. The differences between actual strengths and strengths predicted by the elastic theory are smaller for slender walls than for stockier members, and the 25 per cent increase generally permissible in design is a reasonable allowance for most practical walls and eccentricities of load.

Similar considerations apply to the design of eccentrically-loaded reinforced walls. These should be designed with a permissible concrete compressive stress not more than $33\frac{1}{3}$ per cent greater than the permissible stress in axial compression. When they are designed on an ultimate strength basis the method takes into account the increase of the permissible stress in the concrete.

The results of Building Research Station tests on walls containing 0·4 per cent vertical and 0·2 per cent horizontal mild steel reinforcement in two layers are also shown in Fig. 12.8, which therefore indicates the contribution of the reinforcement for various eccentricities of the load. The test results show that light reinforcement can make a substantial contribution to wall strength, and they support the principle of designing eccentrically-loaded reinforced walls generally as columns.

### Concentrated loads

In designing plain walls to resist local stresses due to concentrated loads, the mean bearing stress may be 50 per cent greater than the permissible stress for distributed loads. The results of tests have supported this concession in design. When axial loads were applied over different proportions of the lengths of dense concrete walls the ultimate mean bearing stress varied, as shown in Fig. 12.9. For high concentrations of the load the ultimate mean stress beneath the load was much greater than the cube strength of the concrete.

The increase of permissible stress may be adopted in designing no-fines walls also. This procedure is supported by the results of tests made at the Otto Graf Institute. Concentrated axial loads and concentrated eccentric loads were applied in these tests to small wall-pieces, not full-size walls, and the results are therefore to be treated with reserve. The ultimate mean stresses beneath the axial loads were relatively greater than those measured in the tests at the Building Research Station on full-size dense walls.

### Lateral (including wind) forces

Concessions are also made in regard to permissible stresses when plain walls are designed to resist lateral forces, including wind forces, in addition to distributed axial or eccentric loads, and when reinforced walls are designed to resist wind forces.

In plain walls the permissible concrete stresses may be increased by 25 per cent above those recommended for axial compression alone, provided

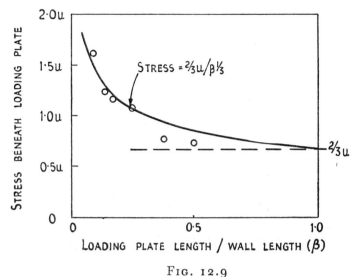

FIG. 12.9

*Strength of walls with concentrated loading*
*(u = 4-in. cube strength)*

that the excess is due solely to lateral forces and any eccentricity of the load. The basis of this allowance when bending occurs with axial compression has been described above in discussing eccentric loads.

In reinforced walls the permissible stresses in the concrete and the reinforcement may be increased by 25 per cent above those specified for vertical loads, bending moments and lateral forces other than wind forces, but the increase must be due solely to wind forces and an upper limit of 30 000 lb/sq. in. is specified for the stress in the tensile reinforcement. In making this concession it is recognized that temporary overstress due to wind forces, which are generally of short duration, is not serious when it is limited to 25 per cent and the steel stress is limited so that wide cracks will not occur in the concrete.

*Door and window openings*

Plain dense concrete walls should have extra reinforcement around door and window openings, in addition to that generally provided for shrinkage elsewhere in the walls. This extra reinforcement is required to give adequate strength and additional resistance to shrinkage and thermal cracking. Minimum quantities of steel recommended for the purpose are quoted in CP.111, and tests at the Building Research Station have shown that these are sufficient to ensure that full advantage can be taken of the strength of wall-columns at the sides of openings. Unreinforced walls with openings are found to fail at loads depending essentially on the distribution of load over the openings. Their strengths were small under uniformly distributed loads, owing to the low bending resistance of the wall-beams at the openings. When the wall-beams were reinforced as recommended in CP.111 collapse did not occur until the full axial compressive strengths of the wall-columns were exceeded.

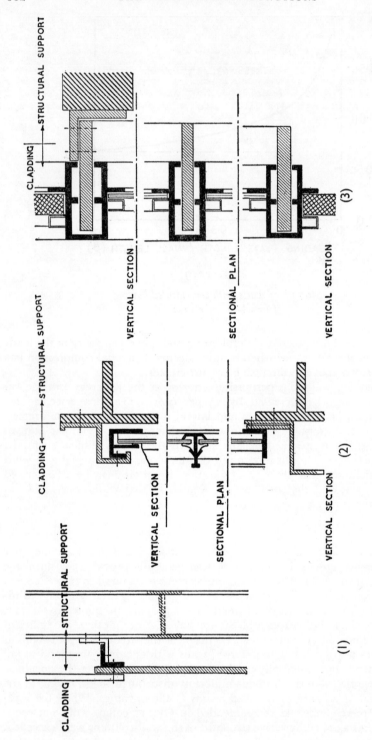

FIG. 12.10
*Curtain walling systems*

## CURTAIN WALLING

In curtain walling systems the walls have no structural role whatever, the object being to sheath the building in a durable weatherproof envelope, providing adequate thermal insulation, yet being as light in weight as possible so as to reduce the dead load on the building frame. The ordinary requirements of strength and stability do not therefore apply, except in so far as the fixings must be strong enough to carry the weights of the cladding systems, and both the fixings and the cladding sheets must be capable of resisting wind loads. With metal panels it may also be necessary either to shape or to back the panels in such a way as to avoid troublesome noises due to cockling movements of the sheets—or 'oil-canning' as the Americans call it.

The principle of curtain walling is old—tile and slate hanging on the outside of load-bearing walls may be regarded as an example of it in a limited sense—but the modern development of the principle is associated particularly with the desire to reduce the weight of the external cladding of multi-storey framed buildings and has, in recent years, been very rapid.

Curtain walling systems ordinarily comprise thin waterproof external sheeting, with lining sheets and air cavities as may be necessary to provide sufficient thermal insulation, the assemblies being carried on or in some kind of light framing which is secured to the structure of the building. Sometimes complete 'sandwich' units are prefabricated, with the waterproof external skin and the insulating backing bonded together. Roofing and glazing techniques are commonly employed for supporting the panels, and the systems may conveniently be divided into three groups (Fig. 12.10):

(1) overlapping sheets fixed externally to a supporting frame which is equivalent to the purlins on a sheeted roof;
(2) patent glazing techniques adapted for use vertically;
(3) rectangular frames with rebates in which the panels are fixed by ordinary glazing methods.

Frequently the external sheeting is actually of glass as this provides a durable and easily cleaned surface completely impervious to water. Colour may then be provided on the back of the glass, or behind it; or the glass may be left clear, and without any insulating backing, in those areas where light transmission is required.

*Chapter 13*

# DIMENSIONAL STABILITY

## THERMAL MOVEMENTS

CAREFUL measurements of coefficients of thermal expansion of most building materials have been made in various laboratories. There would be no point, however, in quoting exact figures. Apart from variations between samples of natural or artificial materials, moisture movements may mask or modify thermal movements, and the range of temperature experienced by a given material in a building will rarely be exactly known. Table 13.1 therefore gives only very rough data; they should be accurate enough, however, for any calculations that can usefully be made by the designer of a building.

TABLE 13.1

*Approximate coefficients of thermal expansion of various building materials*

| | Linear coefficient of thermal expansion within range 0–100°C | |
|---|---|---|
| | Per degree Centigrade | Per degree Fahrenheit |
| | ($\times 10^{-6}$) | ($\times 10^{-6}$) |
| NATURAL STONE | | |
| Marbles . . . . | 1·4–11 | 0·8–6 |
| Limestones . . . . | 2·4– 9 | 1·3–5 |
| Igneous rocks (granites, etc.) . | 8–10 | 4·5–6 |
| Sandstones . . . . | 7–16 | 4–9 |
| Slates . . . . . | 6–10 | 3·5–5·5 |
| BRICKS, BRICKWORK . . . | 5– 7 | 2·8–4 |
| CEMENT MORTARS, CONCRETES (Influenced largely by type of aggregate) | 10–14 | 5·5–8 |
| METALS | | |
| Steel and iron . . . | 11–13 | 6–7 |
| Aluminium . . . . | 25 | 14 |
| Copper . . . . | 17·3 | 9·6 |
| Lead . . . . . | 29 | 16 |
| Bronze . . . . | 17·6 | 9·8 |

*Temperature stresses*

The coefficients of thermal expansion are obtained by measurement on specimens free to move under the effects of variation in temperature. In a building, however, the various parts are more or less rigidly connected.

184

Consequently, thermal or moisture changes tend to set up stresses within the materials under conditions of restraint, and it is the magnitude of these stresses that is usually important rather than the actual free movement under conditions of no restraint.

From a knowledge of the stress/strain ratio and the coefficient of thermal expansion it is possible to calculate the stresses set up by temperature changes under complete or partial restraint, but the results so obtained are strictly applicable only to rapid fluctuation where there is no relief of stress by creep. The stress is directly proportional to the elastic modulus of the material which, as a general rule, is higher for the stronger materials.

The theoretical conditions are easily seen from the four examples given in Table 13.2.

## TABLE 13.2

*Stress due to completely restrained thermal effect in walls (ignoring effect of creep)*

| | Modulus of elasticity (lb/sq. in.) | Coefficient of thermal expansion per °C | Failing stress in compression (tons/sq. ft) | Stress due to 15°C (27°F) rise in temperature (tons/sq. ft) |
|---|---|---|---|---|
| Medium-strength brick in lime mortar . | $0 \cdot 2 \times 10^6$ | $6 \times 10^{-6}$ | 32 | $1\frac{1}{4}$ |
| Medium-strength brick in cement mortar . | $0 \cdot 9 \times 10^6$ | $6 \times 10^{-6}$ | 80 | $5\frac{1}{4}$ |
| Strong brick in cement mortar . . . | $2 \cdot 7 \times 10^6$ | $6 \times 10^{-6}$ | 180 | 15 |
| Granite . . . | $7 \times 10^6$ | $10 \times 10^{-6}$ | 770 | 67 |

From these examples it will be seen that the stresses due to a moderate rise in temperature may be quite high, though less than the working compressive stresses permissible in masonry construction. It is important to note that the temperature stresses rise as brickwork becomes stronger, since the modulus of elasticity increases with strength. For medium-strength brickwork in lime mortar the temperature stress due to a 15°C (27°F) rise in temperature is only about one twenty-fifth of the ultimate compressive strength of the masonry; for a strong brick in cement mortar, however, the stress due to the same rise in temperature may be one-twelfth of the ultimate compressive strength. In practice the change in temperature will usually occur over a period of time sufficient to allow creep of the material to reduce the stresses to one-half or one-third of the values in Table 13.2.

*Curtain walling*

Thermal movements can be particularly troublesome in curtain walling systems in which large panels are fitted into rebates in rectangular frames. The panels and frames are usually of dissimilar materials, and the differential movement complicates the problem of waterproofing, since it may be more than any putty or mastic bedding can continue to accommodate for long periods. The trouble is also accentuated by the fact that lightweight panels and their supporting frames have relatively small heat capacities and are in consequence likely to swing in temperature over a wider range than the more substantial parts of a building. The external panels, in particular, which may be assumed to be separated from the building by a layer of thermal insulation, may closely follow the swing of air temperature. Between night and day in clear summer weather in this country the variation can be up to 40°F, while the total range, between a cold winter night and a hot summer day, may be as great as 90°F.

Panels exposed to sunshine may, unless very light in colour, experience an even greater range of temperature due to the heating effect caused by absorption of the sun's radiation. The temperature of a black panel, insulated at the back, can rise as high as 160°F, even in Britain. The percentages of solar heat absorbed by various surfaces (Table 13.3) give some indication of how materials differ in this respect; it is worth remembering also that, in general, a bright metallic surface will become warmer than a non-metallic surface of the same absorptivity, because it does not so readily *lose* heat by radiation.

TABLE 13.3
*Absorptivities for solar heat*

| Surface | Absorptivity (per cent) |
|---|---|
| Whitewash White paint Polished aluminium | up to 20 |
| Light paints Polished copper | 20–40 |
| Medium paints Aluminium paint Asbestos cement Light red bricks and tiles | 40–60 |
| Dark paints Galvanized steel Tarnished copper Dark red bricks and tiles | 60–80 |
| Black and other very dark paints Asphalt Bituminous felts Slates | 80–100 |

Where prefabricated composite panels are used, with the component layers firmly connected together, temperature gradients across the thickness of the panels and the use of dissimilar materials in juxtaposition may cause deformations which still further complicate the fixing problem. There is much to be said for keeping the exterior waterproof skin separate from the inner insulating layer. Ventilation of the air space may then be useful as a means of keeping down the temperature of the exterior skin in sunny weather, and the presence of the cavity also simplifies the problems of water exclusion and condensation. Even when ventilated, the air space provides a useful increment of thermal insulation.

Special attention must be paid to possible thermal movements where the exterior facings are of glass, for, apart from the problem of sealing against the weather, pinching of the glass by the frame may lead to fracture. Clear glass in those panels through which light transmission is desired presents no greater problem than do ordinary large window panes, and the usual glazing clearances should be adequate. Glass that is coloured, either integrally or by applied colour and with insulating material at the back, presents a different problem, particularly on sunny façades; the radiation energy that is absorbed in or behind the glass (instead of being transmitted to the interior) builds up a higher temperature and larger clearances should be provided to allow for this increased heating effect. A clearance of $\frac{1}{4}$ in. on a dimension of 4 ft seems likely to be adequate in all circumstances, but care may still be necessary to ensure that there are no local points of possible metallic contact with the edge of the glass due to badly placed bead screws or other attachments.

In some circumstances it may be worth using the more expensive coloured toughened glass as an insurance against breakage, though it will then be even more important to avoid damage at the edges.

Clearly, in regard to thermal movements between panels and frames, the advantage lies with those systems of curtain walling defined as falling in groups (1) and (2) (p. 183). These do not depend on putty or mastic fixing and sufficient freedom of movement can be left at the edges of the panels, with overlapping of adjacent sheets where necessary, to accommodate any thermal movements likely to occur.

There is, however, another aspect of the problem of thermal movements that arises with all systems of curtain walling. Although the frame to which the cladding sheets are attached will not, in general, vary in temperature as widely as the sheets, it may vary much more than the main loadbearing structure that carries it. Apart from the effect of differences in heat capacity, the frame will be much more exposed to external influences than will the structure of the building. The latter, too, will probably be kept warm throughout the winter by the internal heating, and may even be stabilized in temperature throughout the year where air conditioning is in operaton. If, therefore, the cladding frame is continuous over a number of storeys, the total movement relative to the structure may be considerable. Of the various materials commonly used for cladding frames, aluminium is likely to give most trouble in this respect because of the magnitude of its thermal movement. Frame members 100 ft long would, for example, if unrestrained, change in length by nearly 1 in. for a 50° change of temperature. Obviously, allowance for such movement must be made in fixing the frame to the structure: this is often done by slotting the holes for the attaching bolts, and ensuring that the bolts are free to slide in the slots. Failing some such provision, the frame must be designed in units small enough for the relative movement not to be troublesome.

## MOISTURE MOVEMENTS

*Causes of changes in moisture content*

Most walling materials have a porous structure and absorb water more or less readily. In winter, during prolonged wet weather, the outer portion of the wall at any rate may be assumed to be in a condition approaching saturation for quite long periods. In the summer, with hot sunshine, drying winds and low humidity, the walls will be very much drier. External walls, therefore, are subject to extreme seasonal variations in moisture content. The only exceptions to this rule are walls covered with continuous impermeable coatings, such as paints or bitumens, walls of highly impermeable materials, such as granite or metal, and curtain walls of impermeable sheet materials. The conditions with internal walls are quite different, the seasonal variations in moisture content being comparatively small.

The first drying stage, when the excess of water introduced during building operations is removed, is particularly important: most of the shrinkage cracking of walls and partitions occurs at this stage. The rate of removal of water by evaporation depends upon a number of factors, of which perhaps the most important in practice is the relative humidity of the air.

*Types of failure*

Failures due to moisture movements take certain typical forms. Most structural elements are free to move to a moderate extent in a vertical direction, but are considerably restrained horizontally. For this reason cracks due to moisture movement tend to take a vertical direction. Walling materials are mostly strong in compression and relatively weak in tension, so that cracking is usually caused by tensile forces set up by shrinkage of materials on drying. There is a marked tendency for cracks to be localized at the weakest points in the section of a wall, usually at door and window openings. Shrinkage cracks commonly run downwards from ground-floor window-sills to the damp-proof course and from upper-storey sills to lintels of storeys below. In internal partitions, often of lightweight materials with relatively large moisture movements, it is not unusual to find vertical cracks dividing up the partitions into areas of about equal sizes. With slab partitions the crack will usually start along a vertical joint, cross the centre of the slab next above, and continue on the next vertical joint, though occasionally the cracking may follow the joints in a 'step' pattern. In partitions with a door opening the cracking will almost invariably run upwards from a corner of the door frame to the ceiling.

*Magnitude of moisture movements*

The first essential for the designer or builder is to acquire a clear picture of the extent of the movement to which various types of material are liable. As a very rough first grouping, that given in Table 13.4 may serve.

The movements of a number of representative walling materials are shown diagrammatically in Fig. 13.1. Most of this information has been obtained by measuring the movement of various materials from the dry to the saturated condition, or vice versa, in the absence of any restraining forces.

In practice, the moisture movement can sometimes be restrained either by the fixing of the materials at the edges or by adhesion to a strong and more stable background. In the absence of experimental data on the effects of restraint, we have only a partial solution of the problem which moisture movements impose. Nevertheless, the knowledge of unrestrained moisture movements identifies those materials that call for special care in use, and there is a good deal of experience to indicate the kind of precautions that must be adopted. General principles were discussed in Part I, Chapter 2, and some further details are given in the following paragraphs.

TABLE 13.4

*Degrees of moisture movement*

| Materials having very small moisture movements. | Well-fired bricks and clay goods*. Igneous rocks. Most limestones. Calcium sulphate plasters. |
|---|---|
| Materials with small moisture movement. | Some concrete and sand-lime bricks. Some sandstones. |
| Materials with considerable moisture movement calling for precautions in design and use. | Well-proportioned ballast concretes. Cement and lime mortars and renderings. Some concrete and sand-lime bricks. Lightweight concrete products. Some sandstones. |
| Slab and sheet materials with large moisture movement calling for special technique of treatment at joints and surrounds. | Wood-cement materials. Fibrous slabs and wallboards. Asbestos-cement sheeting. Plywoods and timber generally. |

*NOTE: Fired clay products may show an initial expansion on wetting that is irreversible and is not revealed by the drying shrinkage test laid down in B.S. 1257: 1945. It has been shown, in Australia, that walls built with 'kiln-fresh' bricks may expand twice as much as similar walls built with bricks that had been exposed to the weather for a fortnight. A slow moisture expansion, greater than that shown by the standard tests may also take place over a period of years. Some striking failures due to this effect have been reported from the United States of America.

*Cement products*

There is such a wide range of materials in which Portland cement is an essential constituent that they demand special consideration; their moisture movements are always important and must usually be taken into account by the designer. These materials necessarily start their existence in a state approaching saturation and will usually become relatively dry in service, except in special works that are always submerged in water or buried in moist ground. This drying results in shrinkage or, where the shrinkage is forcibly restrained, in a condition of stress. The movements due to changes in moisture content of typical cement products are shown in Fig. 13.2.

*First drying shrinkage.* An important fact regarding the first drying process of a cement product is that the shrinkage is about 50 per cent greater than any movement due to wetting and drying at a later stage. Some experimental results are shown diagrammatically in Fig. 13.3. After the first drying the changes in volume due to alternations of wetting and drying are more or less constant. Thus the first large shrinkage is partly irreversible. Subsequent moisture movements proceed indefinitely: cement mortars, renderings and concretes do not attain a stable condition, and if their environments are such that their moisture content changes periodically, as with materials exposed to the weather, their periodical moisture movements must be taken into account.

This first partly irreversible movement calls for an important distinction between materials that are precast and those that must of necessity be made on the job. The precast material can and should be dried out before it is incorporated in the building structure. In this way the large irreversible movement is accomplished without risk of cracking or other injury to the structure.

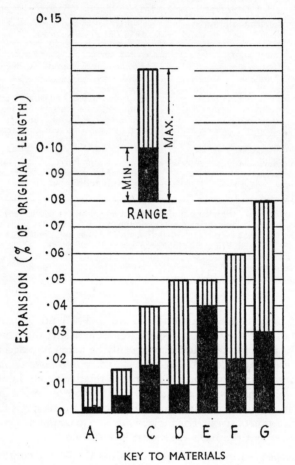

KEY TO MATERIALS

A.  Clay bricks, limestones

B.  Hollow clay blocks, terra cotta

C.  Expanded clay concrete, sintered pulverized-
    fuel ash concrete, plaster partition slabs

D.  Sandstones, sand-lime and concrete bricks

E.  Foamed slab concrete (1:6)

F.  Cast stone, dense concretes, mortars

G.  Autoclaved aerated concrete
    Clinker concrete

FIG. 13.1

*Moisture movements of walling materials*

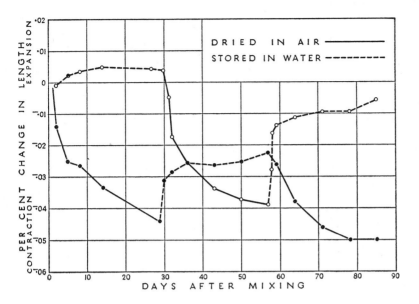

Fig. 13.2

*Length changes of cement mortar specimens due to variations in conditions of storage*

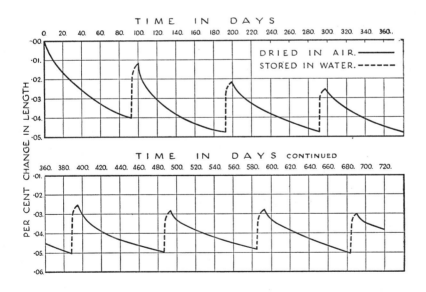

Fig. 13.3

*Changes in length of granite concrete bars over periods of 3-months air drying*

(From Davis & Troxell)

Material cast or applied on the job falls in a somewhat different category. Any restraint to the first, and largest, drying shrinkage must be such that its effects are innocuous. Renderings, screeds and thin coats of mortar are restrained by adhesion to a non-shrinking background. The adhesion must be consistent and good so that any cracking is well distributed. The background must also be strong enough to provide the necessary restraint; the shrinkage of a strong cement rendering has been known to exert sufficient force to tear off the surface layer of rather poor brickwork.

Shrinkage of more massive structural elements in concrete is usually controlled by the use of steel reinforcement. The distribution and design of this reinforcement demands very careful consideration; it does not by any means follow that an arrangement of reinforcement that satisfies the requirements as to strength and stability will be equally effective in dealing with shrinkage (see p. 173).

*Control of quality.* While the designer must take account of the shrinkage of concrete when contemplating its employment, it is also incumbent on the producer of precast units and the designer of concrete mixes to make concrete with a drying shrinkage no greater than it need be. A considerable amount of control in production is possible and should be exercised.

Drying shrinkage is influenced by the following factors:

(1) The proportion of cement in the mix. Drying shrinkage is primarily a property of the cement paste, so that large drying shrinkages are

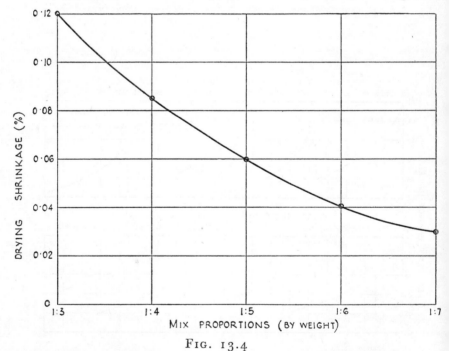

FIG. 13.4

*Variation of drying shrinkage with cement content of concrete or mortar: drying shrinkage of specimens (water/cement ratio 0·5) after 6 months in air at 70°F and 50 per cent relative humidity*

associated with rich mixes. Frequently concrete is made much richer and stronger than is really necessary, with a consequent sacrifice of dimensional stability (Fig. 13.4).

(2) The water content of the mix. Wet mixes usually have a greater initial drying shrinkage than dry mixes; undue wetness of mix generally arises from unwillingness to meet the relative inconvenience of handling the drier mixes.

(3) The nature of the aggregate. The grading and shape of the aggregate may have an indirect effect on factors (1) and (2) above. However, a more important consideration is that dense rigid aggregates such as crushed rock restrain the shrinkage movement of the cement; more yielding types of aggregate, such as are used in lightweight concrete, do not offer so much restraint and so produce concretes with greater drying shrinkage. Lastly, some aggregates themselves have considerable drying shrinkage and this may enhance the shrinkage of the cement. The shrinkage properties of concretes made with lightweight aggregates have been discussed in Part I (pp. 109–13).

The strength of a cement product depends very much upon the proportion of cement, and within practical limits the richer mix will be the stronger. The greater strength, however, is accompanied by a greater drying shrinkage (Fig. 13.4). For many of the purposes for which materials are used in building, undue importance has been attached to high strength, and this tendency persists. For many building components the reduction of moisture movement is far more important than the production of strength beyond that which is needed, and it would be very much better to think less of strength and to concentrate on reduction of moisture movement. For lightweight concretes and partition materials the aim might well be to use as lean a mix as possible, and one important subject for study is to ascertain how weak such materials can be made whilst still being adequate for their function.

*Brickwork and concrete masonry*

The liability of masonry walls to crack depends not only on the moisture movements of the bricks or blocks and of the mortar but on the relative strengths of the two components. Where cracking cannot be completely avoided it is desirable that it should be well distributed so that individual cracks are small in width. Cracks in the joints are not so noticeable as those through the masonry units. It is therefore best to use as weak a mortar as possible consistent with the development of sufficient strength (p. 112).

When using units whose shrinkage is to be reckoned with, such as sand-lime or concrete bricks or blocks, the following precautions can be taken by the user to keep down the shrinkage and to distribute shrinkage stresses in such a way that the risk of major cracking is reduced, or that cracking is confined to mortar joints.

*Storage.* Bricks and blocks should be protected from rain on the site. If stacks cannot be sheeted over, they should at least be sufficiently open to allow air circulation, thereby assisting drying after rain. The more absorbent types of blocks sometimes have to be wetted just before laying, to reduce suction. This should be done sparingly and only when really necessary; the body of the block should never be saturated with water.

*Mortar.* Mortar should be of a relatively weak type. A mix of one part of Portland cement with two parts of hydrated lime and eight to nine parts of sand, all by volume, is generally suitable. A rather stronger mix (1:1:5–6) may be necessary in work carried out in winter or for special conditions. Alternatively, one part of Portland cement and eight parts of sand by volume, with a plasticizer, may be used in place of the 1:2:8–9 mix or one part of Portland cement and five to six parts of sand by volume, with a plasticizer, in place of the 1:1:5–6 mix. Mixes with a lower proportion of cement (e.g. 1:3:10–12) are suitable for internal work carried out in summer. There is in practice a wide latitude in mortar composition that can be used without materially affecting the strength of the wall (pp. 116–7, 160–2). Where a mortar stronger than 1:1:5 must be used for some reason, blocks of very low drying shrinkage should be used if cracking is to be avoided.

*Reinforcement.* Reinforcement has been used in the bed-joints of courses close to windows and door openings, as a means of controlling shrinkage cracking. This does not prevent the formation of cracks, but may stop them from becoming wide and unsightly. Little is yet known about the optimum amount of reinforcement necessary to meet the wide range of shrinkages that can occur in concrete blockwork. Moreover, the durability of reinforcement is likely to be poor in so exposed a position as a mortar joint, especially where cracking occurs.

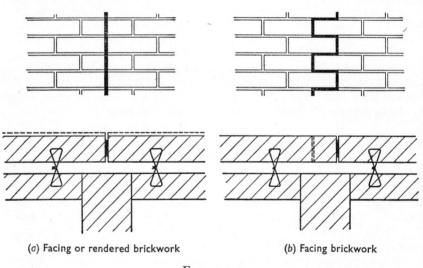

(*a*) Facing or rendered brickwork  (*b*) Facing brickwork

FIG. 13.5

*Arrangements of vertical joints in walls of domestic buildings to allow for shrinkage movement*

*Design.* Dividing the wall into panels with freedom from restraint at the ends will reduce the risk of cracking. Continuous vertical movement joints may be formed at suitable intervals over the length of the wall, as shown in Fig. 13.5. These joints may be situated behind rain-water pipes, or as dividing features between the houses in a terrace. They need to be sealed, to exclude wind and rain. In facing work, a movement joint may be caulked with a mastic compound: this is one of the most satisfactory methods. In rendered work, a strip of damp-proof course felt may be set vertically in the gap as the wall is being built, and the rendering brought up to the projecting felt on both sides of the joint. As an alternative giving absolute exclusion of wind and rain a V-section copper strip may be fixed to the wall so as to bridge the gap, the limbs of the folded strip being subsequently embedded in the rendering. This method gives a neat and pleasing appearance but is somewhat expensive to provide and the strip is rather difficult to fix in position. Another method is to make a vertical break at the midpoint of windows between sills and lintels, leaving dry joints to be mortared up later when the structure has ceased to shrink (Fig. 13.6).

FIG. 13.6

*Dry joints left to accommodate shrinkage movement*

Generally, shrinkage cracking is important only because of its effect on appearance. It does not materially affect structural stability nor, in cavity-wall construction, does it affect the exclusion of rain. The cracks usually develop during the first summer after building. Where an external rendering is to be applied over blocks with a high drying shrinkage, there will be less risk of the rendering being cracked by movements of the background if the rendering is applied when the wall has dried out.

If it is necessary to make good any cracks, the work should be done during the summer months when the masonry has dried thoroughly. The cracked joints should be cut out and any broken blocks replaced, using the same mortar mix as was used for the original work.

*Slab and sheet materials*

A different approach to the problem of moisture movement is possible with slabs and sheets, which are more or less positively fixed by nailing, bolting or clamping along two opposite sides at least, as distinct from masonry units, which are usually bedded on mortar and are stabilized partially by their own

## TABLE 13.5

*Precautions to avoid shrinkage cracking with various materials
due to change in moisture content*

| Material | Magnitude of moisture movement | Precautions in use |
|---|---|---|
| Well-fired clay bricks, blocks and terracotta. | Very small. | Preferably do not lay fresh from kiln. Should be either wetted or exposed to the air for a week or two before use. |
| Concrete bricks. | Appreciable. | Discrimination in choice of bricks; insistence on maturing so that the first irreversible drying shrinkage occurs before erection; protect work in progress in wet weather; do not use a very strong mortar. |
| Sand-lime bricks. | Appreciable; may vary with different types of brick. | Discrimination in choice of bricks; protect work in progress in wet weather; do not use a very strong mortar. |
| Limestones. | Generally very small. | None called for. |
| Sandstones. | Appreciable; may vary with different types of stone. | Discrimination in choice of stone; do not use a very strong mortar; protect work in progress in very wet weather. |
| Cast stone and dense cast concrete products. | Appreciable. | Provide details of cast stone in ample time to allow manufacturers to mature the units; insist on maturing of cast concrete blocks; do not use very strong mortar; protect work in progress in very wet weather. |
| Rubble masonry and flint work. | The volume of mortar in the wall becomes great and shrinkage of the mortar is important. | Do not use very strong mortar; protect work in progress in very wet weather. |
| Lightweight concrete blocks. | Moderate, varying with composition and mix. | Ensure that material complies with B.S. 2028 (Type B for external walls, Type C for internal, non-loadbearing walls); do not use a very strong mortar; allow to dry before plastering. |
| Wood-wool slabs. | Considerable, but readily restrained. | Preferably not used in external panels except for short-lived structures. For internal partitions ensure that shrinkage is restrained by suitable joint treatment. |
| Most building boards, plywood. | Considerable, but readily restrained. | Sealing all surfaces (including edges) by painting may permit external use; otherwise confine to internal use. Fix at all edges. |
| Plaster blocks and slabs. | Small. | Suitable only for internal use, unless specially protected. Build dry and keep dry. |
| Plastics. | Very small. | None called for. |

weight. The class includes such components and materials as storey-height panels, wood-wool slabs, building boards, plasterboard, plywood and even paper and textiles.

With these materials it is usually possible to fix the slabs or sheets so that movement is either concealed or restrained so that there is no opening at the joints.

It may be mentioned here that this principle does not generally hold where thermal movement of metal and glass sheet is concerned (see p. 187).

*Summary*

(1) The designer should carry in mind a broad classification of types of material in terms of their moisture movement.

(2) Types of material that have large moisture movements are unsuitable for use in external walls where seasonal changes in moisture content are likely to be severe.

(3) When it is known that moisture movements with certain types of material are considerable, it is important to ensure that special precautions are taken in their use to prevent failures in the form of shrinkage cracking. Monolithic concrete requires careful design of reinforcement to control shrinkage. Precast concrete units should be matured before erection in walls.

(4) The effect of weather conditions during the progress of building operations is important. Wet weather, especially in winter, makes it difficult to get products properly dried out, and the materials stored on the site are liable to get wet unless they are kept under cover. Work in progress should also be protected from rain. A high moisture content in the early stages results in high shrinkage when the work subsequently dries out.

(5) The effect of drying conditions in the building is important. Where the heating in a new building is run to capacity to get a rapid dry-out before occupation, drying shrinkage troubles are very liable to be accentuated. It would be desirable as far as possible to select non-shrinking materials for a rush job.

(6) The clauses in British Standards and British Standard Codes of Practice that are aimed at control of drying shrinkage should afford a valuable safeguard.

(7) Table 13.5 summarizes the liability to moisture movement of the more common building materials and the appropriate precautions in use.

*Chapter 14*

# EXCLUSION OF WATER

## LATERAL PENETRATION OF RAIN

THE three ways, mentioned already in Part I, of preventing rain water penetrating through a wall to the interior of a building are:

(1) the provision, at the outer face or within the fabric, of a continuous impermeable skin;

(2) the use of a sufficient thickness of materials that are permeable, but allow water to pass so slowly that, under the site conditions of wind and rainfall, it will not reach the inner face before a drying-out period ensues;

(3) the inclusion, within a wall of permeable materials, of a continuous cavity to break the capillary paths along which the moisture travels.

The second is the oldest method. Thick walls and a generous eaves over-hang often ensure its adequacy in buildings up to two storeys high in English weather, especially if masonry construction is finished with a rendering to seal off any through-cracks at joints.

More recently, the cavity wall has been widely adopted. Properly constructed, it is a more certain safeguard against rain penetration, its performance in this respect being independent of unforeseeable extremes of weather or breakdown of materials. The cavity wall also gives an important increase in thermal insulation compared with a solid wall built with the same quantity of material (p. 218).

The first method, although difficult to carry through successfully, has always found favour among designers and suffers no lack of champions at the present time. Its popularity may result from a common-sense approach to the problem of rain exclusion—when it is raining, we wear a mackintosh, so why not treat our buildings likewise? But in practice the provision of a continuous impervious coating all over a building is almost impossible. Buildings are made up of a variety of components, each having its own thermal and moisture movements; at some junctions between dissimilar materials cracking is inevitable. The behaviour of the painted stucco introduced in the Regency period provides an example. Moderate success was achieved by covering the walls first with stucco and then painting the surface, but breakdown of the protective film has been frequent, and maintenance costs are high. When penetration does occur with a construction of this kind there is no way out for the water, which eventually migrates to the inner surface.

Attempts have been made to obtain a water-repellent surface without completely sealing the surface pores. Colourless waterproofers, including those based on silicones, all do this in some degree. The best of these coatings can produce a hundredfold reduction in the rate of absorption of rain, against

198

a fivefold reduction in the rate of evaporation of water from the wall. The balance is sufficiently favourable to make the treatment advantageous unless there are defects that allow water to get behind the water-repellent film.

One way of overcoming the problem of relative movement is by means of lapped joints, as in slate hanging. The vertical lap must be sufficient to prevent water being blown in by a strong wind; it may be calculated from the expected wind pressure (see p. 9–11), which can be readily translated from lb/sq. ft to head of water in inches by dividing by six. Thus if wind pressure is likely to attain 12 lb/sq. ft, the vertical lap will need to be at least two inches.

In the past ten years, the trend has been toward the use of oil mastics for sealing joints where movement is expected (p. 128). These mastics are now used almost universally at the junction between window frames and walls and they play a vital part in the defence against rain penetration in curtain walling. Unfortunately, some designers do not yet appreciate that oil mastics, tolerant though they are of movement, cannot be expected to function satisfactorily if they are stretched or compressed much more than about a tenth of their original width.

## THE SOLID MASONRY WALL

Ordinary masonry units are porous to a greater or less extent, and it is necessary to consider how a solid wall constructed of such material functions in keeping out the rain.

There are two important and quite different ways in which a solid wall may function in this respect:

(1) A relatively impervious unit may be used, set in a dense mortar, with the object of providing a definite barrier to the transmission of water. At first sight this would seem to be the most straightforward way of dealing with the problem. To be successful, however, this method demands a perfection of material and workmanship that is most difficult to secure in practice. The bond between the units and the mortar must be perfect and the wall must be free from even minor cracks and fissures. Even if the wall is built in this way, movement of the units and mortar with changes in moisture content and temperature are likely to produce cracks in course of time.

(2) A porous absorptive unit may be used, set in a mortar having somewhat similar characteristics. In this case, rain falling on the wall will be absorbed at the outer face but will re-evaporate, again at the outer face, when fine weather follows rain. So long as the wall can still absorb water into the pores, the water cannot form a continuous film nor can it run through to the inner face through any cracks and fissures that are somewhat wider than the pores still absorbing water. With porous units and mortar, therefore, workmanship and supervision are much less important.

### Mortars

What is important is to ensure compatibility between units and mortar. The use of a relatively impervious mortar with porous units may lead to a concentration of water just above the horizontal joints, with a corresponding increase in the likelihood of penetration to the inner face. This is demonstrated by Plate 14.1, which shows the back of a test wall built of open-texture lightweight concrete blocks with dense cement-mortar joints, after a period of spraying with water on the front. Water can be seen running down from each of the horizontal joints.

Whilst it is not difficult to select a mortar that has much the same characteristics as the units in respect of strength and porosity, it is not often possible to produce a mortar similar in respect of moisture and thermal movements. Moreover, the mortar will have an initial drying shrinkage. In consequence, there is always a tendency for the mortar to crack away from the units it bonds, especially in vertical joints. This tendency is most marked with strong mortars, when the adhesion to the masonry unit is less than the tensile strength of the mortar itself. Weak mortars crack away more rarely. That penetration occurs at joints rather than through porous units is demonstrated by Plate 14.2 which shows the back of a test wall of porous brickwork after the front has been sprayed with water just long enough to produce penetration.

*Pointing*

There is no evidence that the pointing of brickwork and blockwork after completion of the building has any advantage over flushing up the joint at the time of building, provided that this operation is done with care. If pointing is done as a separate operation, it is unwise to use a pointing mortar stronger than the main body of the mortar; when this is done some of the pointing mortar commonly breaks away after a few years and the risk of rain penetration is increased.

*Renderings*

Porous renderings, by preventing direct flow of water into cracks at mortar joints and elsewhere, greatly increase the resistance to rain penetration. They may still be of some value even when cracked. Dense renderings, on the other hand, serve to keep rain out only so long as they remain crack-free. As soon as cracks develop, rain can gain an entry to the wall behind the rendering, where it is entrapped. This and other aspects of external renderings are treated more fully in Chapter 18.

*Brickwork*

There are still many 9-in. fair-face brick walls giving satisfactory protection against rain penetration, particularly in the drier half of Britain. Penetration has been known to occur through porous headers; these offer less resistance than two stretcher bricks separated by a layer of mortar, where the water has to transfer from brick to mortar and then from mortar back to brick. However, as already mentioned, penetration occurs more often at fine cracks between bricks and mortar; the less porous the bricks and mortar, the more likely is this penetration at joints to occur. Perforated bricks, giving the mortar a positive key, are markedly better in this respect (other things being equal) than solid bricks.

Direct penetration of water through plain brickwork is not as common as is often supposed. More frequently, dampness is associated with local defects such as cracked sills and with badly designed parapets or other architectural features.

Projections properly designed to throw water clear of the wall below can be of considerable help, as, for instance, is an eaves projection in single- and two-storey dwellings. High walls without a projection at the top, or at any levels below, incur an increased risk of penetration. Under such conditions 13½-in. and even 18-in. brickwork have been known to have inadequate resistance to driving rain.

It may be difficult to decide whether a given instance of dampness is due to rain penetration alone or has been aggravated by condensation from within. The thermal insulation afforded by a damp wall is less than that of a dry wall. Before the stage of penetration of rain to the inner surface is reached, heat loss through the wall in cold weather may have lowered the temperature of that surface so much that condensation occurs.

*Natural stone masonry*

The foregoing principles apply also with natural stone masonry in solid walls.

The modern tendency in high-class work in ashlar is to use a relatively thin skin of natural stone, backed up with solid brickwork. The joints are made with great care and the ratio of joint to masonry unit is very much less with the larger stone blocks than with the smaller brick units. Furthermore, the precaution is often adopted of waterproofing the back of the stones to isolate them from any soluble salts in the brickwork backing. It is doubtful, however, whether either precaution helps very much in preventing penetration of rain; entry of water to the backing can still occur at the mortar joints, and an almost impervious coating may then aggravate the dampness by restricting movement of the water back to the face of the wall where it could evaporate.

Rain has been known to penetrate through thick walls of granite masonry. As a rule, the problem of obtaining a dry wall with impervious material of this kind is a difficult one. Owing to the lack of any absorptive capacity in the stones, water tends to stream through any cracks or fissures in an otherwise impervious joint; nor is there sufficient absorption in a porous mortar joint to hold back the rain for any length of time.

With rubble and random masonry, where smaller stones are used, the problem of obtaining a watertight solid wall is essentially the same as with the brick wall.

*Cast stone and concrete units*

The term 'cast stone' is applied to facing blocks, usually manufactured to special order under carefully controlled factory conditions. More generally, precast concrete units are cast in numbers from the same mould with no special attention to decorative value, though in this category it is necessary to include units that are given some embellishment, such as an imitation of the tooled finishes applied to natural stone.

With all materials of this type, watertightness is difficult to attain. Given adequate curing, the initial drying shrinkage of the blocks will have occurred before the units are built into a wall, but there still remains appreciable reversible movement on wetting and drying. Moreover, thermal movement may be double that of clay bricks. These movements, in time, produce cracks at the mortar joints; the bigger the units, the greater the movement that has to be accommodated at the joint and in consequence, the larger or more frequent are the cracks. The use of strong mortars encourages large cracks at infrequent intervals, whereas with a weak mortar the movement is spread over all the joints. Weak mortars are, therefore, generally to be preferred, but even so, a watertight wall of fair-face blockwork may not be attainable without resorting to cavity construction.

If the wall is rendered, both movement of the blocks and the feed of water to the cracks can be much reduced. Given good workmanship, a rendered solid wall may have sufficient resistance to rain penetration where exposure is not too severe.

*Cavity-block walling*

Attempts have been made from time to time to obtain the benefits of cavity walling without recourse to two independent leaves. A fair degree of success has been achieved with some types of cavity blocks, laid with two strips of mortar, one at the outer and one at the inner face (Plate 14.3). The plain walling rarely gives trouble, but the quoins are liable to leak unless special blocks are provided. Furthermore, the provision of efficient cavity gutters above openings is complicated.

## NO-FINES CONCRETE

Walls of no-fines concrete consist essentially of small stones cemented together at their points of contact. They are rendered externally, to keep out the wind, and any water that may be carried by it. They provide no positive barrier to the movement of water through them, but they provide no capillary paths either. Any water penetrating the external rendering will trickle down its inner surface, through the interstices of the no-fines concrete, to where provision is made for it to drain outwards at the foot of the wall or at features such as lintels. If these drainage details are adequately designed, it is most unlikely that rain will penetrate a no-fines concrete wall.

In this respect, the walling is similar to cavity construction. A difference arises in that water trickling down through a no-fines concrete may gradually drift towards the inner face. With dense aggregate the drift appears to be small—four-storey dwellings have been so constructed, and have not shown signs of internal dampness at the base of the walls. With porous aggregate, penetration can occur more readily.

## MONOLITHIC REINFORCED CONCRETE

Monolithic reinforced concrete walling presents the anomaly that, although it is one of the most dense and impermeable materials in common use, the problem of rain exclusion is an extremely difficult one. The difficulty arises from the fact that owing to the impermeability of the concrete all the rain that is blown against the wall runs down the wall face in a continuous sheet and finds its way to the interior wherever there is a crack or a local defect. For this reason the control of shrinkage cracking by a suitable amount of reinforcement properly distributed is absolutely essential, since shrinkage is inevitable. The avoidance of local defects, such as 'honeycombing', depends on care in placing and consolidation of the concrete, and in the choice of a mix that is fully workable without an excess of water. The treatment of construction joints demands special consideration and supervision to avoid planes of weakness or of excessive permeability, as well as to secure satisfactory appearance.

## CAVITY WALLING

The continuous cavity has proved itself to be the most efficient and certain safeguard against the penetration of walls by rain. There have been failures in this respect but, in most cases where it has been possible to investigate, failure has been due to violation of the essential principle in cavity wall construction that there shall be no 'bridge' of solid material capable of transmitting water across the cavity. There is abundant evidence that entirely satisfactory results can be obtained in cavity walling given good design and conscientious and careful work.

It is important that the inner surface of the outer leaf shall not encourage dripping. For this reason, projections extending into the cavity should be avoided. It has been known for water penetrating an outer leaf of concrete units to drip from one projection on to another and then splash across the cavity on to the inner leaf. Care in the design of concrete and other cladding units to avoid this possibility is imperative.

### The ties

From the point of view of obtaining a weathertight wall the ties are a distinct disadvantage. Mortar dropping from the bricklayer's trowel may lodge upon the ties lower down the wall, and thus bridge the cavity. This can be avoided to some extent by drawing a batten up the cavity as the wall is erected in order to catch the droppings, but as a further precaution the design of the ties should be such as to afford the minimum of lodgment for a pat of mortar. There should also be some sort of drip in the centre of a tie, so that water cannot run along the tie from outer to inner leaf.

Three types of tie satisfying these requirements are specified in B.S. 1243 (Fig. 14.1).

### Openings and damp-proof courses

Apart from mortar bridges on the ties, the most common cause of cavity walls failing to exclude rain is bad detailing at openings and at the foot of the wall. Some of the more important points are shown in Fig. 14.2 (good detailing) and Fig. 14.3 (bad detailing).

An efficient damp-proof course over the head of an opening is essential. There are many materials in sheet form that are quite impervious, but it is important that the damp-proof course should be capable of being accurately dressed over at least two sharp bends. If the material cannot be dressed accurately to shape and does not keep its shape, there is a real danger of the formation of mortar bridges over the openings, as shown in Fig. 14.3, No. 6. Sheet lead and sheet copper fulfil the requirements for damp-proof courses of this kind very satisfactorily (but see p. 211 regarding protection of lead in contact with mortar). A stiff bitumen/asbestos sheet material that can be shaped when heated is also being used.

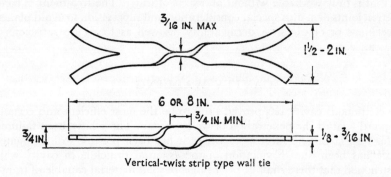

Vertical-twist strip type wall tie

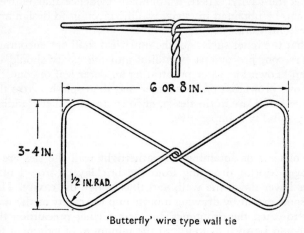

'Butterfly' wire type wall tie

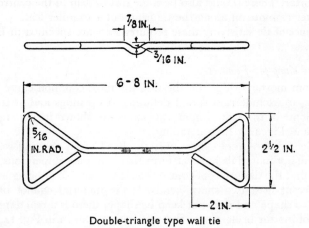

Double-triangle type wall tie

FIG. 14.1

*British Standard (B.S. 1243) wall ties*

*The filled cavity*

Filling the cavity cannot increase security from rain penetration, and it may reduce such security; it is not to be recommended unconditionally.

From time to time, designers have attempted to improve the resistance of a cavity wall to penetration of rain by filling the cavity with bituminous material or dense cement mortar. Such walls have rarely given satisfactory service. For an impervious filling to be effective, it must have no breaks anywhere. If any local defects are present, water can find a way through and will become entrapped behind the impervious filling. An open cavity is very much more effective.

As will be discussed more fully later, filling the cavity with heat-insulating material, either as a loose fill or in quilt or sheet form, would be a convenient way of reducing heat losses through the wall. It is reasonable to assume also that a loose fill of a material that, by virtue of water-repellence, offered no capillary path for moisture transfer between the leaves could cause no trouble (cf. no-fines concrete walling, p. 202); laboratory tests have confirmed that the risk of penetration through a fill of water-repellent nodules of glass silk fibre is very slight. Unfortunately, our knowledge of the long-term behaviour of the water-repellent coating is not sufficient for any guarantee to be given that penetration will not occur in, say, fifty years' time. At worst, the filled cavity wall will be slightly better in respect of resistance to rain penetration than a solid wall of the same thickness; where this type of wall would be expected to give satisfactory service, a filled cavity wall can be recommended with some confidence. For buildings that will have to suffer severe exposure, it would be safer to avoid bridging the cavity in this way.

*Practical treatment*

The primary object of cavity construction in masonry is to ensure that rain does not penetrate to the inner face of an external wall, even under very severe conditions of exposure. The essential requirement is that the cavity shall be continuous and not bridged by any porous material that could conduct water to the inner leaf.

In a cavity wall with a thin 4½-in. outer leaf it must be realized that in very wet weather there is every likelihood that water will reach the inner face of the outer leaf, even in such quantity as to trickle down it, and adequate provision must be made to conduct this water to the outside of the wall.

From the practical building point of view the following are the most important points. Reference may be made to the details shown in Figs. 14.2 and 14.3.

(1) A cavity damp-proof course should be provided over every opening, however small, unless all the brickwork above is entirely protected, and the outer edge of the damp-proof course should be as near the opening as possible.

(2) The least possible amount of masonry should be allowed to project into the cavity (Fig. 14.2, No. 2, and Fig. 14.3, No. 2).

(3) The cavity should never be bridged with a horizontal damp-proof course.

(4) Window-sills should be designed to prevent the collection of mortar droppings or water on the projecting ends (Fig. 14.2, No. 13, Fig. 14.3, No. 8).

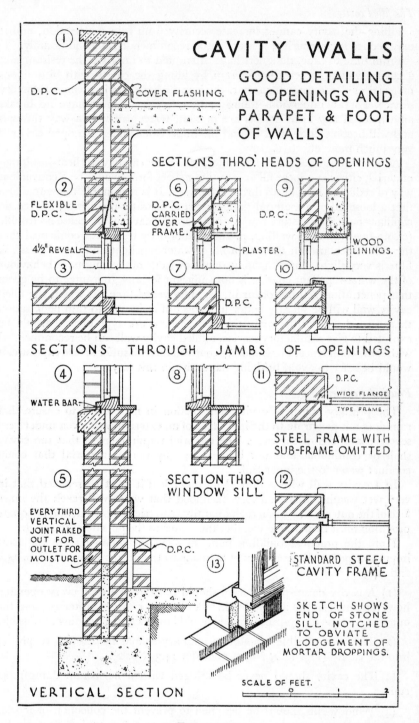

# CAVITY WALLS

## GOOD DETAILING AT OPENINGS AND PARAPET & FOOT OF WALLS

FIG. 14.2

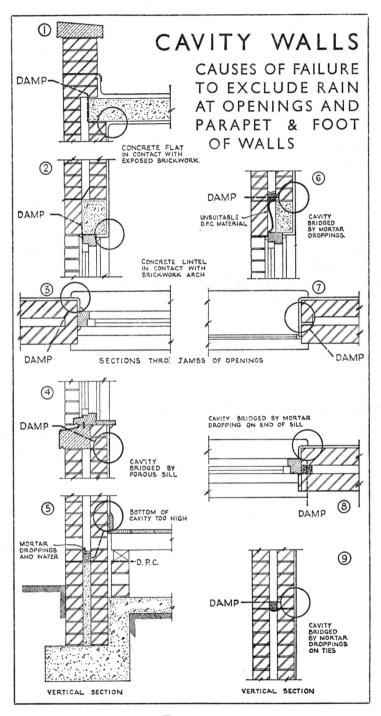

CAVITY WALLS
CAUSES OF FAILURE
TO EXCLUDE RAIN
AT OPENINGS AND
PARAPET & FOOT
OF WALLS

DAMP

① CONCRETE FLAT
IN CONTACT WITH
EXPOSED BRICKWORK.

② DAMP
CONCRETE LINTEL
IN CONTACT WITH
BRICKWORK ARCH

⑥ DAMP
UNSUITABLE
D.P.C. MATERIAL
CAVITY
BRIDGED
BY MORTAR
DROPPINGS.

③ DAMP
SECTIONS THRO! JAMBS OF OPENINGS

⑦ DAMP

④ DAMP
CAVITY
BRIDGED BY
POROUS SILL

CAVITY BRIDGED BY MORTAR
DROPPING ON END OF SILL

⑤ BOTTOM OF
CAVITY TOO HIGH
MORTAR
DROPPINGS
AND WATER
D.P.C.

⑧ DAMP

⑨ DAMP
CAVITY
BRIDGED
BY MORTAR
DROPPINGS
ON TIES

VERTICAL SECTION

VERTICAL SECTION

FIG. 14.3

(5) Cavity damp-proof courses over openings should be long enough to prevent the water discharged from them flowing back to the jambs. High openings thus require longer trays.

(6) Cavity damp-proof courses should be of a material that can be formed to the shape required. The ends should be bent to discharge the water against the outside leaf of the wall.

(7) Outlets should be provided to discharge any water collected in the cavity. Open vertical joints are usually employed in brickwork or masonry (Fig. 14.2, No. 5).

(8) Vertical damp-proof courses should be provided where required at openings, all contacts between the outer and inner leaves being broken by a damp-proof course (Fig. 14.2, No. 6).

(9) Flemish bond should not be specified for 4½-in. walls. The use of snap headers may lead to a dirty cavity and possibly to splashing of water across to the inner leaf, besides being expensive and less efficient than the stretcher bond.

(10) Neither party walls nor partitions should make contact with the outer leaf of the wall.

(11) Where a cavity wall is used partly as an external wall and also becomes an internal wall at a lower level, below a roof projecting from the side of the building, the cavity must be stopped with a cavity damp-proof course at the lowest level of the exposed wall. Outlets should be provided at suitable places to discharge any collected water (Fig. 14.4).

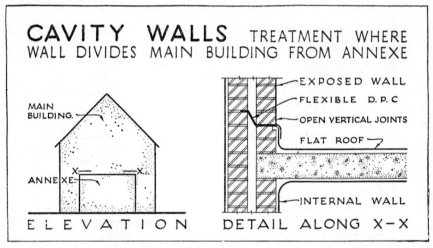

FIG. 14.4

(12) The cavity should be commenced at least 3 in. below the damp-proof course of the inner leaf, and outlets for any collected water should be provided in the outer leaf below the damp-proof course (Fig. 14.2, No. 5). The space thus formed is a precaution against water rising above the inner damp-proof course. It should be clear of rubbish and mortar droppings. Where possible the damp-proof course of the inner leaf may well be at a higher level than that of the outer.

(13) Wall ties must be of a non-corroding material and easily cleansed of mortar droppings. The mortar collected by the ties and cavity gutters should be completely removed. This can be done by leaving holes as necessary at the quoins and cleaning with battens. A batten the width of the cavity is sometimes placed at its base and raised as the wall is built to prevent the intrusion of rubbish or droppings. A combination of these two methods will give added security. It should be realized, however, that careful supervision is essential for clean cavities, for without it no such preparations are of use.

(14) Wall ties should be built square with the cavity, and on no account should they be allowed to slope downwards towards the inner leaf.

## CURTAIN WALLING

In curtain-walling systems reliance is placed on the use of an impervious outer skin for the exclusion of rain. The nature of the joints then assumes primary importance because, with no absorption on the outer face of the wall, all water striking the wall must run down the face and wind pressure will then blow water in through any leaking or badly designed joints. Experience, particularly in the U.S.A., shows that, on high exposed buildings, water may on occasion be forced upwards by wind pressure and penetrate into the buildings at points where this would not normally be expected. Wind-driven snow may also be troublesome where there are unsealed joints.

With all systems there is much to be said for designs that provide an air space immediately behind the impervious skin, with provision for the outward drainage of any water that may penetrate joints (or condense on the inner face of the skin and run down). This provision for drainage is, of course, one of the features of patent glazing design, so that curtain-walling systems in which patent glazing bars are used vertically (group 2, p. 183) are favourably placed in this respect. Care may, however, still be needed to ensure that water or fine snow is not blown in under the bottom edges of the outer sheeting. The ordinary methods of sealing these spaces when patent glazing is used on roofs may not be adequate on large vertical expanses. Foamed-plastics sealing strips are finding some application for this purpose.

Systems with overlapping sheets (group 1, p. 183) rely mainly on the extent of the overlaps for their freedom from leakage. The sheets should not fit together so closely at the overlaps as to form capillary gaps up which water can be drawn, but in practice the fit is seldom close enough for there to be any risk of this.

Systems with panels fixed with putty or mastic in rectangular rebated frames (group 3, p. 183) remain waterproof only as long as the putty or mastic remains in place and in good condition. This is the weakness of such systems, for thermal movements cause constant working at the joints; the ideal requirement, that a compound should stay in place over long periods without slumping and yet remain sufficiently plastic and adhesive to maintain a permanently watertight joint, appears to be beyond practical possibility. This makes it all the more desirable that adequate drainage should be provided at the backs of the outer sheets.

Various modifications of these framed systems are being developed in which the panels are fixed with beads and compressible sealing strips, used sometimes in association with soft mastics to give the final seal. In some systems, too, rubbery sealing strips are formed *in situ* from softer ingredients, to provide good bonding with the surfaces they separate, and the necessary movement, without any risk of slumping. Such methods may provide the final answer but more experience is needed before a definite pronouncement can be made.

## POST-AND-PANEL CONSTRUCTION

The details and types of post-and-panel systems vary widely but all have a common problem, that of making a watertight joint at the junction of post and panel. The design of this joint must take account of the risk of relative movement. The junction at the base of the panel is also vulnerable; the panel will usually be carried on a concrete beam or floor and any flow-off will tend to pass into the building. The resistance of the panel itself will be similar to that of normal walling of the same materials and construction.

The use of cavity construction simplifies the problem especially if the posts are incorporated in the inner leaf only and a continuous cavity is ensured. Otherwise the best design is that which includes a rebate or slot in the posts into which the edges of the panel are built. In this way any crack that opens is protected against direct passage of moisture and is backed by dense concrete. The joint may be filled with a mastic or mortar, or a vertical damp-proof course may be incorporated.

With cavity construction, of course, the base of the wall should incorporate a cavity gutter.

With solid infilling panels the problem of the junction remains but there is also risk of direct penetration through the panels. A rendering is made less effective than it would be on a homogeneous wall because of the cracks that are likely to develop at the junction of the post and panel.

# VERTICAL MOVEMENT OF WATER

Apart from the lateral penetration of rain, it is necessary to prevent water rising in a wall from the ground or descending after penetration through parapets, chimney stacks or other projecting features. This is done by providing damp-proof courses wherever necessary.

## DAMP-PROOF COURSES

The direction of movement of water is important. Some materials are suitable for protection against movement of moisture in any direction; others only against upward movement. Two courses of dense bricks in cement mortar will successfully resist the rise of moisture by capillary action, and it is an advantage to leave the vertical joints unfilled. Good slates are impervious and two courses laid in cement mortar to break joint will also resist capillary rise of moisture. But neither the brick (even with all joints filled with mortar) nor the slate damp-proof course can be relied on to prevent the downward passage of moisture; an impervious material, jointed with laps or welts where necessary, must then be used. (A slate damp-proof course will usually suffice

PLATE 14.1

*Porous blocks laid in dense mortar: moisture penetration concentrated at joints*

H*

PLATE 14.2

*Moisture penetration through brickwork at horizontal and vertical joints*

PLATE 14.3

*Hollow clay bricks* ($13\frac{1}{8}$-in. $\times 8\frac{3}{8}$-in. $\times 2\frac{3}{8}$-in.) *designed to give a cavity effect as regards mortar joints*

PLATE 14.4

Efflorescence on brickwork below cope in sill

to prevent undue horizontal movement of moisture between parts of a structure where there is no difference in water pressure between the two parts.)

The prevention of upward movement of moisture is normally needed only at one level, i.e., just above ground level; prevention of downward movement is needed at many different levels, e.g., in parapets and chimneys, above lintels in cavity walls, etc.

A damp-proof course should remain effective as long as the building. Besides the material being durable, it may need to accommodate some structural movement without fracture.

*Sheet-metal damp-proof courses*

The metals most commonly used are lead and copper.

Lead is very flexible; it will accommodate some movement, can be dressed to complex shapes without fracture and it is highly resistant to sliding. It will not squeeze out under the pressures likely to be met with in normal building construction. It is impervious to moisture; lapped joints are sufficient where moisture movement is upward; for downward movement the joints should be welted. Lead is resistant to ordinary atmospheric corrosion because of the formation of a tough resistant surface film. Fresh lime or Portland cement mortar can cause corrosion and the metal should be protected by a coating of bitumen or of bitumen paint of heavy consistence. It is best to paint first the mortar bed on which the lead is to be laid, the underside of the lead before laying, and then the top surface after laying. Alternatively one of the proprietary products consisting of lead sheet sandwiched between layers of fabric-reinforced bitumen can be used.

Copper is flexible, has a higher tensile strength than lead and will accommodate slight movements. It will not squeeze out and gives ample resistance to sliding. It is impervious and the joints should be treated as for lead. The metal is only very slightly affected by contact with mortars and it does not, in normal use, require any protective coating. There is, however, a risk of staining external walls, especially stone, below a copper damp-proof course.

*Bitumen-felt damp-proof courses*

The British Standard for bitumen felts for damp-proof courses (B.S.743) includes six types, based on hessian, fibre felt or asbestos, with or without a core of sheet lead.

All types are flexible and will accommodate slight movements. They are liable to squeeze out under heavy pressure and they offer little resistance to sliding. The materials are impervious to moisture and the pressure from the weight of material above is usually sufficient to seal the lap joints; the laps should be at least 4 in. wide and may be sealed with bitumen if necessary.

Bitumen itself is a durable material. The only constituents liable to decay are the hessian or felt base, but, provided the bitumen remains undisturbed, the efficacy of the damp-proof course is not impaired even if decay occurs. The materials should be unrolled with care, especially in cold weather.

*Asphalt mastic*

Asphalt needs to be laid by experienced men employed by specialist firms. It can withstand only very slight distortion, it has fair resistance to sliding at ordinary temperatures, and it may be liable to squeeze out under very heavy pressures or in very hot climates. The material is completely impervious and there are, of course, no joint problems. Good asphalt is a very durable material.

*Rigid units*

Two courses of slates or dense bricks in cement mortar form a damp-proof course that will resist upward or, in some cases, horizontal passage of moisture but cannot be relied on to prevent downward movement. Slight structural movements may cause cracking but this is not serious where only upward movement of moisture is to be prevented. Both resist sliding. Good slates and bricks are not affected by contact with other building materials or soil. Particular care is needed in the laying and bedding of slates and bricks in damp-proof courses.

Slates should be at least 9 in. long and have an average water absorption of not more than 0·3 per cent.

Bricks should be of the engineering type and have a water absorption of not more than 4·5 per cent as measured in the boiling test (B.S. 1301, Class A).

Mortar for slate and brick damp-proof courses should be relatively impervious to moisture; a 1 : 3 Portland cement : sand mix is suitable.

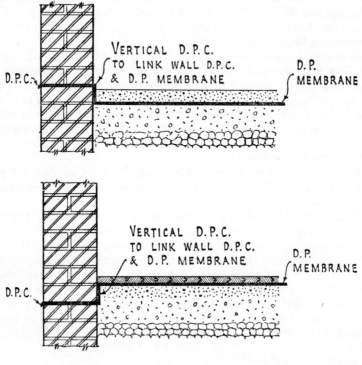

FIG. 14.5

*Linking damp-proof course in wall with damp-proof membrane in solid floors*

*Position of the damp-proof course*

When a damp-proof course is found to be ineffective, usually the fault lies in its position or extent rather than in defects in the material; it may be by-passed in some way, as by a coat of rendering or by pointing (in an ill-advised attempt at concealment—see p. 145), or it may not be joined to adjacent damp-proof courses or membranes.

Fig. 14.5 shows appropriate positions of damp-proof courses in walls adjoining solid floors.

## CHIMNEYS

Chimney stacks may provide routes for moisture penetration unless adequate precautions are taken.

For a chimney at or near the ridge, and extending only slightly above it, good weather protection at the top is sufficient in all but very exposed positions. When the exposed part of the stack is more than a few feet in height a damp-proof course is advisable where the stack emerges from the roof. The simplest and most effective form is a combined damp-proof course and flashing of lead or copper at the level shown in Fig. 14.6. This form is to be preferred to a stepped flexible damp-proof course. Good protection is needed at the top, as at the top of a parapet wall. A precast concrete capping in one piece with sloping top, and ample overhang, properly throated, is adequate. Cappings of brickwork and tile creasing, even though flaunched with mortar, cannot be relied on to keep out moisture indefinitely and require an impermeable damp-proof course immediately below them.

## MISCELLANEOUS FEATURES

Especial care is needed in the design of features that include some horizontal or nearly horizontal surfaces. Much heavy rain falls almost vertically; it misses the normal walling, but falls directly on the copings of parapets, on cornices, projecting string-courses and sills. Unless provision is made to dispose of this large quantity of water, the wall below may become damp.

*Parapets*

Parapets suffer severe exposure; they are high up and exposed on both sides. Moreover, they are not artificially heated, as are many walls below parapet level. Parapets are, therefore, liable to be much wetter than normal walling in periods of inclement weather. For this reason, a parapet more than a few courses high should be separated from the wall below by means of a continuous damp-proof course, terminating at the face of the wall in a metal flashing, as shown in Fig. 18.1 (p. 256).

The parapet itself is usually protected by a coping, which is often considered sufficient to prevent downward penetration of rain. However, there are few, if any, materials that will not develop cracks—usually at the joints between units—when exposed for some years on the top of a parapet. The damp-proof course shown in Fig. 18.1 immediately beneath the coping is intended to guard against penetration through these cracks. Where the parapet is in

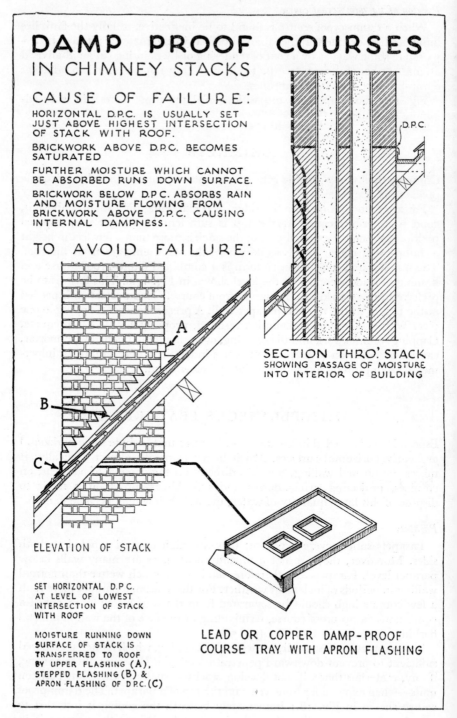

# DAMP PROOF COURSES
## IN CHIMNEY STACKS

### CAUSE OF FAILURE:

HORIZONTAL D.P.C. IS USUALLY SET JUST ABOVE HIGHEST INTERSECTION OF STACK WITH ROOF.

BRICKWORK ABOVE D.P.C. BECOMES SATURATED

FURTHER MOISTURE WHICH CANNOT BE ABSORBED RUNS DOWN SURFACE.

BRICKWORK BELOW D.P.C. ABSORBS RAIN AND MOISTURE FLOWING FROM BRICKWORK ABOVE D.P.C. CAUSING INTERNAL DAMPNESS.

### TO AVOID FAILURE:

D.P.C.

SECTION THRO.' STACK
SHOWING PASSAGE OF MOISTURE INTO INTERIOR OF BUILDING

A

B

C

ELEVATION OF STACK

SET HORIZONTAL D.P.C. AT LEVEL OF LOWEST INTERSECTION OF STACK WITH ROOF

MOISTURE RUNNING DOWN SURFACE OF STACK IS TRANSFERRED TO ROOF BY UPPER FLASHING (A), STEPPED FLASHING (B) & APRON FLASHING OF D.P.C. (C)

LEAD OR COPPER DAMP-PROOF COURSE TRAY WITH APRON FLASHING

FIG. 14.6

cavity construction, the damp-proof course beneath the coping should be continuous across the full width of the wall. Copings should project clear of the wall and have a throat or drip to throw water clear of the face.

*Cornices and protecting string courses*

Any features projecting from a wall should be themselves impervious or should be provided with an impervious covering. Large areas may be covered with asphalt or layers of bitumen felt. Typical details for large cornices are shown in Fig. 14.7. For small projections, a simple strip metal flashing may

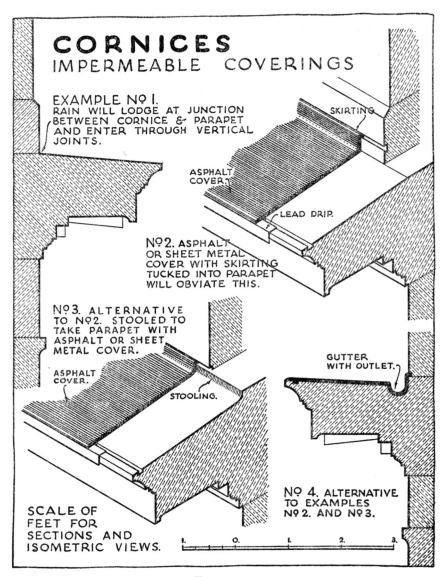

FIG. 14.7

be preferred. It has been found from experience that attention to these details is often far more important than a high resistance to rain penetration in the walling below.

## Sills

Window sills receive the run-off from the windows above and in consequence any slight defect in them can have an effect out of proportion to its size. A fine crack in a sill will permit the entry of a large quantity of rain to the wall below. This is demonstrated in Plate 14.4, where water penetrating by way of the crack in the middle of the sill has saturated the brickwork as far as the festoon of efflorescence. Salts have been deposited on the surface where this water has evaporated.

*Chapter* 15

# HEAT INSULATION

In considering the heat-insulation characteristics of the external walls of a building, their importance should first be assessed in relation to the overall heat exchange between the inside and the outside of the building as a whole. This implies that:

(i) the contribution to the heat exchange by ventilation and by conduction through the enclosing building structure should be compared (p. 39), especially when designing for extreme conditions of external or internal climate for buildings that are to be air-conditioned, or for other atypical circumstances.

(ii) the contribution of the external walling to the conduction heat exchange should be assessed. For example, in a multi-storey building the area of the external walling will be a much greater percentage of the total area of the exterior of the building than it would be in a single-storey building.

Although the planning of a building must take many factors other than heat transfer into account, there are circumstances in which the plan shape and the orientation of the building may justifiably be influenced by thermal considerations. For example a compact plan, reducing the external wall area to a minimum, will reduce heat loss as well as building costs. In climates where solar heat is likely to make a building uncomfortably hot, it may be advantageous to plan the long axis of the building in an east-west direction so that the area of external walling exposed to the direct rays of the slanting sun is kept to a minimum.

As the air-to-air transmission coefficient $(U)$ for a wall can be influenced by the exposure, solar radiation, wind and moisture conditions as mentioned on p. 37, the $U$-value will depend partly on height and aspect. The effect of these factors is normally taken into account in the British Isles in a range of values for the external surface resistance of the wall (see p. 220). Thus the $U$-value for a south-facing wall will be somewhat lower than that for a similar wall facing north.

Having established the relative importance of heat insulation for the walling of any particular building, consideration can be given to the details of the design and construction of the walls. Here again it may be desirable to assess the importance of insulation of various portions in relation to the whole of the walling. For example, if a large part of a wall of a heated building consists of single-glazed windows, through which the rate of heat loss can be comparatively high, the insulation of the remainder of that wall may not be very significant in relation to the overall heat exchange between the interior and the exterior.

This does not mean that the unglazed part should not be well insulated, for any additional cost of improved insulation will of course be related to the

217

area involved: also a well-insulated part may be beneficial to body comfort. Thus it may be desirable to examine the contribution of the wall as a whole to the heat exchange and the effect of this contribution on the size and running costs of the heating or air-conditioning plant. The complete appraisal of the desirable balance between the window and the wall areas must also take account of the daylighting requirements, the cost of artificial lighting, and if necessary the cost of providing blinds or curtaining.


## CAVITY CONSTRUCTION

Cavities within a construction offer resistance to heat flow: this resistance depends to some extent on the width and direction of the cavity but, as a rough guide, the heat insulation value of an unventilated vertical cavity at least ¾ in. wide is approximately equal to that provided by a ⅜-in. thickness of insulating fibreboard.

If one or both sides of the cavity has a surface of low emissivity, such as the surface of aluminium foil facing the cavity, the insulation value of the cavity is nearly doubled.

Ventilation of a cavity will reduce its insulation value to some extent, depending on the ventilation rate. The effect of cavity ventilation on the overall insulation value of a wall will also depend on the proportion of the total heat resistance of the wall provided by the cavity and on the position of the cavity in relation to the temperature gradients across the wall. For example, consider an external cavity wall to a building in which the internal temperature is higher than that outside and the direction of heat flow is therefore outwards: if the bulk of the heat resistance of the wall is on the warmer side of the cavity, normal ventilation of the cavity to the colder external air will not have an appreciable effect on the overall insulation value of the wall, as the temperature of the air in the cavity is likely in any case to be nearer that of the external air.


## WINDOWS

The normal single sheet of window glass offers comparatively little resistance to outwards heat flow from a building but allows considerable heat *gain* at times from solar radiation, depending on aspect, locality, and shielding by trees and buildings. Double glazing, mainly by virtue of the cavity between the two sheets of glass, considerably reduces the outwards heat flow but makes no appreciable difference to the gain from solar radiation. As with any other framed panel construction, however (see below, p. 222), the benefit of the cavity as regards outwards heat flow may be partly reduced if it is bridged to any appreciable extent by framing members of high thermal conductivity.

It was indicated in Part I (p. 39) that, for the purpose of sizing heating plant for a building, heat losses should be calculated from $U$-values that are appropriate for days on which heat losses from the building are greatest. For this purpose it is normally recommended that the $U$-values for single glazing in the British Isles should be assumed to be 1·00 (B.t.u./sq. ft h °F) when the window faces N, NE, E, NW, and the exposure to wind is 'normal', and, for double glazing, 0·50 when the window faces W, SW, or SE, and the exposure to wind is 'severe'. Further values are given in the 'Guide to current practice', 1955, of the Institution of Heating and Ventilating Engineers, for other exposures and aspects ranging from 0·70 to 1·30 for single glazing and from 0·41 to 0·56 for double glazing; in addition, attention is there drawn to the effect of the frame on the overall $U$-value of the window.

As the above $U$-values for windows are greater than those for many wall constructions, for which the values often lie between 0·20 and 0·40, the designed capacity (and hence the capital cost) of a heating installation for a building may be strongly influenced by the proportion of window area in the external walls.

The effect of windows on fuel consumption and hence on the running costs is more complicated for, as already indicated, the heat gain from solar radiation may be very variable and will influence the average thermal transmittance value. In addition, if curtains, blinds or shutters are closed over the windows during the hours of darkness the rate of heat loss through the window areas will be reduced during these periods.

A complete economic appraisal of this window problem should also take into account the following factors:

(1) Solar radiation may not provide heat when it is most needed, e.g. in a dwelling the major requirement for space heating may be during certain hours of darkness in winter.

(2) Although the heat gain from solar radiation will be independent of the temperature inside the building, the rate of heat loss will be directly related to the difference in temperature between the inside and outside of the building. This means that the ratio between the 'ingoing' and the 'outgoing' heat will vary to some extent with the pattern of heating provided in the building.

(3) With some types of building the running costs of the artificial lighting installation will be reduced with an increase in window area. The cost of artificial lighting may be an important factor with the levels of lighting now often required.

(4) The cost of providing blinds or curtaining if required.

(5) Any relevant maintenance costs.

Modern methods of construction allow the building designer great freedom in the fenestration for buildings. Although frequently aesthetic considerations may be paramount in this aspect of design, there is a need for the functional factors mentioned above to be taken into account.

## MATERIALS AND CONSTRUCTION

Table 15.1 gives approximate values for the thermal conductivity and thermal resistivity (see p. 36) of some of the more common structural materials and of materials commonly used for thermal insulation in buildings. It will be seen that, in general, the materials of low density provide better thermal insulation than those of higher density. The values given for common bricks indicate the reduction in insulation value of a material due to increases in the moisture content.

## TABLE 15.1

### Thermal conductivity and resistivity
### of some common building and insulating materials

| Material | Moisture content (per cent of dry weight) | Density (lb/cu. ft) | Conductivity $k$ (B.t.u. in./ sq. ft h °F) | Resistivity $1/k$ |
|---|---|---|---|---|
| Asbestos-cement sheet . | — | 95 | 2·0 | 0·5 |
| Asphalt . . . . | — | 140 | 8·5 | 0·12 |
| **Bricks** | | | | |
| Common bricks . . | 0 | 110 | 5·6 | 0·18 |
| | 2·9† | 110 | 8·0 | 0·125 |
| | * | 110 | 8·4 | 0·12 |
| | 16 | 110 | 11·6 | 0·086 |
| Sand-lime bricks . . | 0 | 115 | 7·5 | 0·13 |
| Concrete (ballast) 1 : 2 : 4 . | * | 140–155 | 10 | 0·10 |
| **Concrete (lightweight)** | | | | |
| Cellular concrete . . | * | 20–100 | 0·58–4·5 | 1·72–0·22 |
| | 0 | 75 | 2·6 | 0·38 |
| | 20 | 90 | 6·0 | 0·17 |
| Clinker concrete . . | * | 95–105 | 2·3–2·8 | 0·44–0·36 |
| Foamed-slag concrete . | * | 65–80 | 1·7–2·35 | 0·59–0·43 |
| Plaster (lime, sand, cement) | — | 90 | 3·3 | 0·30 |
| **Timber (across grain)** | | | | |
| Deal . . . . | — | 38 | 0·87 | 1·15 |
| Oak . . . . | — | 48 | 1·11 | 0·90 |
| Cork slab (baked) . . | — | 9 | 0·29 | 3·45 |
| Hair felt . . . . | — | 5 | 0·27 | 3·70 |
| Fibreboard . . . | 10–15 | 15–25 | 0·37–0·45 | 2·70–2·22 |
| Glass, mineral, rock or slag wool . . . . | — | 3–15 | 0·23–0·30 | 4·34–3·33 |
| Wood-wool slab . . | — | 25 | 0·57 | 1·75 |
| Compressed straw slab . | — | 23 | 0·60 | 1·67 |
| Vermiculite (exfoliated) . | — | 5–7 | 0·45 | 2·22 |

NOTE: Values above are for normal atmospheric temperatures and moisture contents unless otherwise noted.

\*Specimens conditioned in an atmosphere at 64°F and 65 per cent relative humidity.

†A north wall normally exposed.

Approximate $U$-values for many constructions can be calculated if the resistivities and thicknesses of the materials involved are known, together with values for the thermal resistances of the internal and external surfaces and of any cavities within the construction. For a wall, the internal surface resistance is usually taken (in British units) as 0·70 and the external surface resistance as 0·30 if, say, it faces NW, N, NE or E and the exposure is 'normal'. Values for other orientations and exposures are given in the 'Guide to current practice' of the Institution of Heating and Ventilating Engineers.

The following example of an 11-in. brick cavity wall plastered on the inside will serve to illustrate the method:

$k$-value of brickwork (say) 8·00; ($1/k = 0·125$)

Resistance of two 4½-in. brick leaves = 2 × 4½ × 0·125    =    1·13
Resistance of ⅝-in. plaster = ⅝ × 0·30    =    0·19
Resistance of internal wall surface (say)    =    0·70
Resistance of external wall surface (say)    =    0·30
Resistance of cavity (say)    =    1·00

Total air-to-air resistance    =    3·32

$$U = \frac{1}{\text{total resistance}} = 0·30$$

The effect on the $U$-value of different exposure conditions, of high moisture content in the materials or of providing an insulating lining to the inside of the wall can be obtained by substituting or adding the appropriate resistances in the above example and then recalculating the $U$-value for the new total resistance.

Table 15.2 gives $U$-values obtained by calculation or by direct measurement for a number of wall constructions.

TABLE 15.2

*U-values of wall constructions*

| | Construction | U-value (B.t.u./ sq. ft h °F) |
|---|---|---|
| 1 | 11-in. brick cavity walling plastered internally    .    .    . | 0·30 |
| 2 | As 1, but with ½-in. insulating fibreboard behind the plaster   . | 0·21 |
| 3 | As 1, but with ½-in. insulating fibreboard on battens behind the plaster    .    .    .    .    .    .    .    .    . | 0·17 |
| 4 | As 1, but with 2-in. wood-wool slabs behind the plaster    . | 0·15 |
| 5 | As 1, but with aluminium-backed plasterboard on battens behind the plaster    .    .    .    .    .    .    . | 0·19 |
| 6 | As 1, but with ⅝-in. lightweight plaster in lieu of normal plaster | 0·26 |
| 7 | As 1, but with 4-in. lightweight concrete blocks for inner leaf of wall in lieu of 4½-in. brickwork    .    .    .    .    . | 0·20–0·25 |
| 8 | Lightweight concrete hollow block (18 in. × 9 in. × 9 in.) wall, rendered externally and plastered internally    .    .    . | 0·25–0·30 |
| 9 | Steel-framed wall, covered externally with corrugated asbestos-cement sheeting and lined internally with: | |
| | (a) ½-in. insulating fibreboard    .    .    .    .    . | 0·36 |
| | (b) 2-in. wood-wool slabs    .    .    .    .    .    . | 0·21 |
| | (c) 3-in. lightweight concrete blocks    .    .    .    . | 0·37 |
| | (d) ¾-in. wool-quilt, plasterboard and plaster .    .    . | 0·21 |
| 10 | Steel-framed wall covered externally with corrugated asbestos-cement sheeting but without internal lining    .    .    . | 1·15 |

Table 15.2 serves to illustrate that the addition of the same amount of insulation to constructions with different $U$-values does not give equal

reductions in those values. Thus the addition of $\frac{1}{2}$-in. insulating fibreboard and a cavity to constructions 1 and 10 reduces the *U*-values of those constructions by 0·13 and 0·79 respectively (constructions 3 and 9(*a*)).

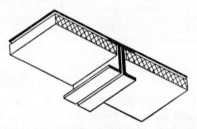

A. Metal external cladding is attached to metal framing members which act as cold bridges and thus increase heat flow.

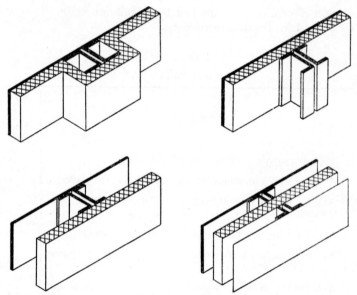

B. Four methods of placing the insulation to prevent the metal framing members from acting as cold bridges. Improved thermal insulation is achieved.

FIG. 15.1

*Influence of framing members on heat transmission through insulated walls (insulation shown by cross-hatching)*

Reference has been made in Part I (p. 38) to the complexity of calculating *U*-values for certain non-homogeneous constructions. This difficulty may arise with modern non-traditional walls if, for example, they have frequent metal framing members that extend through the full thickness of the wall and thus provide many paths for the rapid flow of heat. If the wall is also faced with metal that is in close contact with the framing members, this facing will further assist the rapid transfer of heat through the wall. For such constructions the single calculation shown above will not suffice and the value

must be measured experimentally. In the design of the walling it may however be possible to break the continuity, through the wall thickness, of the
framing members and so to reduce their effect on the heat transmission
through the walling (Fig. 15.1). Alternatively it may be possible to place the
bulk of the insulation so that it separates the framing members from either
the internal or the external face of the walling: in this way the members will
not span from the warm to the cold face of the walling.

Certain standards of thermal insulation have been recommended or adopted for external walling, excluding the window area, in post-war publications;
the economics of heat insulation is discussed in Part I. The desirable standard
of insulation for walls should take into account the basic construction and
the readiness with which its insulation value can be improved. Future
development of materials, methods of application and construction may
justify higher standards of insulation than those acceptable today.

*Summary*

The importance of providing good thermal insulation in the walling of a
building should be assessed in relation to the gain or loss of heat from the
building as a whole.

The effect of the ratio between window and wall area and the desirability
of providing double glazing should be considered in estimating the capital
and running costs of the heating or air-conditioning installation.

Although thermal insulation may not be a deciding factor in the choice of
wall construction, the feasibility of providing the desirable standard of insulation should be considered before the basic form of construction is determined.

The possibility of using load-bearing insulating materials, such as lightweight concrete or hollow blocks, and also the practicability of adding insu-
lants to the basic wall construction should be considered in an early stage of
the preparation of detailed drawings for the building.

# Chapter 16

# SOUND INSULATION

## EXTERNAL WALLS

THE problem as it affects the external wall is primarily one of planning so that rooms where quiet is desirable do not face on noisy thoroughfares. The effective sound insulation of the external walls of a building is largely governed by the window system used. With open windows the insulation is in any case very small and the construction of the actual wall does not matter. With closed single windows it is useful to make the wall insulation a little better than the window insulation, but there is no advantage in making it more than, say, 10 dB better unless the windows are very small. With double windows it is necessary to make the insulation of the walls at least as good as that of the windows and preferably 5–10 dB better, which means that the wall insulation should usually be as high as possible.

TABLE 16.1

*Windows in 9-in. brick wall*

| Type of window, etc. | Net insulation of the wall |
|---|---|
| No openings . . . . . . | 50–55 dB |
| Wide-open windows . . . . . | 5–10 dB |
| Slightly-open single windows . . . . | 10–15 dB |
| Closed 'openable' single windows . . . | 20 dB |
| Sealed single windows (24–32 oz glass) . . | 27–28 dB |
| Sealed single windows (¼-in. plate glass) . . | 30 dB |
| Double windows (24–32 oz glass) incorporating 5 per cent area of permanent 'indirect' ventilation . . . . . . . . | 18–20 dB |
| Closed 'openable' double windows (any weight of glass) . . . . . . . | 35 dB |
| Sealed double windows (24–32 oz glass) . . | 42–43 dB |
| Sealed double windows (¼-in. plate glass) . | 47 dB |

A point to bear in mind about double windows is that if they are made openable for occasional ventilation, their insulation when closed is likely to be at least 10 dB less than that of permanently sealed double windows. To achieve the best possible insulation they must be completely sealed; it is then usually necessary to install an air-conditioning system operating all the year round.

Most of the value of double windows is also lost if permanent natural ventilation is provided, either incorporated in the window itself or elsewhere in the outside wall—unless the ventilation is obtained through properly designed absorbent-lined ducts. Such ducts normally require powered fans to get sufficient air flow through them. Occasionally, with 'through' rooms, it may be possible to have sealed double windows on the noisy side of a building, with natural ventilation by open windows on the other side—if it is quiet enough; but the noise would have to be at least 30 dB less on the quiet side to make this feasible.

Table 16.1 gives the approximate insulation to be expected from external walls with various types of single and double window. The insulation given is the net insulation of the wall, assuming the window area to be about half of the whole wall area, the remainder of the wall being 9-in. brick or its equivalent.

Noise can also penetrate a building through doorways, but as there are usually at least two doors between the outside noise and a particular room this is seldom a serious matter. Separation by two closed doors would normally give an insulation of 45–50 dB, or even more, depending chiefly on the amount of sound absorbent in the intervening hall and corridors.

## INTERNAL WALLS

The sound insulation of internal walls or partitions in normal buildings varies from 15 or 20 dB (given by a single sheet of insulating fibre wall-board or by a light partition with a doorway) up to 50–55 dB (given by a 9-in. solid or 11-in. cavity brick wall). Higher insulation than this between adjoining rooms is practicable only when a fully-discontinuous or 'box' structure is employed. By this is meant that the room (floor, walls and ceiling) is a complete structure in itself, more or less entirely isolated from the surrounding structure. The construction is too complicated for detailed description here; it is only practical for special purposes and on a fairly small scale. Continuous wall cavities unbridged except at the edges (or bridged only by light wire ties) are feasible however and are quite commonly used, but they increase the insulation by only a few dB above that due to the mass of the wall. Enough has been said already about the general principles of sound insulation to enable any necessary level of insulation to be obtained economically. The main problem is to decide upon the standard of insulation required for particular purposes and conditions. This is largely a matter of experience for the designer, with assistance from specialists when necessary. When the problem is a precise one, i.e. the particular noise source has been measured in sufficient detail and the required degree of quiet is exactly known, it is a simple matter to calculate the insulation required; but the majority of problems are general and not precise. In course of time it may be possible to establish satisfactory standards of insulation for all common noise problems of a constant nature; up to the present the work of the Building Research Station has enabled fairly definite recommendations to be made for standards of insulation between houses and flats, but not between rooms in other types of building. Insulation standards for houses and flats will now be discussed in more detail.

## PARTY WALLS

Walls separating dwellings, whether houses or flats, require special attention as regards sound insulation. Families vary in how much noise they make and in how much noise from next door they tolerate, so it is difficult to lay down any single hard-and-fast standard of sound insulation for dwellings. It might be thought that one answer would be to make the insulation between dwellings so high that nothing at all could be heard of the neighbours through the walls or floors, but this is quite impracticable.

It follows, therefore, that some attempt has to be made to provide sound insulation according to the reasonable needs of different people, though obviously it is not practicable to satisfy every individual. A judgment is always necessary as to the economic standard of sound insulation for a particular scheme or group of dwellings. Social surveys on noise in dwellings have provided useful data on which judgments can be based, and these surveys, coupled with measurements made in existing buildings, have enabled a system of grading of the sound insulation for houses and flats to be formulated.

At one time it was assumed that an average sound reduction factor (p. 51) was an adequate criterion for defining standards of sound insulation between dwellings. Investigation has revealed that this is not so. Once insulation is adequate over part of the range of frequencies, further insulation over that part will not offset any deficiency in insulation over another part of the range, although of course it will increase the average sound insulation figure for the whole range. Thus a continuing annoyance at one end of the range can nullify an improvement at the other. The system of grading described here, therefore, is based on curves specifying the minimum insulation at all frequencies; a single numerical value will not define a grade adequately.

*House party-wall grade*

This grade is based on the performance of the 9-in. brick party wall and no economic alternative to it appears to be feasible at present for semi-detached and terrace houses. With this grade the noise from neighbours is reduced to a level that is acceptable to the majority; a lower standard certainly could not be justified on present evidence. A higher degree of insulation remains a desirable aim but is not yet generally practicable by known simple and economic methods. For example, an 18-in. brick wall might give a gain of only 5 dB over a 9-in. wall at all frequencies, but the gain may in fact be less because of flanking transmission (i.e. transmission along surrounding parts of the structure such as side walls or floors). With a 13½-in. brick wall the corresponding gain would be only about 3 dB.

For flats, the Grade I requirements for party walls are set at a level slightly less stringent than that for houses, for the practical reasons indicated below. The grades are as follows:

*Grade I.* This is the highest insulation that is practicable at the present time for flats. It is based on the performance of a concrete floor construction with a floating floor, which gives the best floor insulation obtainable by normal structural methods. Noise from the neighbours causes only minor disturbance; it is no more of a nuisance than other disadvantages which tenants may associate with living in flats.

*Grade II.* With this degree of insulation the neighbours' noise is considered by many of the tenants to be the worst thing about living in the flats, but even so at least half the tenants are not seriously disturbed.

*Worse than Grade II.* If the insulation between flats is as low as 8 dB worse than Grade II, then noise from the neighbours is often found to be intolerable and is very likely to lead to serious complaints by the tenants. With better insulation than '8 dB worse than Grade II' the likelihood of serious complaint decreases gradually, but when there are also other reasons for dissatisfaction serious complaints about noise may occur at any insulation that is worse than Grade II.

*The grade curves.* The levels of airborne insulation that are required to satisfy the grade for houses and Grades I and II for flats are given in Fig. 16.1. To qualify for a particular grading the insulation should be not less than the value shown at each frequency.

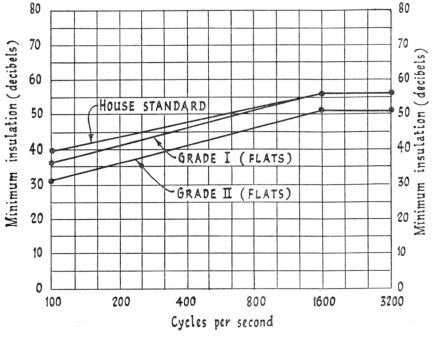

FIG. 16.1

*Grade curves for airborne sound insulation*

The performance in terms of the grades of common party-wall construction is indicated in the following list.

*Satisfactory for houses and Grade I for flats:*
9-in. solid brick, plastered.
11-in. cavity brick, plastered.
7-in. dense concrete, plastered.
12-in. no-fines concrete, plastered.
Two leaves of 3-in. clinker concrete, plastered, with at least 3-in. cavity (butterfly wall ties).

*Grade I for flats, but not satisfactory for houses:*
9-in. no-fines concrete, plastered.
Two leaves of 3-in. clinker concrete, plastered, with 2-in. cavity (butterfly wall ties).

*Grade II for flats; unsatisfactory for houses:*
6-in. no-fines concrete, plastered.
4½-in. brick, plastered.
Two leaves of 2-in. clinker concrete, plastered with 1-in. cavity.

NOTE: In this list, no-fines concrete is assumed to have a density of 100 lb per cu. ft.

*9-in. brick.* As regards sound insulation, the simplest and most reliable construction for party walls is the 9-in. solid brick wall plastered both sides. This construction, as already stated, is the basis of the grade for party walls in houses in relation to which any proposed party-wall construction in houses should be judged.

*Solid concrete.* Any solid party wall of concrete or other material plastered both sides having the same superficial weight as a 9-in. brick wall (i.e. not less than 90 lb/sq. ft) will meet the standard for houses. If ordinary dense concrete is used, either *in situ* or in solid blocks, the thickness required is about seven inches. If the concrete is of an open texture, e.g. 'no-fines' concrete, or most lightweight concretes, it is important that the plastering should not be omitted from any part of the surface and that any flues from fireplaces, etc. should be lined so as to seal off all air-paths through the porous material. The attempt to seal porous concrete walls with linings of wall-board on battens in lieu of plastering is not recommended, as this construction has usually proved to be unsatisfactory for sound insulation. Another construction that should be avoided is dense concrete cast in permanent shuttering of wood-wool slabs, with the surface of the wood-wool plastered. The separation of the plaster from the concrete by a layer of wood-wool rigidly bonded to both materials has been found to cause loss of insulation at an important part of the frequency range.

*11-in. cavity brick.* This construction was recommended at one time for party walls between houses on the basis of its higher average insulation but in fact it need not be preferred to a 9-in. solid wall. Both the 9-in. solid wall and the 11-in. cavity wall, like any other structure, give better insulation at the higher than at the lower frequencies; the 9-in. solid wall is in fact satisfactory at high frequencies, but improvement at low frequencies would be an advantage. The superiority of the 11-in. cavity wall over the 9-in. solid wall, however, is at high frequencies only. There is no consistent difference between the two at low frequencies, which is where improvement is needed; therefore the better insulation of the cavity wall at high frequencies offers no sensible advantage, and there is no basis for recommending it in preference to a 9-in. solid wall between houses. If a cavity wall is used it is important to ensure a cavity not less than two inches wide and to use wire ties of the butterfly pattern, or to omit ties altogether if building regulations permit, otherwise a lower insulation will be obtained.

*Other cavity walls.* Other materials (such as natural stone, concrete blocks or *in situ* concrete) may be used for the leaves of a cavity wall between houses instead of brick, so long as the wall is plastered and the superficial weight of the wall remains the same, namely, not less than 90 lb/sq. ft. If, however, a lightweight (porous) concrete is used, the weight of the wall can be reduced to 50 lb/sq. ft provided the cavity is increased to three inches or more. In all cases the requirements already stated regarding plastering and the use of wall-ties must be met.


# FRAMED STRUCTURES

Any of the constructions mentioned may be built as panels within the bays of framed buildings without affecting the insulation grading, provided the connection between the frame member and the wall panel is made both air-tight and rigid by sealing it with mortar. The practice of inserting strips of non-rigid material (such as cork or felt) round the edges of the panel to separate it from the frame is not recommended; in certain special constructions such strips can be designed to improve the insulation, but in general they are likely to reduce the insulation. In particular, horizontal resilient membranes alone inserted in the walls at floor levels—usually with the object of reducing the flanking transmission up and down the walls—are of no value for the purpose and are best omitted.

*Chapter 17*

# FIRE PROTECTION

## FIRE RESISTANCE OF WALLS

MANY fire resistance tests to B.S. 476 have been made over the past twenty years at the Fire Research Station of the Joint Fire Research Organization. The fire resistance periods assigned for design purposes, from the results of these tests, to some of the more common forms of wall construction are given in Table 17.1.

The fire resistance of solid walls of brickwork or concrete increases in rather more than direct proportion to thickness; walls of lightweight concretes give, weight for weight, higher fire resistance than those made of dense concrete or brickwork; hollow clay or concrete blocks have a similar advantage.

Normal plastering, i.e. with sand mixes, slightly improves the fire resistance of walls provided a good bond to the wall is obtained, but plasters based on perlite or vermiculite can give considerable increases, e.g. the 1-h fire resistance of an unplastered 4½-in. brick wall can be increased to 6-h fire resistance by application of gypsum-perlite plaster ½ in. thick on each side.

The fire resistance of hollow walls with metal or timber studs clad on each side with sheet materials depends on the nature and thickness of the cladding. As normally constructed they do not give more than 1-h fire resistance but if they are specially designed the longer periods of fire resistance can be attained.

## INTERNAL WALLS

The functions of walls in relation to fire protection were indicated broadly in Part I. Detailed requirements vary according to the particular function the wall has to perform, e.g. whether it is a separating wall between buildings, an external wall or, as a special case, a wall enclosing a safe deposit.

Since the separating wall between buildings serves to protect the adjacent owners against each other's hazards, it is clearly desirable to provide a period of fire resistance sufficient to guard against any eventuality. Fortunately the customary minimum separating wall of 9-in. brickwork gives as high a fire resistance as is normally wanted. Where the occupancy on each side of a party wall is known, as in terrace or semi-detached houses, the fire resistance of the party wall can be based on fire load, and for houses 1-h fire resistance is adequate.

It was at one time universal practice to carry the party wall through and above the roof. The practice is still enforced by some authorities; although it entails risk of damp penetration, it prevents the hogging of tiled and slated roofs over the wall which occurs when tiles and slates are bedded on the top of the wall to ensure a fire-tight joint. As the wall is intended to effect a complete separation between buildings, combustible material should not be carried over the top: it is usual to allow tiling battens if they are fully bedded in mortar.

## TABLE 17.1

*Fire resistance (in hours) of some common forms of construction*

| Construction and materials | Minimum thickness in inches (excluding plaster) for period of | | | | |
|---|---|---|---|---|---|
| | 6 hours | 4 hours | 2 hours | I hour | ½ hour |
| BRICKS AND SOLID BLOCK CONSTRUCTION: | | | | | |
| Bricks of clay, concrete or sand-lime built as a solid wall: | | | | | |
| No plaster . . . . . . . | 8½ | 8½ | 8½ | 4 | 4 |
| Built as a cavity wall . . . . . | 10½ | — | — | — | — |
| Concrete blocks: | | | | | |
| Built as a cavity wall: 4½-in. outer leaf: inner leaf of solid or hollow concrete blocks, Class 1 aggregate (inner leaf thickness only) . . . | 4 | 3 | — | — | — |
| Ditto, Class 2 aggregate . . . . | — | 3 | — | — | — |
| Reinforced concrete: | | | | | |
| With minimum concrete cover as reinforcement of 1 in. . . . . . . . | 9 | 7 | 4 | 3 | 3 |
| HOLLOW BLOCK CONSTRUCTION: | | | | | |
| Clay blocks: | | | | | |
| Plastered at least ½ in. thick on each side and shells not less than ¾ in. thick: | | | | | |
| 1 cell in each block and each block not less than 50 per cent solid . . . . | — | — | — | 4 | 3 |
| 1 cell in each block and each block not less than 30 per cent solid . . . . | — | — | — | 6 | — |
| 2 cells in each block and each block not less than 50 per cent solid . . . . | — | — | 8½ | 4 | — |
| 2 cells in each block and each block not less than 30 per cent solid . . . . | — | — | — | 6 | — |
| Concrete blocks: | | | | | |
| Plastered at least ½ in. thick on each side and 1 cell in wall thickness: | | | | | |
| Class 1 aggregate . . . . . | — | 8¾ | 4½ | 3 | 2½ |
| Class 2 aggregate . . . . . | — | — | — | 8¾ | 3 |
| Construction and materials | Minimum thickness in inches for period of | | | | |
| | 6 hours | 4 hours | 2 hours | I hour | ½ hour |
| HOLLOW STUD PARTITIONS, steel or timber studding: | | | | | |
| Plaster on metal lathing: | | | | | |
| Portland cement plaster, Portland cement-lime plaster or gypsum plaster . . . . | — | — | — | ¾* | ½* |
| Plasterboard with or without gypsum plaster: | | | | | |
| ⅜-in. thick plasterboard on each side . . | — | — | — | — | 3/16 (neat, single coat) |
| ½-in. thick plasterboard on each side . | — | — | — | ⅜* | nil* |
| 1-in. wood-wool slab on each side, plastered . | — | — | — | — | ½* |

*Thickness of plaster only.

Separating walls inside buildings (often called division walls) perform precisely the same function as separating walls between buildings, but because they separate parts in the same ownership, there is no need to provide for the contingency of the unknown requirement as happens with the wall separating buildings.

Walls enclosing stairs and lift shafts are one of the main features for protection against vertical spread of fire and in large buildings, where they also provide protected access to upper floors for firemen, they must be effective fire stops. They also protect the means of escape, but where this is the only requirement it is sufficient to provide a fire resistance which will ensure safety only as long as the stairs are being used as an escape route. In general a fire resistance of $\frac{1}{2}$-h or 1-h is then sufficient, as compared with a 2-h or 4-h period if other circumstances have to be considered.

Openings in fire-separating walls need special consideration and doors or shutters which afford adequate fire resistance are needed.

## EXTERNAL WALLS

A load-bearing external wall should have a period of fire resistance sufficient to ensure that it will continue to act as a load-bearing element during a fire, but if it is pierced by numerous window openings through which fire could spread out of or into the building, it would be unreasonable to require it to be of a high standard as a fire stop.

The risk of fire spread between one building and another opposite it depends on the distance between the buildings, their sizes, the amount of opening in the external walls facing each other, on the kind of building, i.e. whether warehouses or offices, etc., and on the construction of the walls. There is, of course, no risk if the buildings are spaced very widely apart and then any amount of window opening can be used safely and, subject to considerations discussed below, the fire resistance of the wall need not be considered. Hence an elevation may consist wholly of glass or of other light construction having little or no value as a fire stop.

Where the distance between the buildings is sufficient to enable the fire services readily to cool a building elevation with water and thus to prevent fire spread, similar considerations apply, but in building to a street line it may be necessary to restrict the amount of opening, because what is appropriate separation for one building may be inadequate for a larger building.

When building elevations are so close together that the full efforts of firefighting cannot be brought into operation, it may be necessary not only to restrict severely the amount of opening but to protect the openings by using fire-resisting glazing, glass block masonry, and in some cases specially designed steel shutters, or by providing a drencher system which enables the elevation to be cooled by a curtain of water running over it. Moreover, the fire resistance of the wall itself must be of a high standard, so that it may act as an effective fire stop.

No single standard of fire resistance for external walls can take into account the possible economies that could be effected by careful consideration of all factors, though some attempt is made to meet the requirements of this complex problem in recent revisions of both English and Scottish building byelaws. Further basic information is needed, however. Thus, when multi-storey buildings are spaced apart sufficiently so that the risk of spread to or from adjacent buildings can be discounted, it remains necessary, if the storeys are fire-separated internally, to consider the risk of spread from storey to storey via windows in the external wall.

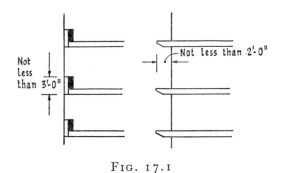

FIG. 17.1

*Wall or fin required to oppose spread of fire upwards from storey to storey*

In normal practice the height of wall between the lintel of a window in one storey and the sill of the window above serves to protect the upper storey against fire passing out of the lower window. If the windows were carried down to floor level this protection would be lost and it is therefore necessary to retain this height of walling of an appropriate grade of fire resistance or to provide other means of protecting the upper storey, e.g. by carrying the floor slab through the wall as a horizontal projection (Fig. 17.1). The minimum period of fire resistance to be specified for the horizontal strip of wall between windows (which is of particular importance in considering curtain-walling systems) is still under consideration at the time of writing (1958).

*Chapter* 18

# DURABILITY AND EXTERNAL FINISHES

THE purpose of this chapter is to discuss the various materials that are used for the external surfaces of walls with particular reference to their durability, their performance in excluding rain, and the changes that may occur in their appearance on weathering. These are all matters that influence the choice of materials.

## BRICKWORK FACINGS

The most important weathering processes affecting brickwork are the following:

(1) Frost acting on brickwork that is saturated or partially saturated.

(2) Disruption by crystallization of soluble salts, deposited in or just beneath the surface of the material by evaporation of moisture.

(3) Expansion of mortar caused by the chemical action of soluble sulphates diffusing into the mortar from bricks containing such salts, when the brickwork remains wet for long periods.

It will be noted that rain is the important factor common to all three. Hence the most general precaution is to design so that, as far as possible, rain is thrown clear of the wall, as discussed in Chapter 14.

*Frost action*

Deterioration of brickwork by frost action is confined to work that freezes while wet. The base of a wall from just below ground level up to the damp-proof course is a critical part, and copings, parapets and other features presenting horizontal surfaces which take up water are even more vulnerable. In England, so far as frost action is concerned, it is usually only for these positions that it is necessary to discriminate in the choice of materials. Any brick that is good enough in other respects should be sufficiently frost-resistant for the main areas of walling.

*Crystallization of salts*

Deterioration of brickwork due to crystallization of salts depends upon the quantity and availability of the salts; they may be derived from the bricks themselves, from the mortar used for jointing and pointing, or by contamination from some source external to the wall itself. Deterioration also depends upon the resistance of the brick itself to the forces exerted by crystallization of salts; this resistance is an important property in good bricks, for it would indeed be difficult to ensure that there will be no contamination by salts in the long life to be expected of a well-built brick wall. It does not seem that resistance is related to any property that can be determined in a simple manner; neither strength, as ordinarily measured by a compression test, nor absorption of water on immersion provides any indication.

Much has been said and written about the behaviour of soluble salts in masonry and brickwork, and a brief digression may be made here to consider the nature and origin of these salts. The salts most commonly found in brickwork are the sulphates of calcium, sodium, potassium and magnesium. These are all soluble in water, though calcium sulphate is considerably less soluble than the others and is less likely on this account to form either a major constituent of efflorescence or to cause disruption by crystallization. Where serious failures of brickwork by salt crystallization have been investigated at the Building Research Station it has nearly always been found that magnesium sulphate or sodium sulphate has been the destructive agent. The presence of nitrates and chlorides is usually an indication of contamination from some external source, such as ground water or material stored in contact with the affected brickwork.

It will be sufficient here to distinguish the various sources from which the salts may originate without too strict an enquiry into the chemistry of their formation:

(1) The bricks themselves. Even if facings are carefully chosen, salts contained in the backing bricks may be transferred to facings by the movement of water in the walls.

(2) The mortar used for jointing and pointing.

(3) Contamination from some external source, such as groundwater, material stacked against the wall, and wind-borne spray from the sea.

(4) Drippings from limestone or concrete dressings conveying calcium sulphate or calcium carbonate in solution.

*Soluble salt content of bricks*

Salts present in the bricks may have been present originally in the clay or tempering water, or they may have been produced during the manufacturing process by the decomposition of compounds present in the clay or by the action of sulphur gases in the kiln. The content of soluble salts of bricks varies enormously, and it would be extremely rare to find any clay brick entirely free from the sulphates of calcium, sodium and potassium. Calcium sulphate, in particular, is very commonly found in bricks but, as already noted, owing to its low solubility it is not an important cause of efflorescence. For any one particular type of brick the salt content may vary over wide limits; certain salts tend to be decomposed and expelled from bricks by hard firing, and in a kiln where close temperature control is not exercised there may be considerable variations in temperature, resulting in a higher concentration of salts in those bricks coming from the cooler part of the kiln. It should be noted that the actual quantity of soluble salts, even in a brick which is quite a bad one in this respect, is very small. Some typical analytical data for the soluble salt content of bricks are shown in Table 18.1 (two samples each of four types) together with brief notes as to the practical implications of these salt contents. It should be noted, however, that the effect of soluble salt content in building materials is so intimately bound up with the capillary properties and pore structure that it would normally be unwise to condemn a material on salt content alone, with the possible exception of the magnesium content.

TABLE 18.1

Results of soluble-salts analyses and efflorescence tests on clay building bricks

| Type of brick | Fletton | | London Stock | | Colliery shale SP common | | Keuper marl WC common | |
|---|---|---|---|---|---|---|---|---|
| | I | 2 | I | 2 | I | 2 | I | 2 |
| Total solubles (per cent by weight) . | 3·70 | 2·39 | 0·20 | 0·77 | 0·96 | 0·29 | 0·86 | 5·70 |
| Composition: | | | | | | | | |
| R₂O₃* . . | 0·06 | 0·02 | nil | 0·02 | 0·11 | 0·02 | nil | nil |
| Ca (calcium) . | 0·97 | 0·62 | 0·06 | 0·18 | 0·06 | 0·03 | 0·21 | 1·40 |
| Mg (magnesium). | 0·01 | 0·01 | 0·01 | 0·01 | 0·03 | 0·03 | 0·03 | 0·04 |
| Na (sodium) . | 0·02 | 0·06 | 0·01 | 0·02 | 0·01 | 0·01 | 0·04 | 0·08 |
| K (potassium) . | 0·02 | 0·02 | 0·01 | 0·05 | 0·03 | 0·03 | 0·05 | 0·17 |
| SO₄ (sulphate) . | 2·13 | 1·42 | 0·11 | 0·42 | 0·29 | 0·08 | 0·49 | 3·38 |
| SiO₃ (silicate) . | 0·04 | 0·06 | nil | 0·05 | 0·01 | 0·02 | 0·04 | 0·03 |
| Liability to efflorescence . . | nil | slight | nil | slight | heavy, iron and potassium sulphates | moderate, magnesium and alkali sulphates | slight | variable, slight to heavy, alkali and calcium sulphates |

SP—stiff-plastic-pressed          WC—wirecut

*$R_2O_3$ is a conventional symbol for the sesquioxides or iron and aluminium ($Fe_2O_3$ and $Al_2O_3$) which are precipitated together in the course of analysis, and are not separated when there is too little to justify the trouble involved.

Portland cement and hydraulic lime mortars may liberate efflorescent salts, usually the carbonates or sulphates of soda and potash. It is now generally realized that efflorescence is likely to appear on new brickwork in cement mortar. Non-hydraulic and semi-hydraulic limes rarely liberate efflorescent salts.

The soil or other filling behind retaining walls may be a prolific source of soluble salts capable of causing efflorescence and decay of brickwork. Ashes and rubble filling in particular can be dangerous; clean crushed stone or brick is to be preferred. Concrete backings may also provide salts. Reinforced concrete lintels and the bearings of reinforced concrete floors may give rise to bands of efflorescence on facing brickwork.

*Calcium sulphate*

It has been mentioned that calcium sulphate is a common constituent of many bricks, but that owing to its low solubility it does not cause much efflorescence. It may, however, cause trouble in another way. In brickwork that remains wet for long periods (of the order of months at a time), cement mortar may be attacked by calcium sulphate from bricks, resulting in expansion and disruption (p. 91). Eminently hydraulic lime mortars may be similarly affected. For sewage works and the like it is therefore desirable to choose bricks free from calcium sulphate. The special case of cement renderings is discussed later in this chapter.

*Selection of clay bricks*

At first sight it would seem a simple matter to specify that bricks should be 'free from soluble salts' or that the 'soluble salt content' should be limited to some definite amount. The first of these alternatives would mean that no clay bricks at all could be used, and the second, unfortunately, would not help either because the total proportion of soluble salts present bears no general relation to freedom from efflorescence and decay. It would be necessary to find the appropriate limit for every particular type of brick throughout the country.

A reliable opinion as to durability and freedom from efflorescence troubles of bricks can be formed from the results of a comprehensive series of tests consisting of chemical analyses of the water-soluble constituents, efflorescence tests and tests of resistance to disruption by crystallization of salts. For an important building an investigation of this kind might be considered by some to be a justifiable precaution.

Failing other means, the architect or builder is thrown back on the age-old practice of observing for himself whether the material he proposes to use is satisfactory. He can inspect buildings in the district where the particular bricks he proposes to use have been employed. In doing this he must ascertain what mortars have been used, for, as has already been mentioned, a perfectly good brick may be marred by an efflorescence derived from the mortar or other material. He can inspect the brickfield, looking out for efflorescence on the stacks (though the absence of this does not necessarily guarantee immunity from trouble in the wall) and the brickmaker will often be prepared to produce evidence of the control he exercises to maintain uniformity in firing conditions.

Finally, an experienced clerk of works or builder's foreman will be able to recognize the presence of underfired bricks in a consignment. Both in salt content and in resistance to crystallization, the underfired brick is the bad one. The so-called 'salmon' should be suspect, even when the colour is one that may harmonize well with the elevational character that the designer wishes to achieve.

The brown staining, mentioned on p.146 as being caused by iron compounds in the brick, is of not very common occurrence but the user may bear in mind its possibility and can guard against it by making enquiry of the manufacturers of the brick. The trouble is confined to comparatively new work, and any precautions taken to prevent the formation of efflorescence in the early life of the wall will tend to minimize the likelihood of its occurrence. Where it is known that bricks are liable to give this trouble, staining can be avoided by delaying the pointing until the wall has been exposed to the weather for a time.

*Selection of sand-lime and concrete bricks*

Sand-lime bricks, if well-made, have ample durability for all normal purposes and are also free from troubles due to a content of efflorescent salts or to deterioration by crystallization of salts derived from other materials. There is a British Standard for sand-lime bricks, and all bricks should be required to comply with it. The Standard specifies three grades of brick:

(1) brick for special purposes, having a high strength and uniformity, and suitable for situations where heavy loads are to be supported, or where conditions of exposure to weathering are particularly severe;

(2) brick of an intermediate grade, of satisfactory durability for external walling;

(3) brick of low grade, suitable for use in internal walls.

A well-made cement concrete product is well established as a durable material and concrete bricks should come in this category. There is also a British Standard for concrete bricks, on lines similar to that for sand-lime bricks.

*Choice of mortar*

The general comments in Part I, on the principles of use of mortars (p. 112) require some amplification here.

There are two main factors by which the characteristics of mortar exert a profound effect on the behaviour of brickwork. These are:

(1) the capillary properties of the mortar;

(2) the content of soluble salts in the mortar.

The ideal at which to aim in the choice of a mortar is to match its properties with those of the particular brick to be used.

If a very dense, impermeable mortar is used with a fairly permeable brick, the flow of water into the wall in wet weather and back again in dry weather will mainly take place through the brick and not through the mortar. In consequence any crystallization of salts will tend to take place on the brick itself and not on the mortar, to the detriment of the appearance of the wall and possibly causing decay of the brick. Generally a choice of mortar strength according to brick strength (p. 160) will give some similarity of capillary properties as well; some general recommendations are given on p. 116.

Soluble salts may be introduced into the mortar either in the cementing material or in the aggregate.

Portland cement and hydraulic limes contain varying quantities (usually small) of soluble salts that may contribute to efflorescence; other limes rarely constitute a significant source of efflorescence. This further supports the case for using cement: lime: sand mixes that are no stronger than necessary.

As a general rule local materials are used for making building mortars; it is rarely economical to transport sands from a distance. Over most of Great Britain there are good deposits of suitable clean sand, but in some districts it is not so easily obtained. Organic impurities in loam and clay are likely to reduce the rate of strength development of Portland cement and hydraulic limes, but will not usually give rise to efflorescence. Sea sand and estuarine deposits may be troublesome unless they are well washed. Ashes and clinker may vary very greatly in their content of soluble salts; the mortars made from them are usually mill-run and a very fine-textured, porous material is produced; efflorescence will tend to be deposited on the joints in preference to the brick. Crushed brick, if clean, is a good aggregate; if contaminated with old plaster and other rubbish it may be very bad.

*Protection of brickwork during construction*

The weather at the time of erection of buildings has an important effect on the formation of efflorescences on brickwork. A very wet winter season will be followed in due course by a crop of reports of trouble in the spring when drying winds arrive. Some of these cases are minor catastrophes, as when a new building in facing bricks assumes a coat of efflorescence so bad as to make it appear that it has been very badly and patchily lime-washed. This has actually happened, and the only remedy that could be suggested was to wire-brush vigorously; this would have the effect of making the deposit look more uniform and would remove the worst of it. The only sure safeguard against such an occurrence is the protection of unfinished work and brick stacks against inclement weather.

*Removal of efflorescence*

Many enquiries are received at the Building Research Station for some simple treatment to remove efflorescence. These are often coupled with the suggestion that some wash with a suitable 'chemical' might effect the desired result. Unfortunately there is no substance that can be recommended for the purpose, and a little reflection will show that this must be so. The efflorescence is a solid deposit and though there are many solutions, including plain water, which will dissolve the deposit, it will only pass into solution and appear again as the excess of liquid evaporates at the surface.

Actually, many of the efflorescences that appear on new brickwork do gradually diminish, by the action of wind and rain, and after a term of years may disappear altogether. The action can be accelerated only by repeated washings with a hose, allowing intervals for the salts to be deposited between washings. Wire-brushing the wall at the times of maximum efflorescence will also help materially, but this is a laborious process; it should not be employed on sand-faced bricks.

*Change in appearance of brickwork facings*

Brickwork offers scope for fine craftsmanship and time deals kindly with it on the whole. In rural surroundings the brick building does not lose its essential architectural characteristics to any important extent. The more porous and absorptive kinds of brickwork acquire a layer of soot in highly polluted atmospheres, but with bricks of the darker tones the colour is obscured but slowly. Texture, which in brickwork can be most interesting, is little altered by exposure; with the softer mortars it tends to be accentuated by weathering.

Light-coloured bricks if rough textured are likely to be defaced by soot deposits more quickly than those of the darker shades. Their use, therefore, is more appropriate for rural and suburban environments.

Modern mortars are much more durable than the old non-hydraulic mixes and the joints may be expected to resist erosion. If emphasis of the brick pattern is required and if it is desired to obtain an effect of relief, this must be produced at the time the wall is built.

In urban districts with highly polluted atmospheres, colour in brickwork may be expected to be masked by soot deposits and should therefore be secondary to form and texture.

## NATURAL STONE

The different natural stones have quite different modes of weathering, depending upon their structure and chemical composition, and as a preliminary it is desirable to attempt some classification; this is given in Table 18.2. In the following notes a brief discussion is presented of the agencies leading to decay of natural stones.

### Effects of frost

The general mechanism of frost action has been described on p. 83. Stones may be injured by this cause, either by the freezing of water in planes of weakness such as the bedding planes or by the freezing of water in the pores. Frost damage in buildings is mostly confined to horizontal surfaces such as the upper sides of copings and cornices, where unprotected stones may be thoroughly soaked. Face bedding of stones where the laminations in the bedding planes are parallel with the exposed face of the stone may accentuate frost decay.

### Soluble salts

The principal cause of the decay of natural stone is the formation of a hard layer or 'skin' due to the deposition of soluble salts. The salts may be formed by the action of atmospheric impurities on constituents of the stone itself, they may be originally present in the stone, or they may be introduced into the wall in other materials. The hard skin has physical properties quite different from the bulk of the stone, and in the course of time it tends to flake off, and the action recurs at the exposed face. The solvent action of acid-laden rainwater, though it will gradually erode the surface of the stone, is not the main cause of stone decay, and is less harmful than the formation of a surface skin with its accompanying exfoliation.

So far as the architect or builder is concerned it will be sufficient to recognize the main sources of the salt deposits that cause decay, and they may be summarized as follows:

(1) By decomposition of the stone itself. Sulphurous acid is a common constituent of polluted atmospheres. Although present in greatest concentration in industrial and urban areas where they originate, the products of atmospheric pollution are carried by the wind far into country districts. Limestones are attacked by the sulphur acids; calcium sulphate is formed with the liberation of carbon dioxide which, in solution, can dissolve away a portion of the limestone and redeposit it in a form in which it is particularly vulnerable to sulphur acid attack. Magnesian limestones are attacked in the same way, with the formation of sulphates of magnesium and calcium. It will be seen that the stones more vulnerable to attack in this way are the limestones (consisting mainly of calcium and magnesium carbonate) and the calcareous sandstones (consisting of siliceous grains cemented by calcium carbonate).

(2) Salts introduced into the stone from materials used in contact with it. It is convenient here to distinguish between the mortar (used for bedding, jointing and pointing) and the backing materials.

It has already been shown in the discussion on brickwork that nearly all cement mortars and some hydraulic lime mortars contain significant quantities of alkali salts. Many cases are recorded where stone decay was undoubtedly due to the crystallization of salts derived from the jointing mortar.

## TABLE 18.2

### Classification of natural stones

| Group | Sub-division | Structure and properties | Exemplified by |
|---|---|---|---|
| Igneous rocks | Acid Intermediate Basic | Mainly crystalline, varying from coarse-grained, completely crystalline to fine-grained, non-crystalline (glassy). | Granite Syenite Diorite Dolerite Basalt |
| Sedimentary | Sandstones | More durable fragments of igneous rocks (quartz, felspar, or mica) cemented together by silica, calcium carbonate, iron compounds, or clay. | |
| | | SILICEOUS SANDSTONES Very durable. Silica cementing material not attacked by water or atmospheric gases. | Craigleith Darney Darley Dale |
| | | CALCAREOUS AND DOLOMITIC SANDSTONES Calcium carbonate and magnesium carbonate are good cements, but are attacked by carbon dioxide and acids in air. Less resistant than the siliceous stones. | Red Mansfield |
| | | FERRUGINOUS SANDSTONES Some weather well; others, where less durable cementing materials are also present, may be less satisfactory. | Corsehill Lockarbriggs |
| | | ARGILLACEOUS SANDSTONES (CLAY-CEMENTED) The poorest type of stone. Suffers bad erosion when wetted. | |
| | Limestones | ORGANICALLY FORMED LIMESTONES Shell or other fragments of biological origin cemented together by calcium carbonate cement. | Hopton Wood Clipsham |
| | | OOLITIC LIMESTONES Oolitic grains cemented at points of contact. No continuous matrix. Oolitic grains in a continuous matrix of crystalline calcium carbonate. | Portland Weldon Casterton Bath oolites Ancaster |
| | Magnesian limestones | Limestones, with a proportion of magnesium carbonate as well as calcium carbonate. In the true 'dolomite' the ratio of calcium : magnesium carbonates approaches that of the mineral dolomite. | Anston Huddlestone Bolsover Moor |
| Metamorphic rocks: may be igneous or sedimentary rocks changed from their original form by heat or pressure. | Marble Quartzite Slate Gneiss | Crystalline, by metamorphism from limestones. Crystalline from sandstones. Crystalline from clay. Crystalline from igneous rocks. | |

Natural stone is commonly used as a facing material with a backing of brickwork or concrete. Bricks containing a considerable proportion of soluble sulphates must be regarded as a potential source of danger to the stone. The ashlar facing to a wall is usually of such thickness that rainwater will not penetrate sufficiently to transfer the salts from the backing to the facing, but where moisture penetrates into the wall from above, salts may be transferred to the face as the wall dries out, and decay may result. This emphasizes the need for proper protection of horizontal surfaces, such as sills, copings and cornices. It is now a common practice to coat with bitumen the back of all masonry that is to be in contact with brick or concrete; such a coating should provide an efficient barrier to the movement of salts from the backing into the facing. Lime and cement washes, which have occasionally been used, are relatively inefficient for the purpose.

An effect has often been noted in buildings where one or other of two natural stones in juxtaposition has decayed prematurely. In particular this tends to occur when limestones and sandstones are used together. The acid gases in the atmosphere react on the limestone, forming soluble salts which are washed down and deposited on or in the surface of the sandstone. In certain circumstances the sandstone may then decay rapidly. The same effect may occur with cast stone and sandstone in juxtaposition, and brickwork has been seen to be injured in the same way. Care is required where different materials are to be combined in a wall. The problem is very likely to arise when repairs are being made to an existing wall.

(3) Salts from the soil. Extensive decay of stonework has often been found to be associated with salts from the soil. The presence of nitrates and chlorides is common in ground waters, and walls should always be provided with damp-proof courses at ground level. Retaining walls and similar features demand particular attention; unless the stone is known to be virtually indestructible a careful waterproofing treatment at the back is a very desirable precaution.

(4) Salts from the air. Sea salt may be air-borne up to some miles inland, and it is as well to select particularly durable stone for use near the sea.

*Mechanism of decay*

The mechanism of stone decay can briefly be summarized as follows:

(1) In the great majority of cases decay is due to the deposition of soluble salts at or immediately below the surface of the stone.

(2) The salts responsible for the decay are formed by attack on the stone by acid constituents of polluted atmospheres or are derived from adjacent materials, from the jointing mortar, from the ground or from the air.

(3) The accumulation of salts is less likely to take place in areas that are freely washed by rain. Stone decay is nearly always worst in sheltered parts of the walls.

(4) The deposited salts form a hard surface skin with properties different from the main body of the stone. This skin tends to flake off through further crystallization taking place beneath it or as a result of other volume changes.

*Preservation of natural stone*

The preservation of natural stone is a subject on which many varied and controversial opinions have been expressed, but one fact is certain and cannot

PLATE 18.1

*Failure of dense cement rendering applied to brickwork containing soluble sulphates*

I*

be too strongly emphasized—that ill-advised attempts to arrest the decay of stone have in the past inflicted grave injuries. There is a very real danger that the decay may be accelerated by unsuitable treatment.

It has been shown that the decay of stone is usually associated with the formation of a surface skin with a high salt content. Liberal washing with water, and nothing else, is calculated to remove the salts by solution, and periodical treatment in this way is the best known method of keeping natural stone in good condition, as well as of enhancing the good appearance of the building.

Nothing but plain water should be used. In the past there have been frequent cases where detergents have been employed in cleaning down masonry buildings and gross decay of the stone has resulted. Although the building may seem cleaner after their use, alkalis and agents of undisclosed composition should under no circumstances be allowed. Soda ash, caustic soda, sodium peroxide, or soap powders may be mentioned as substances that are likely to be very harmful.

Where a building is heavily discoloured by grime the 'steam brush' process is valuable. In competent hands this is quite safe, provided, as with washing by water, that no chemicals are used.

Façades of limestone buildings can be cleaned very advantageously by a fine spray of water. The spray is directed on each area to be cleaned, for an hour or so, when all dark deposits, if not actually washed clear, will be so loosened that they can be removed by gentle brushing. With a very fine spray an excessive amount of water need not be used. The deposit is usually cemented to the face of the stone by calcium sulphate—a salt which is sparingly soluble. Provided the spray is allowed to act for a sufficient length of time the calcium sulphate is dissolved and the deposit is loosened. The process is not likely to be effective on siliceous sandstone buildings, where the dark deposits will not contain significant quantities of calcium sulphate.

The provision on the building of facilities for washing, such as permanent supports for cradles, would be useful.

Many treatments, based on a variety of theoretical reactions, have been proposed. Some are claimed to harden up the loose and friable material, to form hard and resistant skins, or to waterproof the surface of the stone. The subject has been extensively studied and, up to the present, no treatment has been found that can be regarded as a universal panacea; many of the treatments that have been proposed are definitely injurious in the long run and others have no significant effect either in arresting decay or in accelerating it. Special circumstances may arise in which an application of a silicone solution or other 'colourless' waterproofer seems worth trying, but in such cases the treatment should be selected only under expert advice and with full awareness of its probable limitations.

Where a drastic change in the appearance of the wall is not an insuperable objection a completely waterproof treatment such as a good oil paint, applied after cleaning off all friable material when the wall is thoroughly dry, will provide complete protection for as long as the paint is properly maintained. There are a number of high quality imitation stone paints (described towards the end of this chapter, p. 262) which would be equally suitable; these also would require periodical renewal, but probably not so often as ordinary oil paint. Preparations of unknown composition should never be used.

*Selection of natural stone*

There is no simple cut-and-dried procedure that can be recommended for the selection of natural stone. In the past the user has been in the habit of making a careful study of the weathering properties of any particular stone in existing buildings, and this is a valuable method on which to base a selection. It involves one particular difficulty, however, and that is to associate the stone in the building with a particular quarry or bed in that quarry. It is not unusual to find that the different beds in any one quarry have widely different weathering properties.

Chemical analyses have often been produced as evidence of the durability of a stone. Such analyses, though easily obtained, afford singularly little relevant information, since they take no account of the structure of the stone.

Microscopical examination by an expert may be very useful when a thorough study has been made of the weathering of a particular type of stone. The structure is revealed under the microscope and when the characteristics that influence durability have been established a good weathering stone can be identified. In association with simple confirmatory tests this may be sufficient. Investigations at the Building Research Station have enabled durable Portland stone to be identified in this way.

Where the studies of the weathering of a type of stone have been less thorough it is possible to form an opinion of the durability of a particular sample by a comprehensive investigation of its various physical and chemical properties; these are considered in comparison with the properties of similar material of known durability. When a new quarry is opened up an investigation of this kind is the only satisfactory basis for judging the probable durability of the stone.


*The staining of limestone*

It was mentioned on p. 146 that limestone masonry sometimes develops a brown or yellow stain, due to alkali compounds from the mortar passing into the stone and reacting with organic impurities to form soluble compounds; these come to the surface as brown stains, which often persist for years. The association of the stains with the jointing is usually quite apparent to the eye. A simple test for the production of the stain has been devised. A cube of stone is allowed to stand on a cube of mortar with a layer of clean washed blotting-paper between them. The cube of mortar is placed in a shallow dish or tray containing distilled water and the water rises by capillarity through the mortar cube and into the stone, where it evaporates at the surface. The relative tendency for staining of any particular combinations of stone and mortar can be observed in this way. No rule can be laid down as to the relative merits of different mortars in respect of staining, for the effect depends not only on the amount of alkali present but also on its availability. Bad stains have been produced in this test on Portland stone by normal and rapid-hardening Portland cements, and considerably less staining by a white cement and very little indeed by a specially prepared alkali-free cement. The probability is that high-calcium (fat) lime mortars and similar limes with moderate cement gauging (preferably white cement) will cause less staining than straight cement mortars. For an important building a series of staining tests on the actual mortars proposed to be used is well worth while.

*Choice of mortar*

The tendency at the present time is for natural stone masonry to be used as a decorative facing to walls of which the main body is composed of brickwork or concrete. Hence it is very important to ensure that the surface of the stone is not disfigured by efflorescence or staining; it has already been shown that the choice of a suitable mortar can exert an important influence in determining whether or not these defects do occur.

We can define the requirements of a good mortar for masonry as follows:

(1) In colour and texture the mortar must harmonize with the stone to be jointed.

(2) It must be plastic in order that the stones may bed down evenly.

(3) The permeability of the mortar must be considered in relation to that of the stones. There may be some justification for the use of a dense, impervious mortar with a very dense stone, but there is certainly every reason to avoid the use of a dense mortar with stones of fair permeability.

(4) The content of soluble alkali should be as low as possible.

The same considerations apply to mixes for bedding and jointing and for pointing.

There are masons' mortars in general use that fulfil these requirements very well, and typical mixes are as follows:

(1) 16 parts fine crushed stone,
    4 parts lime putty or hydrated lime,
    1 part Portland cement.

This mix has been used in some panels in Portland stone ashlar at the Building Research Station and has made a good hard joint. The mix is a little on the lean side and might suffer somewhat in plasticity on that account.

(2) 12 parts fine crushed stone,
    3 parts lime putty or hydrated lime,
    1 part Portland cement.

This second mix would be rather stronger than the first, but would probably be quite satisfactory.

(3) 7 parts fine crushed stone,
    5 parts lime putty,
    2 parts Portland cement.

This mix is recommended by a firm of stonemasons. It would be highly plastic and rather stronger than either of mixes (1) or (2) above. It might perhaps be criticized for general use as one with which shrinkage might conceivably be troublesome in certain cases.

*Appearance*

The appearance and quality of natural stone as considered in these notes must perforce be confined to the more commonly used British building stones. These materials are chiefly used for buildings of a public or monumental character, for it is only in districts where stone is the natural and available building material that we find stone used in domestic work. Stone is used in the more important permanent buildings and its appearance over long periods of time is at least as important as its appearance in newly erected buildings.

As with other materials, it is desirable to know what changes in colour and texture stone will undergo in the course of time.

The problem of predicting the changes in appearance of natural stone walls involves two main considerations. First is the obscuring of colour by the collection of soot and grime, which essentially is a problem for urban sites, and secondly the emphasis of the masonry pattern by differences in the mode of weathering of individual stones.

*Changes in colour*

The close-textured, impermeable stones, such as the igneous rocks, do not provide lodgment for soot and grime to the same extent as the more porous stones; most of them, moreover, are rather dark in colour, which makes the staining caused by soot less apparent. The rate at which light-coloured stones are obscured by soot deposits depends upon their porosity, upon their resistance to acid-laden atmospheres and upon the extent to which they are washed by rain. The cleansing effect of rain washing is dependent to some extent on aspect in relation to the prevailing winds. Certain limestones, such as Portland stone, are washed clean on the areas exposed to rain—an effect which, no doubt, is aided by slight surface erosion by atmospheric acids. The sandstones generally appear to collect a more uniform coating of soot which is not removed by normal weathering. They do not in fact weather in the same interesting manner as limestone.

*Changes in texture*

The tendency is for differences in texture of individual stones to become more pronounced by weathering. This constitutes the most important single factor in giving interest to masonry. It is virtually impossible to attempt to set out any rules for guidance in predicting the extent of this action, and observation of existing buildings is necessary. If, however, the effect is very pronounced in a moderate period it may be a serious disadvantage for some kinds of architectural treatment. On the other hand, a stone which is so durable that it shows no sign of individuality in its weathering over a period of 30 to 50 years may give a rather dull and uninteresting wall, especially when the colour is obscured by a uniform coating of soot.

# CAST STONE

Cast stone may be defined as a synthetic structural material intended to be used in a similar manner to and for the same purpose as natural stone, and consists essentially of an aggregate bound with some sort of cement. Various synthetic compositions have been used or have been suggested for the cement: for example, stones have been made in which the binding material was lime, hardened by treatment with carbon dioxide, magnesium oxychloride, or a chemically hardening mixture containing silicates. None of these has obtained general acceptance and to-day the cement used consists almost invariably of Portland cement.

Frequently, cast stone is made to represent a particular natural stone. Reproductions of Portland and Bath stone, sandstones and granite are commonly made in this way. Often the reproduction of the natural material is so good that the difference is inappreciable, except to the expert.

*History of cast stone*

Although the use of cast stone made with Portland cement as the binding medium is of recent date, it is older than is sometimes supposed. There are several buildings in London where cast stone fixed in the year 1900 may be seen. In Scotland there is a much older example: at the village of Loanhead, near Edinburgh, the village church was built in 1875, the masonry being cast stone made by local labour. Generally the condition of the work is good, the surface being clean and without noticeable crazing. The effect of the weather has been so slight that the pattern impressed in moulding is still practically perfect. There are some large cracks in the walls, but these are due to coalmining subsidences. Yet it cannot be said that the stone was of the highest possible quality, for the aggregate contained a proportion of very inferior material—shale from a burnt-out coal shale bing—and some surface defects have occurred from this cause. A rather interesting feature is that under the arch of the doorway the cast stone is blistering in a manner similar to that often seen with natural stone in similar positions, showing that the weathering properties of the natural and synthetic material have something in common. During the long period of weathering the stone has developed lichen growths.

The oldest example of cast stone on record is at Carcassonne. This dates to about the year 1138, when the Visigoth walls were repaired. Viollet-le-Duc says (1878) of this stone:

'We must not omit to mention a very curious fact concerning the history of the construction. Most of the gates and windows of the towers of the castle on the yardside are coped with lintels in the concrete. Those factitious stones have resisted atmospheric influences much better than sandstones; they are composed of perfectly hard mortar mixed with pounded pebbles, large like an egg, and must have been fashioned in wooden boxes. After having observed on the spot some of those lintels, my attention being roused, I found a pretty large number of those concrete blocks in the outward restorations of the Visigoth walls undertaken in the twelfth century. It would seem that the builders of the latter period, when they wanted strong materials of comparatively large dimension, made use of that process, which proved perfectly successful; for none of these lintels got broken, as happened frequently to the stone lintels.'

These lintels were considered of such interest in relation to the history of building that through the courtesy of the French Government some samples were obtained. From these it was possible to obtain more accurate knowledge of their composition than that given by Viollet-le-Duc's general description. The material consisted of large fragments (up to two or three inches) of sandstone, cemented with a mixture of lime with crushed potsherds. Whether a hydraulic or non-hydraulic lime had been used could not be determined, but evidently the cement was essentially a pozzolanic mortar. Microscopic examination showed around the burnt clay fragments a zone where combination with the lime had occurred. The cement mixture contained an abundance of combined silica; so much that, on cautious treatment of the material with dilute acid, masses of gelatinous silica, preserving the shape of the original fragments, were obtained. The cementing medium in these lintels is thus not entirely dissimilar from hydrated Portland cement in the modern product.

## Crazing

Crazing consists in the development of network of fine cracks on the surface, and it is this effect that often, after a lapse of time, reveals the true character of a material that otherwise might not be recognized as artificial. Crazing of concrete products is a very variable phenomenon. The scale of the network may vary from about four or six inches between the cracks, down to a spacing so fine that it can only be seen under a microscope. The cracks are generally narrow; in the larger crazing they are only of the order of 1/500 in. wide. The majority of well-made concrete products do not craze, but a proportion develop the defect after various periods: sometimes before a concrete product is sufficiently mature to be sold; sometimes after exposure to the weather for months; sometimes after years. Although the art of making cast concrete products is as old as Portland cement itself, until recently no method had been discovered by which crazing could be controlled, though by trial and error some manufacturers had discovered means of limiting the frequency of its occurrence.

There has, however, been an element of uncertainty in these methods; thus it was found that of a batch of blocks made from the same aggregates, with the same proportion of cement and at the same consistence, all cured, it was thought, in an identical manner, some blocks might craze while others remained indefinitely unblemished. 'Remedies'—often proprietary materials of secret composition and used either as additions to concrete or solutions or emulsions for surface application—have always abounded, but in course of time the comparative ineffectiveness of most methods has been amply demonstrated.

The main cause of crazing has recently been shown to be differential moisture shrinkage between the surface layer and the adjacent layer underneath. Control thus depends upon so adjusting the several variables in the manufacturing process as to avoid steep moisture gradients arising in the stone facing, when it is on the building.

In choosing cast stone finishes it is important to inspect as large a specimen as possible. Generally speaking, the rather coarser textures are likely to be the more satisfactory from the point of view of freedom from crazing, and they will generally look well in the building, though they may not be so attractive in very small samples. A very fine, smooth texture calls for the use of fine aggregate and surface trowelling, both of which tend to promote crazing. Suitable mortars for cast stone are indicated on p. 116.

## Weathering

It is not possible to generalize on the durability of cast stone, for its properties can be varied to suit the condition of exposure required. There is now a British Standard for cast stone (B.S. 1217: 1945), whose requirements are adequate to secure structural stability and weatherproofness. But the actual degree of permeability, upon which the weathering properties depend, may be varied, within the limits imposed, over a wide range. Some types have a rather porous, open texture, resembling some of the softer natural stones. Others have a dense structure and a correspondingly high resistance to weathering. The weathering properties of the former more resemble those of natural stones. The only caution that should be given is that the more porous and absorptive types of stone should not be used in highly polluted atmospheres, because acid from the atmosphere may produce surface softening and dusting.

*Appearance*

The colour and texture oi cast stone can be controlled in the process of manufacture and it is possible, by suitably adjusting the mix, to determine to some extent how the material will weather.

Colour is determined by the use of coloured aggregates, white cement and pigments. Texture can be controlled by the choice of aggregate and by the method of finishing the surface after casting. The rate of accumulation of soot and grime depends, as with most other walling materials, on the porosity and roughness of the stone.

As a general rule there will be distinct differences between the weathering characteristics of natural and cast stone. It will have been noted that the tendency is for natural stone to acquire an individuality in the wall by subtle differences in the mode of weathering of individual blocks, which, provided the effect is not exaggerated, undoubtedly enhances interest in the work. The denser and more impervious cast stone, carefully controlled in the process of manufacture, is likely to be uniform in its mode of weathering, so that the contrasts between individual blocks, which enhance the attraction of natural stone masonry, may often be lacking.

The more open-textured cast stones, particularly those made with semi-dry mixes, are likely to show definite variation on weathering, for small alterations in any of the conditions of manufacture of a semi-dry mix may result in quite wide differences in the properties of the finished product.

Being moulded, cast stone lends itself to ornamental effects—not to intricacy in small details, but broad effects can be obtained satisfactorily. By suitable adjustment of the mix and by working at the appropriate age it is possible to carve cast stone with good results. Close co-operation between the manufacturer and the carver is desirable to achieve the best results, and it seems possible that the potentialities of the material in this direction have not by any means been fully explored yet. Cast stone can be made to resemble natural stone in colour, texture, and finish, but the modern tendency is to allow the true cast stone technique to emerge, which has its own characteristics of colour and texture.

## PLAIN CAST CONCRETE UNITS

Cast concrete blocks may be of dense concrete made from gravel or crushed rock or of one of the lightweight concretes described on pp. 110–2.

*Dense concrete blocks*

There are two principal types of dense concrete units. The first, generally a block moulded from a semi-dry mix, has a porous, open texture and makes no pretensions to impermeability. When used in external walling it is intended to be protected by a rendering, for which the rough, open-textured surface provides an excellent key. Blocks of this type have the advantage of low shrinkage, for they are generally lean and their porosity allows them to dry quickly in the stack before delivery to the building site. The second type, which may be of block or slab form, is intended to be used as a facing. These are made from richer concrete and moulded from a wetter mix than the former type. As a result there is a greater liability to shrinkage. Concrete slabs have been made with an exposed-aggregate finish, giving the effect of roughcast or pebble-dash.

Concrete blocks and slabs are used for a variety of purposes, particularly the following:

> external walls of houses and factories, rendered or unprotected according to type,
> as a backing to brickwork in external walls,
> for partitions,
> for panels in steel frame buildings.

Recently there have been great advances in the design of concrete blocks, but units of very poor patterns have been produced. A block intended to be laid by hand might reasonably be expected to possess the following qualities:

(1) It should bond with ordinary sizes of bricks, the length, height and breadth being suitable multiples of brick plus joint dimensions.

(2) It should be light enough to be lifted and laid by one man.

(3) It should be cored to reduce weight and impede moisture penetration.

(4) The design of joints should allow of a break in the capillary moisture path at these points.

(5) If used for facing, it should have a suitable texture and colour, or if intended for rendering should provide a good key for the rendering.

The precautions to be taken to avoid or minimize shrinkage cracking in concrete block masonry have been outlined on p. 193 and suitable mortars on p. 116.

*Lightweight concrete blocks*

The main types of lightweight concrete and their properties have been described in Chapter 11 (pp. 110–2). On account of the seproperties, blocks of lightweight concrete cannot at present be recommended for external use in climates such as that of the British Isles unless some protective coating is applied to reduce moisture absorption. It is the properties of this coating that will then determine the durability. The durability of rendered and paint finishes is discussed later in this chapter.

# TERRA-COTTA

Terra-cotta has a fired clay body which may or may not be coated on the surface with a glaze. In some parts of the country the term 'terra-cotta' is restricted to unglazed ware, other material being known as 'faience' or 'glazed ware'. It is manufactured mostly in the form of hollow pieces, purposely made to the design of the architect.

Terra-cotta can be extremely durable; in Northern Italy many examples of medieval work are in a perfect state of preservation. Any deterioration that does occur is similar to that of other clay products: erosion of the surface by the crystallization of soluble salts or by frost action. It is probably fair to state that the chief reason to doubt the durability of terra-cotta was the poor behaviour of a pinkish-buff material for which there was rather a vogue in the late nineteenth century. This would be termed 'underburnt' by present-day criteria.

As terra-cotta blocks are usually hollow and may be filled with concrete before fixing, the use of unsuitable materials for filling has caused a certain amount of damage. Only sound aggregate, such as would satisfy the relevant British Standard, should be used.

A somewhat unsightly disfiguration sometimes results from the crazing of the glaze on glazed terra-cotta, to form a network of fine cracks in which dirt and grime collect. This may be due to differences in properties between the glaze and the body, so that thermal movements result in differential stresses which are relieved by cracking of the glaze, or to stresses caused by shrinkage of a cement mortar used in fixing the material to the wall.

As with many other materials, the architect or builder may satisfy himself by inspection of existing buildings that the product of a particular manufacturer is durable.

The same conditions govern the choice of mortars for terra-cotta as for natural stone and brickwork.

*Cleaning*

Since the crystallization of soluble salts is one of the agents that may cause decay, it is most undesirable in washing terra-cotta to use any detergent containing soluble alkali compounds. Soap powders, soda ash, caustic soda, or sodium peroxide or any cleaning preparation of undisclosed composition should be rigorously excluded. Clean water or the steam brush alone should be used. One of the outstanding advantages of the smooth, glazed varieties of terra-cotta lies in the fact that the relative impermeability of its surface minimizes the collection of dirt and grime, so that a façade is easily cleaned by washing.

*Appearance*

Good terra-cotta has unsurpassed weathering qualities and remains virtually unchanged for centuries. In its earlier medieval development in Northern Italy it was essentially a medium for fine modelling. In the revival of the use of terra-cotta in the nineteenth century, ornament in relief was a main feature, and the potentialities of the material to receive colour still remained to be exploited. In recent years the trend has been towards the suppression of ornament and the development of light-coloured ware with almost limitless possibilities in the way of coloured glazes.

In an urban atmosphere where sheltered by projecting features, terra-cotta will acquire a coating of soot. Where freely washed by rain the light-coloured modern ware keeps clean. The developments in modern glazes are such that brilliant colours can be obtained, and these may be expected to be highly durable.

Terra-cotta differs to a marked extent from the walling materials previously discussed in that there is very little tendency for the blocks to develop an individuality on weathering. The architectural appeal must therefore be based on uniformity of colour and texture, colour contrast deliberately introduced, and form, since, for the time being at any rate, fine modelling in relief seems to have been abandoned.

To summarize, terra-cotta is a material that loses very little of its essential characteristics on exposure. It cannot therefore be expected to gain in interest by weathering as do some other materials.

## RENDERINGS

The external cement-rendered (stucco) wall has produced some very disappointing results and a number of particularly bad failures. It is interesting to note the stages in the evolution of the external renderings in Great Britain which have led up to the present unsatisfactory condition.

The earliest material in common use was probably a plain lime plaster with no hydraulic setting properties. Such plasters have been used for centuries in country districts. Liable to deteriorate rapidly when exposed directly to rain or frost, they were protected with a coat of paint or, more often, simple washes made from lime and tallow or lime and linseed oil. So long as the protective coatings remained in good condition and were regularly maintained, the lime plasters were sufficiently durable for use on buildings with good eaves protection and where conditions of exposure were not too severe.

The next step forward was the use of hydraulic plasters; these usually consisted of hydraulic limes, 'natural' cements or 'Roman' cement. These had definite hydraulic setting properties and developed fair strengths when suitably handled, though, doubtless, there would be very great variations in the actual strength obtained. We still have left to us a great deal of eighteenth- and early nineteenth-century work, especially that of Nash in London and Brighton, and much of this is in good condition. The work of this period was painted, almost without exception, in a good oil paint, and it is quite usual for leases to contain clauses requiring repainting at two-year intervals. A close inspection of these renderings is interesting. It will often be found that redecoration has included a host of minor repairs, in the form of patches and stoppings; where the paint has been allowed to fall into disrepair, deterioration of the rendering has been rapid.

Up to this stage there was no attempt to produce an unprotected external plastered finish. Towards the latter part of the nineteenth century, the first attempts were made to obtain unpainted external renderings using Portland cement. The roughcast finish was perhaps the most successful, and a great deal of work of that period is still in very good repair to-day.

After the first World War came the introduction of white cements; originally these were of foreign origin and there were intensive advertising campaigns for certain materials. At the same time there were rapid advances in the rate of hardening and strength development of Portland cements. These changes were of the utmost service to the structural engineer, but they were disadvantageous as regards external cement renderings. A smooth, trowelled surface in white cement was very attractive; a brilliant uniform whiteness could be obtained and a new style or architectural treatment was in progress of evolution in which many traditional features were suppressed and the use of bold, unbroken areas of uniform colour and texture was becoming common. The uncovered, dense external rendering in Portland cement became accepted as a working possibility. Unfortunately it was very often disappointing in practice. Surface crazing and shrinkage cracking developed which, at times, were so bad as to render the walls unserviceable. The disadvantages of a relatively impermeable skin, when it cracks, have already been mentioned on several occasions in this book.

*Failures of dense cement renderings*

Renderings are applied in a wet state with an excess of water; as they dry they tend to shrink. This sets up stresses—partly tensile stresses in the rendering and partly shear stresses where the rendering adheres to the backing. The tensile stresses tend to cause cracks, and the shear stresses may cause failure of adhesion. Failures often occur in both ways. If the adhesion of the rendering to the backing is uniformly good, however, the restraint provided in this way may be sufficient to take up the shrinkage stresses; where dense renderings prove successful it will nearly always be found that the adhesion is very good.

In addition to the shear forces tending to break down adhesion, there is a further process that may contribute to failure: differential moisture movement between the outer and inner faces of the rendering. This is most severe where the wall behind the rendering gets saturated by rain penetrating through cracks or by way of some structural defect. When there are drying conditions at the outer face and damp conditions at the back, the front of the rendering shrinks and the back expands, and as a result it tends to assume a curved form and this is another factor leading to a breakdown of adhesion. When a rendering has cracked badly it will very often be found that it is hollow and curling away from the wall at the cracks, the curvature being visible to the eye.

There is a particular type of failure that results from rain penetrating cracks in a rendering that is too dense to permit subsequent rapid drying, or perhaps from interstitial condensation within the wall (see p. 42). With bricks containing a high content of soluble sulphates there is a reaction with the cement of the rendering under damp conditions (p. 91) which leads to progressive breakdown of adhesion (Plate 18.1).

*Types of mix to use*

It has been shown that there are fundamental difficulties in obtaining renderings free from shrinkage cracking in plain cement-sand mixes. They are too strong for their job and the margin of safety against cracking is at best a very small one. Mixes of cement, lime and sand, in various proportions, give a wide range of strength, frost resistance and permeability, from which a finish appropriate to a given background and degree of exposure may be selected. Suitable mixes for a variety of finishes and conditions are given in Table 18.3.

Replacement of part of the cement, in a cement-sand mix, by lime has several consequences. Workability is improved, and water is more readily retained against the suction of the background. The material being weaker,

## TABLE 18.3

### Mixes for external renderings

Recommended composition of mix, as proportion of cement-lime-sand* (parts by volume) for the following conditions:

| Treatment | On strong or moderately strong backing materials | | | On weak or moderately weak materials | On wood-wool building slabs |
|---|---|---|---|---|---|
| | Severe exposure | Moderate exposure | Protected | | |
| Spatter-dash . . . | 1:0:2 to 1:0:2½ | 1:0:2 to 1:0:3 | 1:0:2 to 1:0:3 | not recommended | not recommended |
| Pebble-dash (undercoat and finish coat) . . . | 1:0:3 | 1:0:3 to 1:1:5 | 1:1:5 | not recommended | 1:0:3 to 1:1:5 |
| Roughcast undercoat . . . finish coat . . . | 1:0:3<br>1:0:3† | 1:0:3 to 1:1:6<br>1:0:3† to 1:1:6† | 1:0:3 to 1:1:6<br>1:0:3† to 1:1:6† | 1:1:6<br>1:1:6† | 1:1:6<br>1:1:6† |
| Scraped and textured (undercoat and finish coat) . . . | 1:1:6 | 1:1:6 to 1:2:9 | 1:2:9 | 1:1:6 to 1:2:9 | 1:0:3 to 1:1:6 |
| Smooth (floated) (undercoat and finish coat) . . . | 1:1:6 | 1:1:6 to 1:2:9 | 1:2:9 | 1:1:6 to 1:2:9 | not recommended |
| Machine applied undercoat . . . finish coat . . . | 1:1:6 | 1:1:6 to 1:2:9<br>as for undercoat or proprietary mixes | 1:2:9 | 1:1:6 to 1:2:9 | 1:1:6 |

*The proportion of sand given is for a well graded material. With very coarse or uniformly fine sands use 8 instead of 9, and 5 instead of 6 parts.

†This refers to parts of sand plus gravel or crushed stone; the ratio of sand to stone or gravel should be between 1:1 and 2:1 according to the texture required.

shrinkage if not entirely restrained by the background tends to result in the formation of a multitude of tiny hair cracks rather than a few big ones; being more absorbent, it takes up water falling on its surface or entering fine cracks, and water so held will not reach the background; being more permeable, it permits the ready evaporation of any water that does penetrate.

Recently it has been found that similar advantages result from using aerated mortars, discussed on p. 115, for renderings. At present they are at the trial stage, and it would be premature to form any general conclusions about their performance and durability.

*Brickwork for rendering*

The view has sometimes been held that, since it will be covered up, any brick is good enough for a wall that is to be rendered. Enough has been said to show that this must be wrong and that the requirements actually are exacting. The brick must be well fired and hard, to resist the shrinkage stresses in the rendering. The surface of a rather poor brick may be pulled off by a strong rendering. Adhesion is all-important; a good sand-lime brick or a London stock are examples of types of brick with which excellent adhesion is developed by renderings. These are characterized by a medium to rather high'suction'. Grooved and 'keyed' bricks, where the key is definitely undercut, favour adhesion.

To lay down limits for the content of soluble sulphates would be to exclude large sources of supply of cheap bricks which, otherwise, are very useful products. Perhaps the safest line to take is to bear in mind that sulphate attack on renderings is nearly always associated with access of damp behind a dense skin and, if we cannot limit the sulphate content of the bricks, then we must keep out the damp. Parapets, gables, and garden walls are the worst offenders, and some suggested details are shown in Fig. 18.1. Bricks of high sulphate content should not be chosen for exposed features of this kind that are to be rendered, even if a less exacting choice is decided on for the main area of walls in the building.

*Technique of application*

Applying a plastic mix by means of a trowel is skilled work, and there is little doubt that the degree of skill is one of the factors that make for success. Unfortunately this craft skill cannot be put into words, nor can explicit instructions be laid down in a specification. To obtain good adhesion with a plastic material applied to any surface it is necessary to expel the film of air that tends to remain at the interface. This depends upon the porosity of the background, on the consistence of the plaster mix and on the force expended by the plasterer. Generally, a mix that is thrown on, by hand or machine, adheres more securely to its background than does a similar mix smoothed on from a trowel. The techniques of machine application, by 'spattering box' or pneumatic 'gun' have been widely adopted in this country since 1945.

*Finishes for renderings*

Care should be taken to avoid working up a rich skin to the surface. Wood-float finishes are to be preferred to the steel trowel. Scraping has two main advantages: it gives a uniform finish and at the same time removes all the rich, fatty skin which comes up even with the wood-float. The finishing

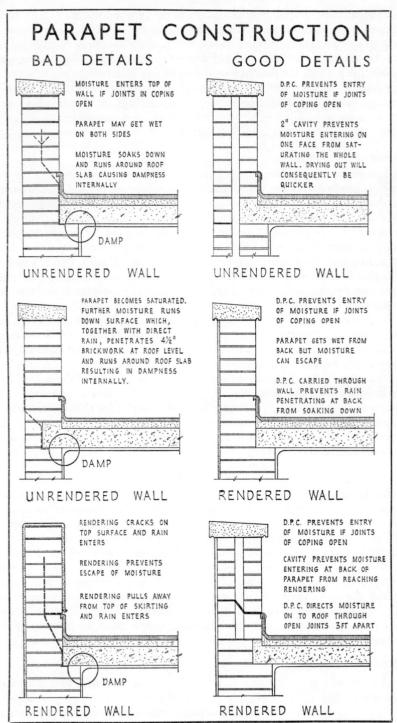

# PARAPET CONSTRUCTION

## BAD DETAILS

MOISTURE ENTERS TOP OF
WALL IF JOINTS IN COPING
OPEN

PARAPET MAY GET WET
ON BOTH SIDES

MOISTURE SOAKS DOWN
AND RUNS AROUND ROOF
SLAB CAUSING DAMPNESS
INTERNALLY

DAMP

UNRENDERED WALL

PARAPET BECOMES SATURATED.
FURTHER MOISTURE RUNS
DOWN SURFACE WHICH,
TOGETHER WITH DIRECT
RAIN, PENETRATES 4½"
BRICKWORK AT ROOF LEVEL
AND RUNS AROUND ROOF SLAB
RESULTING IN DAMPNESS
INTERNALLY.

DAMP

UNRENDERED WALL

RENDERING CRACKS ON
TOP SURFACE AND RAIN
ENTERS

RENDERING PREVENTS
ESCAPE OF MOISTURE

RENDERING PULLS AWAY
FROM TOP OF SKIRTING
AND RAIN ENTERS

DAMP

RENDERED WALL

## GOOD DETAILS

D.P.C. PREVENTS ENTRY
OF MOISTURE IF JOINTS
OF COPING OPEN

2" CAVITY PREVENTS
MOISTURE ENTERING ON
ONE FACE FROM SAT-
URATING THE WHOLE
WALL. DRYING OUT WILL
CONSEQUENTLY BE
QUICKER

UNRENDERED WALL

D.P.C. PREVENTS ENTRY
OF MOISTURE IF JOINTS
OF COPING OPEN

PARAPET GETS WET FROM
BACK BUT MOISTURE
CAN ESCAPE

D.P.C. CARRIED THROUGH
WALL PREVENTS RAIN
PENETRATING AT BACK
FROM SOAKING DOWN

RENDERED WALL

D.P.C. PREVENTS ENTRY
OF MOISTURE IF JOINTS
OF COPING OPEN

CAVITY PREVENTS MOISTURE
ENTERING AT BACK OF
PARAPET FROM REACHING
RENDERING

D.P.C. DIRECTS MOISTURE
ON TO ROOF THROUGH
OPEN JOINTS 3FT APART

RENDERED WALL

FIG. 18.1

coat is scraped with a wooden or steel straight-edge just as it is beginning to harden off, about $\frac{1}{16}$ in. to $\frac{1}{8}$ in. thickness of material being removed. Where a coloured aggregate is used this is well exposed and a great variety of textures can be obtained by varying the size and grading of the aggregate. By using rather coarse pebbles in the finish a kind of 'travertine' texture is produced by scraping. When specially shaped blades are employed for the scraping tool the finish can be patterned in various ways. An ordinary saw gives a ridge and furrow effect which can be quite interesting.

Roughcast and pebble-dashes are well-tried finishes for strong renderings. They provide a surface that is virtually discontinuous, and shrinkage stresses may be relieved by the formation of fine cracks round individual pieces of aggregate. These cracks are visible to the eye on close inspection. Scraped finishes with mixes containing a rather coarse aggregate give much the same effect, the continuity of the surface being broken up by movement of the larger grains under the scraper.

*Rendered parapets*

The rendered parapet has produced some very bad failures indeed, especially when the rendering has been carried over the top and a coping dispensed with. These parapets nearly always go wrong. The conditions of exposure are such that a rendering on a horizontal surface is very liable to crack and, once it has cracked, the rain enters. Thereafter, the rendering hinders evaporation and the wall remains waterlogged and, gradually, the adhesion of the rendering breaks down. This effect is particularly marked with bricks which contain a high amount of soluble sulphates. There are plenty of bricks which are quite satisfactory uncovered but which contain too high a proportion of sulphate to take a rendering in a position such as a parapet. The top of a parapet should incorporate a continuous impermeable membrane (Fig. 18.1) and the rear face of the parapet, at least, should be left unrendered.

*Appearance*

With external renderings it is necessary to consider very carefully indeed what alterations in appearance are likely to take place on exposure. There are many buildings on which rendered finishes must be regarded as unsuccessful on account of the patchy or drab appearance they have developed.

The rendered surface, uniform in colour and texture, is an important adjunct to architectural essays in pure form. Uniformity of colour and texture is the first essential, but the colour must be attractive none the less. It would require a superlative effort in form to carry off a drab and dingy colour. In such cases colour and uniformity of colour, therefore, are of the greatest value.

Texture is a secondary consideration and not very much in evidence in modern external renderings, though highly textured finishes have been obtained by manipulation of the trowel, by dragging twigs or sacking, and in other ways. It is hardly necessary to remark that texture becomes predominant with roughcast and pebble-dashed finishes.

The important factor that outweighs everything else is the change of colour with the accumulation of soot and grime. The lighter the colour the more rapidly will this change occur.

As on other surfaces, the collection of soot depends on roughness, porosity and absorptive properties. Rain streams over dense, non-absorptive surfaces and washes away soot deposits, but tends to do so irregularly, and a streaky appearance results. In smoke-laden atmospheres, open-textured, porous finishes will collect grime rapidly and will lose much of their attractiveness. Roughcast work collects grime very much in the same way as other rendered work; if anything the action may proceed more rapidly on account of the lodgment for dirt afforded by the rough surface. Pebble-dashing retains its original appearance over a longer period than almost any trowel-applied coating. The surface of the pebbles is so smooth and dense that soot deposits are washed off by rain, and, moreover, the original colour is dark and not nearly so readily obscured as with lighter renderings.

The provision of proper flashings and drips can do a lot to control the pattern of weathering, as has been mentioned on pp. 215-6.

*Discolouration due to vegetation.* There is a tendency for the more open-textured finishes to take on a greenish discolouration due to growth of algae or other forms of vegetation, particularly on north-facing walls and other areas where dampness may persist for long periods. This form of green discolouration can be removed, and its recurrence inhibited, by a simple wash of a dilute copper salt made up as follows: copper carbonate, 1 oz; ammonia solution (sp. gr. 0·880), 10 fl. oz; water, 10 gallons. There are also proprietary algicides available.

## MONOLITHIC CONCRETE

Precast concrete walling units, blocks or decorative cast stone, have been dealt with earlier. It remains here to discuss the problems presented by monolithic reinforced concrete as a walling material.

### Resistance to weathering

In 1954, a survey was made, jointly by the Building Research Station and the Cement and Concrete Association, to collect evidence as to the durability of reinforced concrete in parts of buildings exposed to the weather. The ages of the buildings examined varied from under twenty to over fifty years: the types and exposures from office blocks in clean atmospheres to gas works, chemical works and the like in industrial areas by the sea. Some even among the oldest buildings seen, when properly designed and constructed, had not begun to show signs of deterioration; others, in a much shorter life, had suffered badly from corrosion, nearly always because the concrete cover to the reinforcement was too thin or of poor quality. Two general conclusions were drawn: that most of the defects observed could have been avoided had greater care been taken during construction; and that, even in those buildings which had seriously deteriorated, effective repairs were nearly always possible and economically justified.

### Protection of reinforcing steel

Steel rusts in the presence of air and moisture; the action proceeds the more rapidly in the presence of acids in the moisture or air and also in the presence of certain salts. A highly polluted industrial atmosphere will often give rise to specially corrosive conditions because of the presence of sulphur acids derived from the combustion of coal, and sea-water exposure has a similar effect due to the chlorides present. Something less drastic than actual sea-water exposure exists in buildings near the sea, where salt spray may be carried in the air during gales.

The concrete covering to the reinforcing steel affords protection in two ways. First, it prevents the access of air and moisture to the steel; and, secondly, it is strongly alkaline and hence has a corrosion-inhibiting effect. The alkalinity is soon lost in a porous concrete however, as carbon dioxide combines with the alkalis, including free lime, liberated in the setting of the cement.

The essential conditions, therefore, for the protection of the steel in reinforced concrete are the following:

(1) The concrete cover over the bars must everywhere be sufficiently thick—at least $1\frac{1}{2}$ in.

(2) The concrete mix must be dense throughout and care must be taken especially to avoid local weak spots at construction joints and the like. Rigid supervision is necessary, and since it is virtually impossible to tell whether a concrete is good simply by looking at it, some system of methodical testing is valuable.

(3) Shrinkage of the concrete must be controlled and distributed by suitably designed reinforcement, so that wide cracks are avoided, since these would allow the access of air and moisture to the steel. This is the most difficult condition to fulfil and it calls for a highly specialized technique (see p. 173).

As regards the concrete itself, the cement is slowly broken down by the solution of certain of its constituents in water that is slightly acid, as is rain water. This action is very slow indeed in a good concrete, and is usually manifested only by the removal of the cement film and exposure of the sand grains on the surface after a long period of weathering.

*Appearance*

The good appearance of monolithic concrete walling depends more upon the treatment of the formwork pattern than on any other single factor. It was at one time thought that the ideal arrangement would be to construct the formwork so that no trace of its structure appeared on the concrete face. This, however, is not easily achieved, in many cases would be ruled out on economic grounds, and in any case is found not to achieve the effect aimed at by the designer. Large sheets of waterproofed plywood or other material are sometimes used to line the formwork with the object of reducing the number of joints, and sheet-metal linings have also been developed. An alternative is to admit the board pattern but to control it with care. Thus boards should be matched for width; vertical joints should be staggered and lined up one above the other; and the finished building would then have a neat and workmanlike appearance. To keep the board pattern subdued it is necessary to use wrought boarding and to ensure that the boarding is matched for quality. A mixture of old and new timber may give an unhappy result owing to unequal absorption of the water from the setting concrete, which may give startling textural differences in the concrete. Yet another alternative is to emphasize the board pattern, and this has been done in some buildings.

The day-to-day construction joints in the concrete present a difficult problem. However carefully the joints are made it is inevitable that they will appear on the face of the wall as strongly marked lines. If no precautions are taken these lines will be irregular and are then very unsightly. The first step is to ensure a regular, horizontal joint line. This will improve the appearance of the joints, but will not eliminate them, and it remains so to dispose the joints that they are regularly spaced and bear some relation to other architectural features of the building elevation, such as sills and lintels of openings. The joint planes can be concealed at string courses and cornices. This implies that the position of the construction joints will be as much a part of the architect's design as any other elevational feature. Another feature that tends to give unwanted emphasis to the construction joint arises from the fact that when the wet concrete is poured and consolidated in the forms the pressure on the forms is greatest at the bottom of the lift; this tends to make the forms bulge slightly at the bottom of the lift and the concrete projects somewhat immediately above each construction joint. This can be overcome by using stiffer forms, but to do so may not always be economical. If, however, the construction joints are uniformly spaced in relation to the design of the elevation the effect may not necessarily be objectionable.

It is possible to obtain various textures by treatment of the surface when the framework is stripped. Bush hammering, picking and working up with mason's tools have been used, but interesting textures are now more usually obtained by brushing or scrubbing to expose the larger aggregate; some very pleasant effects, both of colour and texture, have been obtained by the use of specially selected aggregates. If, however, the colour of the aggregate is drab, these treatments cannot be expected to produce any interesting effects in colour.

## PAINT COATINGS

Here we are concerned with paint coatings for masonry, concrete and cement products generally, as distinct from those for metal or timber.

As a general rule a paint coating combines the functions of a waterproofer and a decorative medium. It is important in any given case to consider carefully whether the waterproofing function is essential or merely subsidiary to decoration.

Most of the materials available fall into one of four groups: cement paints, emulsion paints, normal oil paints and 'stone' paints, and silicate paints.

Any of these coatings requires periodic renewal, and it is obviously important that there should be a clear understanding with the building owner as to the frequency at which renewals will be necessary. In comparing the costs of different external facings the appropriate sum should be capitalized to make adequate provision for renewal. Another aspect to be considered is the ease of renewal; the different treatments vary considerably in this respect.

### Cement paints

Cement or cement-lime slurries for colour washing have been largely superseded by proprietary brands of cement paint. These paints consist of Portland cement, lime, pigments, waterproofers and also accelerators which made the cement set more quickly; the mixture is supplied as a dry powder ready for mixing with water immediately before use.

Cement paints can be applied to reasonably strong porous surfaces, such as bricks and cement products generally. These surfaces should be well wetted with water before applying the cement paint and, in order to permit full hydration of the cement, the paint should not be allowed to dry too rapidly. On the other hand, the coating should not be exposed to rain before the cement has set. Painting, therefore, is best carried out in cool, but not rainy weather.

Cement paints should not in general be applied to non-porous surfaces (e.g. over old paint, or over colourless waterproofers), because adhesion is frequently poor and there is a risk that the applied film will dry out too rapidly and be soft and powdery.

Most cement paints are also unsuitable for application, especially under damp conditions, to surfaces containing excess sulphates (e.g. calcium sulphate plasters and some types of bricks) since the sulphates may cause the paint to lose adhesion and to blister or flake off. It is claimed, however, that this difficulty has been overcome by the use of special additives and that some paints can be used successfully on sulphate-bearing materials, provided the conditions are not too severe.

On suitable backgrounds, cement paints provide a hard matt surface of high durability; chalking or dusting away occurs gradually over a period of up to ten years. The chalking is, however, too slow to prevent dirt from accumulating on the surface. In urban atmospheres, cement paintwork tends to develop dirty patches and runs, especially in areas sheltered from rain. Repainting may thus be needed after a few years to preserve a fresh appearance, even when the coating itself is still quite sound. In country districts the surface will remain clean for a much longer period. Only pale colours are suitable for exterior use, since there is a tendency to form a white 'bloom' shortly after application.

Surfaces decorated in cement paint can be repainted in the same material without removing the old coating.

*Emulsion paints*

An emulsion is a suspension of very small globules of one liquid, say oil, in another liquid, say water. In emulsion paints the paint medium—oil, bitumen or synthetic resin—and any pigments are finely dispersed in water, with other ingredients to keep the emulsion stable. When brushed on to a surface, the emulsion 'breaks', the suspended globules running together to form a more or less continuous film, the water being absorbed or drying off.

Most oil-bound emulsion paints, or distempers, are intended for interior use, but some are formulated for use on exterior surfaces. A distemper exposed out of doors is likely to require recoating every two or three years. It should weather uniformly by chalking and this helps to preserve its fresh appearance. The coating, however, is rather susceptible to damage by alkalis, by efflorescent salts and by repeated wetting and drying. Persistently damp conditions are also liable to lead to disfiguring growths of moulds or algae. For these reasons the use of oil-bound water paints should generally be confined to surfaces that can be expected to remain fairly dry.

Bitumen and tar emulsions, which are rather restricted in range of colour, were used extensively during the last war for camouflage work. They are resistant to alkalis. Other paints should not be applied over them, as the bitumen tends to bleed through and to disfigure the new finish.

In the most recent forms of emulsion paint, the medium is a synthetic resin, sometimes combined with a drying oil. They offer a wider range of gloss and other properties than do the other distempers.

Properties of various types of emulsion paint, with indications of the surfaces for which they are suitable, are set out in Table 18.4.

### Oil paints

A wide range of oil paints is available, including types specially formulated to be resistant to the attack of alkalis present in cement products. A large variety of surface textures can be obtained, and there are, for example, imitation stone paints which, as the name implies, are intended to give a finish resembling in colour and texture that of natural stones (see below).

Most oil paints are impermeable to water; some flat paints, in which flatting is achieved by the use of a high proportion of pigments and fillers, are exceptions but this increase in permeability generally entails a corresponding shorter life under external exposure. Impermeable paints are likely to fail if they are applied to damp walls, since the trapped moisture may force off the paint film. Very unfavourable conditions may be created if both sides of a wall are sealed with impermeable films. The painting, therefore, should not be begun until the weather conditions are such as to ensure that the wall is reasonably dry. Any defects that might allow moisture to find its way to the back of the paint film must be made good beforehand. Good durability is most likely to be achieved where the paint film is impervious and, in conjunction with the damp-proof courses in walls and parapets or cornices, it effectively insulates the wall against re-entry of moisture.

These precautions to ensure that the walls are dry and remain dry should also provide a safeguard against chemical attack and efflorescence, but it is a useful additional precaution to apply at least two coats of an alkali-resistant primer to surfaces that could produce chemical attack if wet. It should be emphasized that the use of such priming coats is not a substitute for adequate drying before painting.

The success of this type of paint finish depends on satisfactory maintenance. If the wall is rubbed down and repainted with an oil paint before cracking of the old film permits the entry of moisture, it is possible to build up paint coats almost indefinitely. In general no other form of coating is likely to be successful on top of oil paint.

Similar types of paints are based on materials other than drying oils, e.g. chlorinated rubber, which has a high resistance to alkali attack.

### Stone paints

Several special paints for masonry surfaces give a finish resembling certain natural stones in colour and texture. These paints consist of pigmented emulsions or solutions of drying oils and resins or gums, with coarse fillers to produce the desired texture, which can be enhanced by stippling. They are supplied with suitable primers the use of which is essential for the stability of the coating.

TABLE 18.4

*Properties of emulsion paints*

| | Oil-bound distemper | Bitumen or tar emulsion | Alkyd emulsion | P.V.A. emulsion | | Styrene emulsion |
| --- | --- | --- | --- | --- | --- | --- |
| | | | | Gloss, egg-shell or less | Semigloss or glazed | |
| Porosity to water vapour . | High | Moderate | High | High | Low | High |
| Resistance to alkali in surface decorated | Moderate | Good | Moderate or poor | Good | Good | Fairly good |
| Resistance to mould growth . | Rather poor | Good | Insufficient experience | Variable; can be good | | Insufficient experience |
| Resistance to efflorescence . | Poor—flakes | Poor—flakes | Poor—flakes | May blister without flaking, flake or (rarely) permit efflorescence to grow on surface without damage. | | Insufficient experience |
| Outdoor durability (suitable formulations) | 2–3 years | 3–5 years | 2–4 years | Variable. Have been known to remain sound up to four years on brick or cement rendering. | | No suitable formulation as yet |
| Resistance to bleeding of creosote or bituminous materials | Poor | — | Poor | Fairly good | | Poor |
| Redecoration:<br>With same paint . | Satisfactory | Satisfactory | Probably satisfactory | — | — | Insufficient experience |
| With other materials . | Satisfactory | Unsatisfactory | Probably satisfactory | — | — | — |

When properly used, paints of this type are capable of giving a waterproof coating of good durability and appearance. Several of them, moreover, show a high resistance to attack by alkalis and hence are suitable for use on Portland cement rendering or concrete. Precautions in use are much as for ordinary oil paints. It should be realized that, as these coatings are somewhat thicker and less flexible than those of ordinary exterior paints, they are more liable to deteriorate by flaking or scaling unless they are firmly bonded to the surface—hence the importance of adopting the recommended priming treatment. It is essential also to prevent moisture from gaining access to the back of the paint film. Chimney-stacks and parapets in particular call for special care in excluding rain from access at the top.

Owing to the rough texture of these paints they may tend to collect dirt in smoke-polluted atmospheres rather more readily than ordinary paints; on the other hand, they also chalk more readily, so that the dirt is washed off by rain on the exposed areas of the wall.

*Silicate paints*

Silicate paints are those in which the binding medium consists essentially of sodium or potassium silicate. The majority are intended for interior use only, but one or two special proprietary brands can be used successfully out-of-doors as colour washes for cement, asbestos cement and brickwork. Like lime-washes and cement paints they are not damaged by the alkalis in cement and they are porous enough to allow water to dry through them. They are not generally affected by sulphates, but if efflorescent salts are present, the application of silicate paint sometimes tends to promote the efflorescence.

When redecorating surfaces painted with silicate paint it is advisable to continue to use the same type of paint.

# TILE AND SLATE HANGING

The main advantage of slate or tile hanging and the main reason for its survival is that a dry wall can be obtained with certainty. Slates or tiles may be fixed to a timber frame or to a wall of brick or masonry. On occasion slate or tile hanging is resorted to as a remedy for damp penetration through an existing wall.

*Exclusion of rain*

The principle on which the rain-excluding mechanism of tiling is based differs from that of any of the alternative methods of walling. With slating or tiling the water is shed from one course of tiles to the next, as on a pitched roof, and for the fullest efficiency there are two essentials:

(1) that the joint between any two tiles or slates should be backed by underlying tiles;

(2) that there should be no capillary channel to convey water from a wet tile or slate to any other porous material in the building structure.

The conditions for penetration of rain are very much less severe for vertical tiling or slating than for work on sloping roofs. The quantity of rain falling on the tiles is very much less in vertical work and the amount of water running down the wall will be relatively small. Consequently it is not necessary to provide a generous lap except on very exposed sites, and 1½ in., which is the lap usually worked to, should be ample.

Good slates are relatively impervious and are sometimes laid vertically in a mortar bed. Provided the joints are properly lapped there is no reason why this should not be satisfactory. With no lap at the joints there would be a grave danger of cracking of the mortar bed at the joints, which would allow water to enter the wall. Clay tiles have a porous structure and it would be undesirable to lay them on a mortar bed, since this would provide a capillary path for moisture through to the body of the wall.

*Durability*

With vertical tiling or slating the conditions of exposure as regards frost action will be less severe than on roofs. The deterioration of many slates is most commonly due to acid attack by sulphur compounds in polluted atmospheres and is most likely to occur on the sheltered part of the slate. The requirements of the British Standard as regards the durability test are therefore particularly important for slates and it would be unwise to assume that an indifferent slate is good enough for vertical hanging.

With either tiles or slates, vertical hanging imposes considerably more severe conditions on the nails than work on sloping surfaces. By using battens the weight of the tiles can be taken on the nibs, and this is a feature which makes battening worth while. The practice of nailing into the joint in brickwork or masonry presupposes the use of a weak, non-hydraulic mortar which, though often quite adequate, may in certain cases by a disadvantage. The use of nailable concrete fixing blocks laid in courses is an alternative; these should be of aerated concrete or a lightweight concrete containing an aggregate other than clinker, which might have a corrosive effect on the nails.

The composition of the nails used should be considered carefully. The materials available in an ascending order of durability are galvanized steel, galvanized wrought iron, zinc, copper or yellow metal. For buildings in rural districts, galvanized nails may have a useful life of many years, but they are not suitable for use in highly polluted industrial areas. Galvanized nails and zinc nails should not be used in coastal districts, since zinc is readily attacked by chlorides. Yellow-metal nails consisting of an alloy of copper, zinc and tin are likely to be more durable than any of the others and have the advantage that they are hard and can easily be driven.

# SHEET MATERIALS

It is the joints that present the main problem in assessing the durability of sheet claddings and curtain walling, especially where the jointing material has to accommodate movement (p. 128). Little more can be said here than that much development work is in progress on jointing materials for this purpose; the designer proposing to use this form of construction needs to study existing experience and also to seek expert advice on most recent knowledge.

The sheet materials themselves, having very little structural function, will naturally be chosen principally for their durability with due account being taken of appearance and cost. Here it is not necessary to add much to what has already been said in Chapter 11.

Materials that are intrinsically durable have a considerable advantage here over those that require protective coatings, periodically maintained. External painting, though inconvenient, is practicable and can be allowed for in weighing initial costs against maintenance costs, but the unexposed surface of the sheeting is inaccessible and any protective coating needed there must have an indefinite life. This holds also for any metal framing on which sheet finishes are supported. Fortunately the protective coating over the concealed areas does not have to be decorative. Pretreatment and priming in the factory is generally desirable, at least with steel sheets and sections, followed by a robust protective coating (pp. 88–90) applied on the site. The risks of damage to coatings in transport and in fixing must be kept in mind.

*Chapter* 19

# SPECIAL CONSTRUCTIONAL FEATURES

## CHIMNEY FLUES, STACKS AND FIREPLACES

THE main purpose of a chimney flue and stack is the removal of smoke and gases from a fire in the fireplace, but it also assists in ventilation. The following notes relate to chimneys serving domestic fires; chimneys for industrial units and large appliances such as central-heating boilers are not considered.

The principles governing the proper functioning of flues are quite simple. The fuel requires some air (sometimes referred to as 'primary air') to enable it to burn, and this it obtains from the room at or near floor level. In addition some air ('secondary air') is drawn directly into the flue by the draught.

The two currents thus set up carry the smoke up the flue. The amount of air required by different types of solid-fuel appliances varies considerably. For a normal open fire it ranges from 4000–6000 cu. ft/h, roughly three to four times the volume of a room; some open fires require more, others take more, even up to 12 000 cu. ft/h if air can enter the room at that rate through other openings. A free-standing inset-convector type of open fire, fitted with an adjustable throat restrictor, requires only half as much air as the normal open fire, i.e. 2000–3000 cu. ft/h; an openable stove may require a little more than this when open but when closed the air flow is reduced to about 800–1000 cu. ft/h. The efficient functioning of a fire and its flue is largely dependent, in the first place, upon a continuous and sufficient supply of air. As, however, the purpose of a fire is to heat the room in which it is situated it is not sufficient to provide a flue that will merely remove smoke and hot gases regardless of other factors, for all hot air that passes up the chimney in excess of what is actually needed represents a waste of heat.

*Sources of air supply*

The air supply for a fire enters the room either from the outside or from inside the building. It enters mainly through windows, ventilators and doors when these are open, but when these are shut the air continues to enter through gaps around windows and doors, through gaps between floor-boards of suspended timber floors and through any other cracks or openings to the outside or to the remainder of the house. This flow of air often leads to uncomfortable draughts; various devices are available for incorporating in a fireplace to provide the necessary air without causing draughts, but it is essential to ensure that these sources of supply can provide the requisite amount of air for the fire to function efficiently.

*Design of the open fireplace*

The correct design of a fireplace and the entry to the flue, i.e. the throat, is more important than is commonly realized; there is reason to believe that, assuming an adequate supply of air, it is, in fact, the most important factor in preventing chimney smoking.

The throat should not be more than 4 in. from back to front, 6–8 in. from top to bottom, and not more than 10 in. from side to side (Fig. 19.1). Where conditions are particularly adverse, e.g. on the top floor of a block of flats, it is often desirable to reduce the dimensions of the cross-section even more; an adjustable restrictor will then be necessary, as permanent restriction would cause difficulty in sweeping. Throat restrictors have the further advantage of reducing the amount of warm air drawn from the room.

All internal surfaces of the throat should be smooth. The bottom of the lintel should always be rounded as shown in Fig. 19.1. At one time, emphasis was laid on the provision of a horizontal smoke shelf level with the top of the throat. This is still considered desirable but it does not appear to be indispensable if all other features are properly designed. Fears are often expressed that accumulations of soot on the smoke shelf may lead to frequent chimney fires but there is no evidence to support these fears and, in any case, the shelf should be cleaned regularly if it is to fulfil its purpose.

The tiled fireplace surround can have some effect on the functioning of the flue, and Fig. 19.2a shows a common feature that can contribute to a smoky chimney; care should be taken to ensure that the gap between the lintel and the surround is either filled and finished to a smooth curve or closed by means of a curved plate as shown in Fig. 19.2b.

*Position of fireplace in a room*

In designing a building it is not always possible to place fireplaces and flues in the positions most suitable either for thermal efficiency or for reducing the risk of downdraught. Where there is a choice of position the following factors should be taken into account.

The thermal efficiency of any appliance, particularly an open fire, is considerably increased if the flue is on an internal wall, since the heat recovery from the flue into the building is then much higher than when the flue is on an external wall. Fireplaces built against external walls are more likely to smoke than those on internal walls. There are several reasons for this. First, many chimneys rise from the eaves of a sloping roof, a position where there may be a zone of pressure due to wind, as described later (p. 272). Secondly, the back of the fire breast and flue may be of very thin masonry, so that there is considerable loss of heat, especially in windy or wet weather, and cold air may infiltrate through unfilled masonry joints. Thirdly, chimneys in an external wall often contain long single flues, with three of the flue walls exposed to cold and damp.

The choice of the position of a fireplace in a room must be influenced by considerations of comfort and heating efficiency, but positions permitting draughts across the fireplace should be avoided if possible; such positions often give rise to intermittent downdraught, especially if the draught is usually sluggish. The placing of a fireplace without due regard to details of construction may involve sharp bends, flat slopes and restrictions in flues; these features impair the draught.

*Flues*

The word 'flue' is used rather loosely; here it will be taken to refer to the actual passageway enclosed by the stack. The size of the flue should preferably be the normal 9 in. by 9 in. square section or 8 in. diameter circular, and

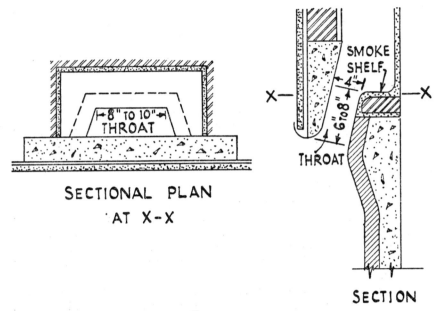

FIG. 19.1

*Open fire-place design—details at throat*

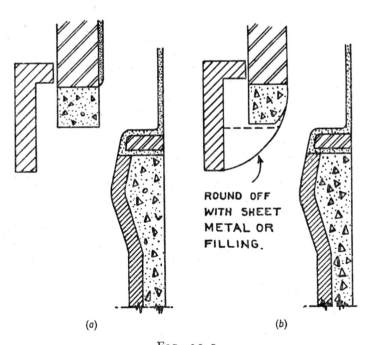

FIG. 19.2

*Open fire-place with tiled surround—detail of finish to avoid smoking*

should certainly not be less than 7 in. unless only smokeless fuels will be used. Bends, when necessary, should be at an angle of not less than 45° to the horizontal and preferably not less than 60°; they should be rounded and care should be taken not to reduce the section in forming them. Unless lined with clay liners the sides of the flue should be made smooth by careful parging.

In houses, and in flats other than those on the top floor, the length of the flue is generally sufficient to obtain a satisfactory draught, but the length of the flue of a bungalow or of a top floor flat, especially if there is a flat roof, might be insufficient. This disadvantage can frequently be offset by the use of a throat restrictor.

### Chimney stacks and terminals

The materials used in chimney construction demand care in selection, for in addition to their exposure to more severe weather conditions than other parts of the building, the heat of the fire and the chemical effect of the products of combustion must be considered. In particular, the effect of the condensation of flue gases from some types of stoves needs careful attention.

Moisture penetration in a chimney-stack may increase the risk of disintegration of bricks and mortar by frost action, sulphate attack or efflorescence. Moisture flowing down the stack may cause dampness and staining inside the house. Moreover, by lowering the heat resistance of the masonry and by the cooling action of evaporating moisture, dampness may cause heat losses from a flue, resulting in smoke nuisance and premature condensation of flue gases. A chimney must therefore be designed and constructed with particular care to avoid damp penetration. A waterproof head is necessary, preferably overhanging sufficiently to protect the stack. Masonry materials must be chosen with due regard to their weather-resisting properties and damp-proof courses must be provided as necessary (p. 214).

Many chimneys have been built of brickwork rendered with cement mortar, quite plain and devoid of pots, flaunching and caps. Trouble with these is almost inevitable, for a cracking of the rendering at the top surface—a most probable occurrence—results in damp penetration, failure of rendering, perhaps failure of brickwork and generally in serious disfigurement, internally and externally.

Masonry is usually sufficiently fire-resisting to withstand the temperatures reached in ordinary flues, and flue linings of fireclay are therefore not generally used except in special cases. Flue linings, however, serve many useful purposes and might well be used more often. Among the advantages possessed by flue linings are added heat insulation, air-tightness, uniformity of section and smoothness, all of which favour a good draught; they also protect the masonry to some extent from the deleterious effects of the flue gases and heat, and they assist in fire prevention.

### Smoky chimneys

The natural tendency is for the warm air, gases and smoke to rise in a flue. Under certain conditions, however, there may be a downdraught and smoke may enter the room.

Apart from blockage by debris or soot, there are three factors that can prevent a flue operating properly: (1) an insufficient supply of air entering the room to replace the air passing up the flue; (2) adverse flow conditions caused by poor design of the passages through which the smoke has to pass, including the throat and the gathering; (3) the development of pressure by the wind at the top outlet of the flue (influenced either by the building itself, by adjacent buildings or trees or by the topography of the site) which cannot be overcome by the rising flue gases. These three factors acting singly or together cause downdraughts. Good design should ensure the absence of all three, though it is obvious that adverse site conditions cannot always be remedied.

*Internal factors.* The problem of insufficient air supply is closely related to general comfort conditions in the room. Measures taken to eliminate draughts usually reduce the air-supply to the room and may do so to a point where the reduced pressure in the room can only be brought to normal by means of air (and smoke) drawn down the flue.

There are two ways of dealing with a deficiency of air. The first is to provide special means of entry for the continuous supply of air needed by the fire; the second, to restrict the amount of air passing up the flue by fitting a throat restrictor.

Apart from the obvious solution of leaving the door or window open sufficiently to prevent smoking—a remedy which is probably out of the question because it would already have been adopted had it not caused excessive draughts—additional air can be admitted by means of ventilators fixed either in the external walls or in the partition wall separating the room from the hall, or by underfloor ducts. The position of the ventilator should be carefully considered as it may also cause draughts and in some positions there is the risk that the suction effect may operate.

*External factors.* Wind affects the action of a flue in several ways. It may on the one hand be directly helpful when, blowing across the flue outlet, it creates a suction in the flue. Other effects of wind, however, are probably much more important.

Fig. 19.3a shows a section of a house with the chimney rising from an external wall, the roof slope being greater than 30°. When the wind is in the direction shown a zone of high pressure is set up on the windward side. If the chimney head is within this zone the chimney is liable to smoke. The limits of this zone cannot be accurately defined and it is a matter for trial and error to determine at what height the outlet would be outside the zone. Experience suggests that the chimney stack should be carried through the ridge and to byelaw height above it (although it should be noted that the byelaw requirements regarding chimney height have been imposed for reasons that have nothing to do with ensuring a good draught). If it is not possible to arrange for the chimney to pass through the ridge, it should be carried up at least as high as the ridge, and in some circumstances a still greater height may be needed. A tall pot may add sufficient height to take the outlet outside the zone of high pressure.

Another point is that the wind creates a suction on the leeward side of the house; if there is an opening to a room on this side, air may be drawn from the room and pressure reduced at the fireplace, thus tending to cause downdraught.

On roofs of a slope less than 30° (Fig. 19.3b and c), a wind produces suction, which increases towards the ridge; for roofs approximating to a 30° pitch, pressure or suction produced by wind on the roof may be neglected. In both cases however, the pressure on the windward walls and the suction on the leeward walls must still be considered.

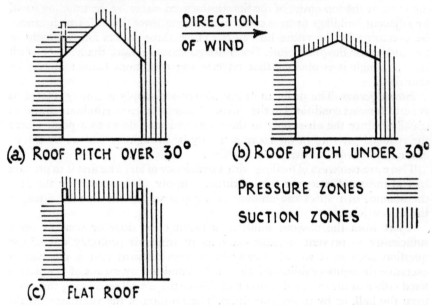

(a) ROOF PITCH OVER 30°          (b) ROOF PITCH UNDER 30°

PRESSURE ZONES

SUCTION ZONES

(c)  FLAT ROOF

FIG. 19.3

*Position of chimney head in relation to pitch of roof—wind pressure and suction zones*

The pattern of wind pressure can be influenced by other buildings, trees, hills, and the projections on roofs, depending on the size, height, shape and nearness of such objects. This is an old problem in built-up areas but it has recently given rise to trouble in newly built estates of mixed development, especially where low buildings are close to tall buildings. On one estate the chimneys of the two-storey houses functioned satisfactorily until the three-storey blocks were erected. Then every two-storey house adjacent to a three-storey block developed smoky chimney trouble despite the design of the fire-place and flue being reasonably good. Unfortunately no general guidance can yet be given as to the form of layout that will minimize the effect of the adjacent buildings and it is necessary therefore to rely on careful attention to other factors, and in particular to include throat restrictors in the fireplace design.

*Slow-combustion boilers*

Flues and stacks serving slow-combustion boilers and stoves present a special problem and if not correctly designed and built are subject to a distinct type of failure which may show itself by gross disintegration of the mortar, frequently causing the chimney stack to bend, or by stained areas of plasterwork on the chimney breast or the ceiling adjacent to it (Fig. 19.4). Stoves and boilers of this type are often burning for long periods at a very low temperature—in many cases damped down by house refuse—and the heat generated in the flue is not sufficient to prevent the condensation on the flue walls. The resultant deposit may contain sulphur compounds, tar, ammonia and soot in addition to water. The contaminated moisture is readily absorbed by most mortars and many types of bricks and stones, often resulting in unsightly staining of external and internal walls and of ceilings and also in an unpleasant smell. The condensed water, supplemented by any rain water penetrating from the exposed face of the stack, may, moreover, set up sulphate attack in the mortar by sulphur compounds in the condensate or by transferring to it sulphates contained in the bricks. Mortar attacked by sulphates expands and since the expansion is frequently uneven the stack will often lean over. Any rendering on the stack will generally crack and may fall off.

As the cure for this type of failure is expensive, often necessitating the demolition and renewal of chimney-breasts and stacks, it is recommended that flues to be used with any type of slow-combustion grate should be lined with an impervious material such as glazed stoneware or ceramic pipes or clay flue liners (Fig. 19.5). The joints of the pipes should be as fine as possible to minimize chemical action, and pipes of the spigot and socket type should be laid with the collars upwards. A great reduction in the amount of condensation may be made by admitting extra air into the flue, preferably through a ventilator fitted into the chimney breast near ceiling level in the room in which the appliance stands. The provision of thicker external walls, partly built of heat-insulating materials or constructed so as to prevent excessive heat losses, is desirable in some cases. As an impervious lining will increase the amount of the deposit flowing to the fireplace, some form of catch-pit is advisable at the base of the flue, with a removable receptacle and an airtight door.

The effects of damp penetration, frost and action of flue gases are all more likely to be serious if the construction is light. It is unwise to build the external walls of flues in half-brick thickness; moreover, the lack of thermal insulation provided by this thickness of masonry has a noticeable effect upon the efficiency of some flues.

*Avoidance of fire risks*

Badly designed or constructed fireplaces and chimney stacks are often the cause of serious fires, though to a large extent this risk is guarded against by the precautions demanded by byelaws. One source of danger is the concrete hearth; concrete is incombustible but it is possible for a fierce fire, especially when burning directly on the hearth, to raise the temperature of the concrete sufficiently to cause the ignition of wood in contact with it. Also, the concrete may crack and so allow flame to reach adjacent wooden members. For this reason hearths should be sufficiently thick and large to provide at least nine inches of concrete between the fire and the nearest woodwork, no metal should be in contact with both hearth and wood members, and hearth shuttering or strutting should be removed when the concrete is set. Some reinforcement of concrete hearths is desirable, to prevent the formation of large cracks through which flame may pass.

Careless construction of flue walls permitting the escape of flame is obviously a source of danger, and, if only for this reason, parging or a flue lining should on no account be omitted.

Cases have been known where wood beams built in contact with hearths have been 'protected' by sheets of asbestos cement. It should be made quite

## CONSTRUCTION

## COMMON EFFECTS

CHIMNEY: 4½" BRICKWORK
RENDERED EXTERNALLY &
PARGED INTERNALLY.

COLD FLUE PRODUCES
CONDENSATION OF WATER VAPOUR.
THE WATER AND OTHER COMBUSTION
PRODUCTS ARE ABSORBED INTO THE
FLUE WALLS CAUSING DISINTEGRATION
OF MORTAR AND PARGING; CRACKING
AND STAINING OF RENDERING.

EXTERNAL WALL:
BRICKWORK RENDERED
EXTERNALLY AND
PLASTERED INTERNALLY.

STAINING OF RENDERING AND
PLASTERING AND OBJECTIONABLE
SMELL.

FLUE: 4½" BRICKWORK
RENDERED ON EXTERNAL
FACE, PLASTERED ON
INTERNAL FACE AND
PARGED.

DISINTEGRATION OF PARGING,
MORTAR AND PERHAPS OF BRICKS.

FLUE BASE: CONCRETE
SLAB PIERCED FOR
SMOKE PIPE.

DEPOSIT COLLECTS ON FLUE BASE
AND RUNS DOWN SMOKE PIPE
INTO STOVE.

SECTION

TYPICAL PLAN

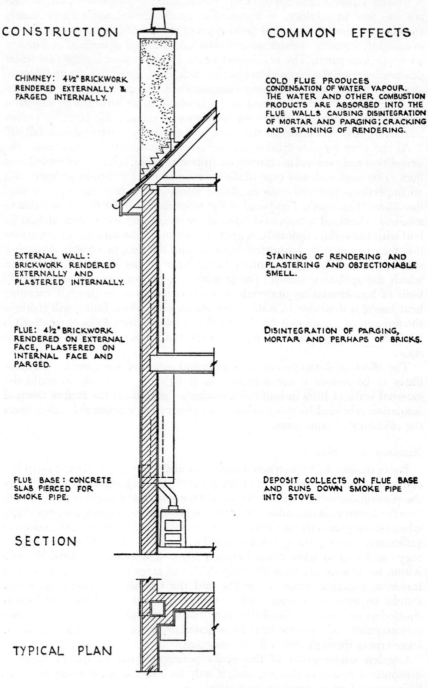

FIG. 19.4

*Slow combustion stoves: failure of conventional flue construction*

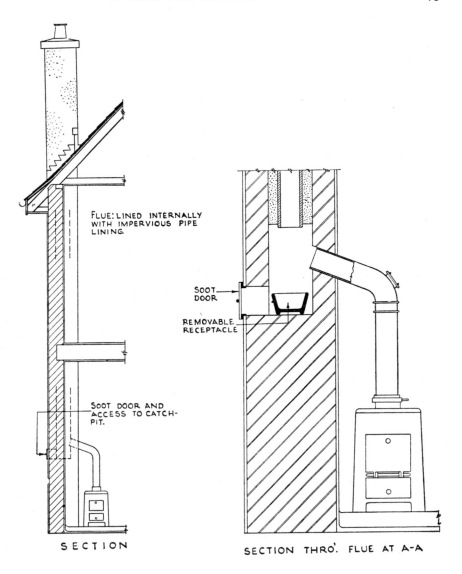

FLUE: LINED INTERNALLY
WITH IMPERVIOUS PIPE
LINING.

SOOT
DOOR

REMOVABLE
RECEPTACLE

SOOT DOOR AND
ACCESS TO CATCH-
PIT.

SECTION

SECTION THRO'. FLUE AT A-A

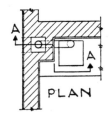

PLAN

FIG. 19.5

*Slow combustion stoves: recommended construction of flues*

clear that although this material is incombustible it is possible for it to become hot enough to ignite wood and it may also crack and so allow the passage of flame. Asbestos board and asbestos blanket, without the addition of Portland cement, are more appropriate for this purpose.

*Flues for gas fires*

The use of coal gas as a fuel and the consequent elimination of smoke and soot have fostered the installation of special types of flues to remove the steam and gases produced by the combustion of coal gas. Two notable examples are asbestos-cement flue-pipes and cement concrete flue blocks, both of which are usually quite satisfactory in use for small domestic gas fires and are often very convenient.

Reference should perhaps be made to the danger arising from downdraught when coal gas is used as a fuel. Its effects are not so apparent as in the case when coal and wood are burnt, owing to the absence of visible smoke, but they may be more dangerous in their consequences. The evil effects of carbon monoxide and carbon dioxide are well known and, unless a flue connected to a gas fire has an efficient draught, considerable quantities of these gases may flow into the room. As much care should therefore be taken to prevent downdraught in gas flues as in ordinary chimneys. Owing to the light construction of these flues the amount of heat insulation of their walls is often small. This, combined with the fact that gas fires are often in occasional use, may result in the flues being often cold and therefore more subject to downdraught and excessive condensation. In addition, at times the flues near the fire may become excessively hot, since some of the special flue blocks have very thin walls.

It would appear, therefore, that some form of thermal insulation to flues of this kind may be advisable, for, although ordinarily no serious consequences need be expected, in exceptional cases the heat near the fireplace and the condensation of flue gases further away from the fire may be sources of trouble. This may be most noticeable in the case of boilers or water units of high thermal efficiency. The most likely result of either excessive heat or condensation will be failure of decorations.

Flues from gas appliances should never be permitted to discharge into wall cavities or roof spaces; the danger from fire, fumes and condensation of flue gases makes it essential that such flues should discharge in the open air and then in such a position that no ill effects from these sources occur. A discharge near ironwork is especially bad, as the action of the condensed moisture, which is invariably slightly acid, may lead to rapid corrosion.

Gas flues are usually provided with baffles to prevent downdraught, but, as stated previously, this cannot be relied upon to give absolute security; the precautions suggested for smoke flues should be taken also with flues used for gas.

## SOME TRADITIONAL WALLING METHODS
## OF PARTICULAR LOCAL INTEREST

There are several methods of construction that are almost obsolete, but which survive locally, being still used to a limited extent particularly where it is necessary to build in harmony with existing groups of old buildings. The reason for the obsolescence of many of these old forms is not far to seek;

usually they were based on the exploitation of local materials in a time when transport facilities were very primitive; modern transport has made available more economical and more efficient materials and, despite their aesthetic attractions, the old forms are hard put to it to survive. Owing to their obsolescence little or no scientific work has been devoted to these old methods of construction and the Building Research Station has no considerable contribution to offer on the subject. A few points, however, have been raised from time to time, and it is believed that these may be of sufficient interest to warrant some discussion.

*Rammed earth walling*

Chalk walling is widely distributed in the chalk country in Wiltshire and Hampshire, cob is to be found in Devon and parts of Somerset and clay lump in East Anglia. All these methods are based on the fact that when certain finely divided materials are tightly compressed they cohere to form a fairly hard, strong solid body. The presence of a certain small amount of water assists in the packing of the particles. The cohesion developed in this way lasts only so long as the materials are kept dry. Once they become thoroughly saturated they revert to mud and lose most of their strength and cohesion. With all these methods, therefore, it is of first importance to keep the walls dry. A wide overhang at eaves is essential. Roofs must be carried out over the verges at gable ends or, alternatively, gables can with advantage be built in brick or stone. Chimney-stacks must be built in brick or stone. Rainwater gutters and rainwater pipes must be of generous size and the pipes should be blocked well out from the wall. One case was known where a waterbutt, fed by a rainwater pipe, was carried away in a gale, taking the pipe with it; the rain poured down the wall of rammed chalk and the whole corner of the house fell out. Originally these old earth-walled buildings will often have been erected by the occupants, who would know their limitations and be zealous in making repairs as they became necessary.

These walls are by no means stable in volume when their moisture content changes, but by following the traditional methods of construction an excess of water is avoided; drying shrinkage is relieved by cracking round individual particles or lumps so that stresses are not built up high enough to crack the wall as a whole. The introduction of a certain amount of cement, in chalk walling for instance, with the object of obtaining a certain degree of hydraulic strength which will survive subsequent wetting, has not been found very successful in the monolithic walls. Drying shrinkage stresses are built up and the walls tend to crack right through.

A certain amount of weather protection is obtained traditionally by coverings of various kinds, such as lime-tallow washes on the wall direct or on lime plaster. Lime-cement slurries or cement paints, brush applied, might also be useful and rather more durable. Strong cement renderings are not suitable; the walling is not strong enough to restrain the volume changes of the rendering due to changes in moisture content, and the rendering soon breaks away from the face of the wall and becomes loose.

*Flint walling*

Owing to the irregular shapes of the flints the proportion of mortar in a flint wall is high in comparison with that of other forms of masonry. The properties of the wall will approach more nearly those of a mass of concrete and, in particular, volume changes with changes in moisture content must be taken into account. Today, flint work is nearly always used as facing backed up with brick, and the problem confronting the builder is to reconcile the very different characteristics of the facing and backing. Brickwork has a low moisture movement, whereas flint work may be expected to shrink considerably as it dries owing to the mass of mortar in it; it is very probable that a certain amount of cracking will occur, whatever reasonable precautions are taken to prevent it. This need not be of any great consequence, except that the cracks may conduct rain into the interior of the wall and lead to penetration of moisture to the inner face. To avoid building up high shrinkage stresses in the flint facing, a very strong mortar should not be used.

## 'Dry' stone walling

By 'dry' stone walling is implied walls erected of stones or blocks without the use of mortar. The aim is to obtain a wall with no capillary channels for the penetration of rain to the inner face. Any water passing into the wall simply runs down between the stones to the foot. There is great art in the erection of walls of this kind; bond stones must be used to tie the faces together, and these must be inclined so that they do not conduct rain across the wall; the inclination of the upper surfaces of all stones is carefully controlled. The essential feature of this kind of work is that success depends upon craft skill which cannot be put into the formal wording of a specification, but the principle is logically sound, and the walls are dry and the buildings habitable. It is probably a sufficient recommendation from the point of view of weather resistance that dry walling in one form or another has been mainly developed in mountainous districts where exposure is severe and stone plentiful, but skilled craftsmanship is essential.

## *Appendix 1*

# GLOSSARY

Most of the technical terms used in special contexts are defined as they arise in the text. The following notes refer mainly to terms that recur in more than one context.

*Coefficient of variation and other statistical measures*

It is often useful to have some way of describing the degree of variation found between a number of comparable measurements. In a sample of a dozen bricks, for example, no two will have exactly the same length, weight or strength. The most familiar statistical measure, the average or mean, gives no idea of how much individual measurements may deviate from the average.

Suppose strength tests on samples of six specimens of some product give numerical values (the units are unimportant here) as follows:

|           |     |     |     |     |     |     |
|-----------|-----|-----|-----|-----|-----|-----|
| series (a) | 100 | 105 | 113 | 118 | 123 | 128 |
| series (b) | 65  | 123 | 124 | 125 | 126 | 127 |
| series (c) | 100 | 113 | 115 | 116 | 118 | 128 |

The mean for each series is 115, but the type of variation about this mean is different for each series. In (a), the values are fairly uniformly spread over a *range* of 28. In (b) the range is greater, 62, but this spread is largely attributable to the one very low value. In (c) the range is the same as in (a), but some of the values are clustered more closely about the mean.

This last characteristic, the degree to which scattered values deviate from the mean, is an important one, and it is measured by the *standard deviation* (usually symbolized by the Greek letter $\sigma$), which is calculated as follows.

Using series (c) as an example:

| The deviation of each value | 100 | 113 | 115 | 116 | 118 | 128 |
|-----------------------------|-----|-----|-----|-----|-----|-----|
| from the mean is obtained by | 115 | 115 | 115 | 115 | 115 | 115 |
| subtraction: | | | | | | |

| | | | | | | |
|---|---|---|---|---|---|---|
| | $-15$ | $-2$ | 0 | 1 | 3 | 13 |
| These deviations are squared: | 225 | 4 | 0 | 1 | 9 | 169 |

and added together: $\qquad$ 408

Dividing by the number of values: $\qquad 408/6 = 68$

and taking the square root: $\qquad \sqrt{68} = 8.25$

yields the standard deviation: $\qquad \sigma = 8.25$

Finally, to obtain a measure of variation that is independent of the scale of measurement, the standard deviation is divided by the mean value, giving the *coefficient of variation*: $8.25/115 = 0.0717$. This last is often expressed as a percentage—here, 7.17 per cent.

For comparison, these forms of statistical description of the three series given above are:

|                          | (a)    | (b)    | (c)    |
|--------------------------|--------|--------|--------|
| Mean                     | 115    | 115    | 115    |
| Range                    | 28     | 62     | 28     |
| Standard deviation       | 9.75   | 22.4   | 8.25   |
| Coefficient of variation | 0.0848 | 0.195  | 0.0717 |
|                          | or     | or     | or     |
|                          | 8.48%  | 19.5%  | 7.17%  |

279

## Emulsion

Certain paints, waterproofing materials, jointing materials and other preparations may be in the form of emulsions when they are applied, and this generally has some influence on their performance.

An emulsion is a dispersion of minute droplets of one liquid in another (usually water) when the two do not, properly speaking, mix. The most familiar example is milk. Among building materials, there are oil-bound distempers and emulsion paints generally, bituminous emulsions, and rubber emulsions (rubber latex). With such materials, the purpose of emulsification is usually to increase fluidity for convenience in application by brushing or pouring.

Fluidity may also be increased by adding a liquid that does dissolve or mix with the material to be applied. Thus, thinners may be added to oil paint or to bitumen (a bitumen thus thinned is known as a 'cutback'), and both rubber solution and rubber latex are in common use.

Whether an emulsion or a solution is to be preferred in given circumstances depends on several factors, only one of which need be mentioned here. As the water dries out after the application of an emulsion it will generally leave a fine pore structure in the residual film. This may be an advantage, as where a background needs to continue drying out after the application of a decorative finish. It would be a disadvantage where a coating needs to provide a positive barrier to the movement of water vapour. For this reason a cutback bitumen, or a bitumen made more fluid by heating, is preferable to a bitumen emulsion if a really efficient damp-proof membrane is required.

## Phon

As mentioned on p. 51, the decibel is an objective measure of sound energy intensity, obtainable by the use of physical instruments. The phon is a measure of loudness—i.e. of a human experience. Briefly, the equivalent loudness of any sound is said to be $n$ phons if it is judged by a normal observer to be as loud as a pure tone, of 1000 cycles per second, of which the sound intensity is $n$ decibels above a fixed level corresponding to the threshold of audibility for a normal observer.

It is worth noting that reference to a 'normal observer' and to 'judgment' implies a type of inexactness that is not encountered with inanimate measuring instruments—a difficulty that inevitably arises when interpreting objective measurements in terms of human experience. This does not lessen the value of attempts to bring the two together, so long as there is full awareness of what assumptions and approximations are being made—for example, that the 'normal observer' is merely a useful fiction.

## Units and abbreviations

Most of the units of measurement used in this book are familiar and their abbreviations self-explanatory. Some may be rather confusing—particularly the group relating to heat transmission. For example, the $U$-value of a construction (p. 36) is expressed as

(a) B.t.u./h ft² °F (or B.t.u./h sq. ft °F),

while the thermal conductivity of a material is expressed as

(b) B.t.u. in./h ft² °F.

The first expression is usually *spoken* as 'British thermal units per hour per square foot per degree Fahrenheit difference in air temperature', and it is still quite commonly printed as

(c) B.t.u./h/ft²/°F,

with each 'per' represented by a stroke '/'. This is unsatisfactory, as the stroke generally represents division and, in (c), it is not clear what is divided by what— an important matter, for

$$\frac{\frac{1}{1}}{2} = \frac{1}{2} \text{ while } \frac{1}{\frac{1}{2}} = 2.$$

The form of the expressions (a) and (b) can be a helpful guide in elementary design calculations. For example, in calculating conductivity from measurements of the amount of heat transferred (B.t.u.), the thickness of the specimen (in.), the period of the experiment (h), the area of specimen involved (ft²), and the difference in temperature between the faces of the specimen (°F), one multiplies the first two together and divides by the product of the other three values. Conversely, the designer, knowing the conductivity of the material and wanting to know the surface-to-surface heat transfer, divides the conductivity by the thickness of the material and multiplies by the time (h), area (ft²), and temperature difference (°F).

Generally, abbreviations used in this book for the names of units are those recommended in British Standard 1991: Part 1; 1954, 'Letter symbols, signs and abbreviations'.

*Appendix II*

# FURTHER READING

Various references have been made throughout this volume to British Standards, British Standards Codes of Practice, and to Building Research Station Digests and other publications.

Full lists of British Standards Institution Publications are contained in the *British Standards Yearbook* or are available from The Institution, Newton House, 101–113 Pentonville Road, London, N.1.

Details of publications published by H.M.S.O., and of papers in the B.R.S. *Current Papers* series, are available on request from the Librarian, Building Research Station, Garston, Watford, Herts.

# INDEX

(138029) Dd. 501432 K. 40 7/70 Hw.